Desk Copy

# Time
# to Wonder

# Time to Wonder

Bernard J. Weiss

*Educational Consultants*
Janet Sprout
Jack P. Henderson

*Related Satellite Books*
Lyman C. Hunt/*General Editor*

**The Holt Basic Reading System**

Level 13

Holt, Rinehart and Winston, Publishers
New York · Toronto · London · Sydney

# Acknowledgments:

*Grateful acknowledgment is hereby made to the following authors, publishers, agents and individuals for their special permission to reprint copyrighted material.*

American Book Company, for "The Friendly Cricket," a Costa Rican folk song, copyrighted 1948.

Atheneum Publishers, for "Ululation," from *It Doesn't Always Have to Rhyme,* copyright © 1964 by Eve Merriam.

Atheneum Publishers, and The Bodley Head, Ltd., and Erika Klopp Verlag, for "The Would-Be Cowboy," adapted from *Grandmother Oma* by Ilse Kleberger, copyright © 1964 by Erika Klopp Verlag, Berlin; English translation copyright © 1966 by The Bodley Head, Ltd.

Kenneth C. Bennett, Jr., as agent for Rowena Bennett, for "The Witch of Willowby Wood," from *Poems of Magic and Spells* by Rowena Bennett.

Brandt & Brandt, for "Wilbur Wright and Orville Wright," from *A Book of Americans* by Rosemary and Stephen Vincent Benét, published by Holt, Rinehart and Winston, Inc., copyright 1933 by Rosemary and Stephen Vincent Benét. Copyright © renewed 1961 by Rosemary Carr Benét.

CBS Radio, for excerpt from "The Queen Who Couldn't Make Spice Nuts," copyright © 1975 by CBS Radio, a division of CBS, Inc.

The William Collins & World Publishing Co., Inc., for "The Animal Parade," adapted from *Rainbow Book of Nature* by Donald Culross Peattie, copyright © 1957 by Donald Culross Peattie.

Coward, McCann & Geoghegan, Inc., for excerpt from *Amelia Earhart—First Lady of Flight* by Peggy Mann, copyright © 1970 by Peggy Mann.

Doubleday & Company, Inc., for "The Boy Who Wouldn't Talk," from *The Boy Who Wouldn't Talk* by Lois Kalb Bouchard, copyright © 1969 by Lois Kalb Bouchard. For "Periwinkle Jones," from *Periwinkle Jones* by Doris Estrada. Text copyright © 1965 by Doris Estrada. Illustrations copyright © 1965 by Jo Ann Stover.

Doubleday & Company, Inc., and Newspaper Enterprise Association, for "The Fun They Had," from *Earth Is Room Enough* by Isaac Asimov.

Doubleday & Company, Inc., Hughes Massie, Ltd., and Paul Gallico, for "The Day Jean-Pierre Went Round the World," adapted from *The Day Jean-Pierre Went Round the World* by Paul Gallico, copyright © 1965 by Paul Gallico.

Field Enterprises Educational Corporation, for adaptation of excerpt on "Spider" from *The World Book Encyclopedia,* copyright © 1975 by Field Enterprises Educational Corporation.

Follett Publishing Company and Chatto, Boyd & Oliver, for *The Story of Lengthwise,* copyright © 1967 by Ernestine Cobern Beyer, published in Great Britain 1969 by Chatto, Boyd & Oliver.

Harcourt Brace Jovanovich, Inc., for "Anansi's Hat-Shaking Dance," from *The Hat-Shaking Dance and Other Tales from the Gold Coast* by Harold Courlander and Albert Kofi Prempeh, copyright © 1957 by Harold Courlander. For "Little Girl, Be Careful What You Say," from *Complete Poems,* copyright 1950 by Carl Sandburg. For "How To Build An Ant Village," from *Science In Your Own Back Yard* by Elizabeth Cooper, copyright © 1958, 1970. Reprinted with some changes.

Harcourt Brace Jovanovich, Inc., and Curtis Brown, Ltd., for "Haiku" by Shiki and Soin, from *Cricket Songs: Japanese Haiku,* translated and copyrighted © 1964 by Harry Behn.

# Art Credits:

Joseph Phelan, pages 458–464
James Barkley, pages 471–486
George Solonevich, page 487
Career Graphics by Sven Lindman

Cover and Unit Opener designs by Pellegrini, Kaestle & Gross, Inc.

Cover photography by Dick Frank

# Photo Credits:

# Table of Contents

UNIT 2
# THE GIFT OF LANGUAGE

UNIT 3
# THE WONDER OF LIFE

UNIT 4
# A DIFFERENT DRUMMER

UNIT 5
# A WORLD OF WONDERS

## UNIT 6
## TO CATCH THE HIGH WINDS

# Books Fall Open

Books fall open,
you fall in,
delighted where
you've never been;
hear voices not once
heard before,
reach world on world
through door on door;
find unexpected
keys to things
locked up beyond
imaginings. . . .
True books will venture,
dare you out,
whisper secrets
maybe shout
across the gloom
to you in need,
who hanker for
a book to read.

*David McCord*

# Books Will Venture

# The Magnificent Brain Concocts a Recipe

CLIFFORD B. HICKS

### All Flibbertyneedled

It had all started on a rainy, blustery day in March. They were alone in the house because Mrs. Fernald, Alvin's mother, was at a club meeting.

Daphne, Alvin's sister, was there—and Shoie, his best friend. Shoie was half a head taller than Alvin, although they were almost the same age. Around Roosevelt School he was known as the Great Athlete. He could run faster, stand on his head longer, and throw a baseball farther than any other kid. His real name was Wilfred Shoemaker, but early in life he'd been nicknamed Shoie.

Daphne was eight years old. She worshiped her big brother Alvin, and constantly showed it. She was always trying to do everything that Alvin and Shoie did. Although Alvin would never admit it, he admired his little sister's determination. His father called it "spunk." And Daphne's spunk had often come to Alvin's rescue when he landed in a scrape.

The kids sat in the living room arguing about whether Miss Hootens, who taught third grade, wore a wig, whether Shoie was a good enough ballplayer to make the major leagues, and whether, if you were trapped in a falling elevator, you should jump up and grab the light fixture.

Alvin was growing tired of the arguments. He was, as he put it, all *flibbertyneedled* inside from the long winter and the bad weather. Alvin often made up words to describe how he felt, and today *flibbertyneedled* seemed to fit just right.

He had picked up one of his mother's magazines and was turning the pages when his eye suddenly stopped at an advertisement that announced, "You can win any one of a thousand valuable prizes." He was reading the rules of the contest when Shoie glanced at him. Alvin's face was scrunched into a frown, and his eyes were glazed. It was a sure sign the Magnificent Brain was working.

"What's up?" asked Shoie, who was immediately interested.

Alvin didn't even hear him. Shoie went over and bonked him lightly on top of the head, which he knew was the only way to unplug the Magnificent Brain. Alvin's Magnificent Brain was a separate part of his mind over which he had no control. When it took over, his eyes glazed and no one could get through to him. Shoie had named it the Magnificent Brain because the phrase seemed to describe some huge computer, always flashing with new thoughts.

"What's up, Alvin?"

Alvin stood up and shook his head to clear the circuits. "We're going to win a contest. It says here that we can win any one of a thousand valuable prizes for inventing a new candy."

"Inventing a new candy," repeated Daphne. She had a habit of repeating the last few words anyone said, and a conversation with Daphne always sounded like there was an echo in the room. "We ought to put chocolate in it."

"And cinnamon," said Shoie. "Cinnamon has a good flavor."

There was a pause as they thought it over. Then they all headed for the kitchen at once.

## Globbledy Gook

"Who's running the contest?" asked Daphne, as she got out a big pan.

"The Kitchenmate Appliance Company," replied Alvin. "They make all kinds of ranges and refrigerators and stuff. Where's the sugar?"

"It's inside the bowl over there, but you need a little butter first," Daphne said. Alvin started taking things out of the refrigerator. He brought Daphne the butter. She put a little butter in the pan and turned on the burner. "Now put in some milk and sugar, Alvin."

Alvin dumped in enough sugar to cover the bottom of the pan about an inch deep. He poured in a little milk.

Meanwhile Shoie had found the baking chocolate, and now he stood halfway across the room, flipping in the squares one by one as though he were tossing free throws on a basketball court.

Alvin went through the kitchen cabinets.

"Corn syrup," decided Daphne. "And a little brown sugar."

"And cinnamon," repeated Shoie.

They dumped in these ingredients, paying no attention to the amounts.

"Sometimes they put cereal in candy," suggested Shoie. He imitated the voice of the TV announcer. " 'I eat Good Omens because they start off my day with a smile on my lips and a song in my heart.' "

A cup of Good Omens disappeared into the pan, followed by half a dozen marshmallows.

Alvin found an envelope half full of powder to make grape-flavored frozen suckers and tossed it to Shoie, who dumped it all in. Alvin had come across a small bottle of orange-colored liquid. "Tabasco," he read off the label. "Anybody know what it is?"

The other kids, searching for possible ingredients, were too busy to answer, so Alvin shook some of the colored liquid into the pot, which by now began to bubble. He turned down the burner, and then he shook in a few more drops of the liquid.

"It's getting kind of *globbledy*," he reported to the others. "Maybe we ought to add some water or something."

Daphne had been exploring the refrigerator. Now she came up with half a glass of lemonade which she had stored in there the week before. She dumped it into the pot instead of water. "Just to give it a little better flavor," she said.

"Cinnamon," said Shoie. "More cinnamon." Alvin shook the rest of the can of cinnamon into the pot. And for good measure he added something called allspice that he'd found in the cabinet.

Looking into the slowly bubbling pot, Daphne shook her head. "It's got kind of an awful purplish color, Alvin. There's some food coloring on the shelf over there. Let's see if we can make it look better."

First she tried red, but that seemed to work badly with the purple powder, turning the candy a sickening violet. Yellow helped a little but not much.

"This stuff labeled 'Tabasco' is bright orange," said Alvin. "Maybe if we used a little more of it—" Again he shook the bottle into the pot. It didn't seem to help much. He tried adding some green food coloring. The purplish mess turned to a rather odd brown.

"How long do you suppose we ought to cook it?" Shoie asked Daphne, who was slowly stirring the bubbling contents of the pot with a wooden spoon.

"Soft-ball stage," she said. It was clear to Alvin and Shoie that she didn't know what soft-ball stage was, but it sounded good. The three kids stood around the pot watching the mess thicken.

Daphne lifted the spoon out and let a clump of the candy drop into the pot. Suddenly, as though the wooden spoon were a magic wand, the candy stopped bubbling and turned solid before their eyes. At the same moment a horrible burning smell rolled up from the pot.

"Quick, turn off the burner!" shouted Alvin. Daphne dropped the spoon back into the pot and turned off the heat. "Now we've got to beat it," she announced brightly, "like Mom beats the fudge."

"What do you beat it for?" asked Alvin.

"To make it smooth."

"Here," said Alvin, taking charge. "Let me do it."

When he grabbed the spoon, he found that it was stuck. He pulled harder, with no success. Finally, Shoie stood on the pan while Alvin tugged upward on the spoon. There was a sudden pop, and the candy, with the spoon still stuck in it, went sailing up toward the ceiling, flew across the room, and plopped down on one of the kitchen stools.

Alvin looked at it for a long moment, then walked over and picked up the spoon. The entire stool came off the floor.

"That's the worst mess I ever saw," said Shoie. "But we ought to taste it." He got a sharp knife from a drawer, managed to saw off a piece, and popped it into his mouth.

"Arrrrrrgh! Arrrrrrrgh!" He ran for the sink and swallowed a full glass of water without stopping. "That stuff," he gasped, "is living fire!"

"Let me try some," said Daphne.

Alvin sawed off a piece for her, and she slipped it into her mouth. Trying to show off in front of the boys, she didn't run for the sink, but big tears appeared in her eyes, and she snorted in great gasps of air.

By now the sticky mess had settled a bit across the seat of the stool. Alvin knew the other two would call him chicken for weeks if he didn't try a piece himself, so he sawed off a glob, took a deep breath, put the piece in his mouth, and bit down hard.

The trouble was, as he said later, the stuff not only was burning hot, but stuck his teeth together. He stood there making choking sounds deep in his throat as he tried to pry his jaws apart. Meanwhile Daphne was hopping around on one foot with tears streaming down her face, and Shoie was fanning his open mouth with both hands.

It was at that moment that Mom walked into the kitchen.

### Fernald's Fireballs

After they'd cleaned up the mess as well as they could, Shoie was sent home, and Alvin and Daphne were sent to their rooms to "think about"

ruining the kitchen stool. Alvin went to his desk, took out a pencil, and sat there staring at the contest entry form he'd taken to the room with him. He had to admit it wasn't very good candy, but maybe somebody would like it. He began filling in the form.

"Name of Candy" was the first line. Alvin sat thinking for a long time. Finally he licked the tip of the pencil and carefully printed "Fernald's Fireballs."

The next line said: "Ingredients." Here he was lost. He couldn't possibly remember everything they'd put in. He wrote down a few of the ingredients, and after each of them he wrote "one cup" or "three teaspoons" or "two pinches, to taste," which was a phrase he'd picked up from one of his mother's cookbooks. He couldn't remember the name of the orange stuff in the strange little bottle, so he left that out.

Finally, under "Cooking Instructions," he wrote: "Let simmer over low heat to soft-ball stage, stirring constantly. Then put the pan in cold water and beat it—I mean the candy, not the pan. Can be rolled into balls or wrapped around ice cream sticks." He thought for a moment, then smiled to himself and added a final line, "Either way, it has a very unusual taste."

He placed the entry form in an envelope, sealed it, and waited for Dad to come home. He knew he was in for a lecture about that stool.

2 cups

1 cup

Marshmallow

4 tablespoons

3 teaspoons

a pinch.

Two months later, when he'd forgotten all about the contest, the letter came announcing that he'd won a prize. He stood there in the hallway with Shoie and Daphne, hardly believing what he'd read.

"Do you suppose they *really* liked that awful stuff?" he asked in a low voice.

"I can't believe it!" said Shoie.

"Can't believe it," said Daphne.

"Did you write down everything we put in?" asked Shoie.

Alvin tried to remember. "No. No, I couldn't remember it all. And besides I had to guess at the amounts." Suddenly everything clicked into place. "That's it!" he said. "I couldn't remember everything, so I must have invented a new candy right out of my head—"

"The Magnificent Brain did it again!" shouted Shoie.

"—and won a prize!" finished Alvin.

"Won a prize!" echoed Daphne.

### Reflections

1. What other name might you give for the separate part of Alvin's mind called the Magnificent Brain?
2. Have you ever felt "flibbertyneedled"? What was the feeling like, and how did you get over it? How did Alvin get over it?
3. Where was Alvin's mother? Why is that fact important to the story?
4. Does the color of food make you like it or dislike it? Give examples. How do you form an opinion about food before you taste it?
5. What name would you have given the horrible candy?
6. Why did Alvin smile as he added the final line to his recipe: "Either way, it has a very unusual taste"?

# Sarah Cynthia Sylvia Stout

SHEL SILVERSTEIN

Sarah Cynthia Sylvia Stout
would not take the garbage out!
She'd boil the water
and open the cans
and scrub the pots
and scour the pans
and grate the cheese
and shell the peas
and mash the yams
and spice the hams
and make the jams.
But though her daddy
would scream and shout,
she would not take the garbage out.
And so it piled up to the ceilings:
Coffee grounds, potato peelings,
stale bread and withered greens,
olive pits and soggy beans,
cracker boxes, chicken bones,
clamshells, eggshells, stale scones,
sour cream and soggy plums,
stale cake and cookie crumbs.

At last the garbage piled so high
that finally it reached the sky.
And none of her friends
would come to play.
And all the neighbors moved away.
And finally Sarah Cynthia Stout
said, "I'll take the garbage out!"
But then, of course, it was too late.
The garbage reached beyond the state,
from Memphis to the Golden Gate.
And Sarah met an awful fate,
which I cannot right now relate
because the hour is much too late.
But, children, think of Sarah Stout
and always take the garbage out!

# Periwinkle Jones

DORIS ESTRADA

The two boys rocked lazily in the porch swing, occasionally giving a push with their feet to keep going.

"I reckon this is the dullest place in the world," Oscar said with a big yawn.

"Yep. I reckon it is," Sam agreed.

"Why, there's my cousin Periwinkle Jones out in California," said Oscar. "You should hear the exciting things that happen where she lives. Earthquakes at least once a month. One last month shook down a forty-story building. Missed her by inches. One before that opened up a crack twenty feet deep right in her back yard. She filled it with water and stocked it with fish. Only trouble now is the poachers sneaking in at night."

"Little dangerous out there, I'd say."

"But challenging."

"Yup. Challenging. Never gets dull like this."

Mr. and Mrs. Jarvis came out on the porch. "You'd better be thinking about how to entertain Periwinkle when she comes here next week," said Mrs. Jarvis.

Mr. Jarvis chuckled. "Well, judging from the letters she writes, I don't think we'll have to worry much about how to entertain Cousin Periwinkle."

"I do." Oscar kicked the floor peevishly. "After the exciting life she lives out there in California, she won't be able to stand it here for a week," he said.

"Nothing to do," Sam agreed.

"Sure," Oscar said. "Dullest old place on earth."

## Cousin Periwinkle Arrives

It was a hot, drowsy afternoon. Periwinkle had arrived the night before. Oscar and she were resting on the front lawn and drinking lemonade.

"Oscar, what kind of boards are holding up that plant?" asked Periwinkle. She pointed to a corner of the yard where honeysuckle grew six feet tall, and spread itself almost thickly enough to hide whatever was under it.

"They're the framework of an old well," he answered. "My great-grandparents had it dug when they were first married. When they quit using it, they let the honeysuckle take over."

"I wonder if the water is any good after all these years."

"No one knows. The well has been closed such a long time. Once it was fine for drinking, though. I've heard that back in those days lots of people came off the road to get water here. At first they stopped in wagons and buggies. Later they started coming along in the old-time cars. Those cars would heat up something awful! They'd pull over to the side with their radiators asteaming, and the driver would ask for some water. During the First World War, a train loaded with soldiers broke down on the tracks across the way. The soldiers came over here to rest and get drinks."

Periwinkle's voice was filled with awe. "You know, Oscar, this farm is simply seething with history!"

Oscar was speechless with pride. After a long sigh, he found his voice. "Yes, I guess it is. Why, even bands of gypsies stopped and got water from that well. One time a gypsy woman told my grandmother's fortune—free."

"What did she say?"

"She said that a treasure was buried in these fields."

"Did anyone ever find it?"

"We-ll," he drawled, "Grandma said she supposed that if a person worked the soil especially hard and was lucky enough to have good crops, the crops would be the treasure. Funny thing though—"

"What?"

"The night after the gypsy told the fortune, the folks saw a light in the field. When they went there the next morning, they found that someone had been diggin'. Whoever it was must have left before he found anything, because the hole was shallow."

### Digging for Treasure

That night, the sound of tapping woke Oscar from a deep sleep.

"Sssssst," a voice whispered.

He got out of bed and went to the window. Periwinkle was standing outside with her index finger in a shush position across her lips.

"Ssshhhh. Oscar, don't make a sound, but come out here. There's a light down in the east field." . . .

"You're joking."

"No, I'm not. I've been sitting in a tree watching it. I'll bet someone is digging for the treasure."

Oscar slipped out the window and climbed the tree with his cousin. Far off in the east field, a light was jerking back and forth.

"We'd better go there before he gets away," Periwinkle said.

They climbed out of the tree and tiptoed across the yard and down the trail leading past the chicken coops. After creeping softly down a ditch toward the light, they turned into a grove of trees and hid behind some bushes.

"Look. There are two men, and they're digging with shovels. What did I tell you!" Periwinkle said, nudging Oscar. "They're after that treasure, all right. Maybe they've discovered the exact spot where it is. We have to get them away from here before they find it."

"How?"

"Let me think." She watched the diggers closely as she tried to plan some way to make them leave. "Oh, I know. A wolf would scare them away."

"But we don't have a wolf. If we did, it would scare me away, too."

"Not a real one. Listen, Oscar. I'm good at animal calls. I'm going to give a hair-raising wolf howl that will send those men flying out of here about three feet off the ground."

One man sank a shovel into the earth with a push of his foot. At that moment, Periwinkle tipped back her head, opened her mouth toward the sky, and sent a wild wolf call into the night. The man's hand fell from the shovel.

"What was that?" he asked gruffly.

"I don't know," the other one answered. "It came from over there."

Both looked curiously at the wooded area fringing the edge of the field. They walked slowly toward it. Leaning over and staring at the ground, they began to part the undergrowth and search it. One man stood erect and faced the bushes and trees near the lane. Then he went straight to the spot where Periwinkle and Oscar were hiding.

He heard a rustling movement back in the brush, but unseen by him were two children who went flying through the trees and down the lane about three feet off the ground.

Turning to the other man who had joined him, he asked, "Did you find anything over there?"

"Nothing at all. That was a strange kind of yowl. Sounded like a little lost calf."

"Maybe Mr. Jarvis can find it in the morning when he comes to weed."

"I guess. Well, if we're going to go fishing before daylight we'd better dig some more worms."

### Pirates

Sunshine was dazzling the next morning when Periwinkle discovered pirate tracks down by the creek.

"Those were pirates we saw in the field last night," Periwinkle informed the boys. "They've had word of that treasure, you can be sure. News like that gets around."

Sam spoke in a tone of complete bewilderment. "I tell you, pirates are the last things I ever expected to turn up around here."

"Once upon a time they operated out of New Orleans, but too many people there are on the lookout for them now," she said. "They've had to change ports. This is an ideal place. No one is looking for pirates in Oklahoma."

"Where do you suppose those pirates are, Periwinkle?" asked Sam.

"There's no telling," she answered.

"This creek goes on and on," Oscar said. "It goes all the way to Infinity Hole, right smack against the side of a mountain. At that spot, it's so deep that no one has ever touched the bottom."

"The creek ends against the side of a mountain?" asked Periwinkle.

"Mmm hmmm."

"That's where the pirates are!" she exclaimed excitedly. "The creek only appears to end there. Actually it goes into the mountain, which is partly hollow. Inside, the whole bottom is filled with water."

"If they knew about the hole, they'd be a scared bunch," Oscar said. "Being strangers around here, they probably don't realize how dangerous it is."

Periwinkle took a stick and began drawing a picture of a mountain on the ground. In front of it she drew wavy, circular lines to represent water. "They're in greater danger than you know. Infinity Hole is deep because that mountain is sinking. Every time it settles a little, it pushes down all the ground around it and shoves the bottom of the stream farther into the earth."

"What will the pirates do if the mountain goes completely beneath the water?"

"Before it goes under, they'll have to cut a hole in the top and sail out."

"Wonder how long it will take to finish sinking?"

"Years. Until then, they have the best hiding place in the world. No wonder they haven't been discovered before."

"When do you suppose they'll come out again?" asked Sam.

"Oh, they'll be petrified after last night and won't do anything for a while," answered Periwinkle. "But you can be certain that after they lay low for a week or two, they'll come roaring out of the side of that mountain and make another try for the treasure."

Periwinkle snapped her fingers in disappointment. "Worse luck! I'll be back home by then."

Beckoning the boys to come closer, she lowered her voice and looked intently into their eyes. "Oscar Jarvis and Sam Hopper, I want you to promise me to keep your eyes open for pirate tracks. Watch for a disguised pirate to come into the store for supplies."

"How will we recognize him?" Sam asked.

"By a severe squint in one eye. They usually wear a black patch on one side of the face. When they take it off, the eye on that side squints because it isn't used to the light."

Sam squared his shoulders bravely. "We'll look straight into the eyes of everyone who comes into that store."

"Also, boys, you must watch for anyone who tries to pass a gold doubloon in his change. Take turns stalking him like a lynx night and day. If he does any digging, don't let him out of your sight. It may be years before he locates the treasure."

A flash of lightning tore at the sky, and thunder crashed around their ears. After the sound had died away, they heard Oscar's mother calling.

"We'd better go see what she wants," he said.

. . .

Several days later, the two boys swung lazily in the porch swing, occasionally giving a push with their feet to keep going.

"I suppose Periwinkle is back in California by now," said Oscar.

"Most likely," agreed Sam.

"As for me, I guess I'll spend the rest of my life on some little old farm around here."

"Me too. Pretty exciting place to live."

"Yep. History all around us."

"Mighty interesting place to be."

"Most interesting place in the world."

### Reflections

1. Why was Oscar worried about entertaining his cousin, Periwinkle Jones?
2. What did Mr. Jarvis mean when he said, "I don't think we'll have to worry much about how to entertain Cousin Periwinkle"? Was he right?
3. Did Periwinkle's visit change the boys' idea about living on a farm? How?
4. What new and exciting adventures might Periwinkle write about in her next letter to Oscar? How might Oscar answer her letter?
5. Would you like to have Periwinkle as a cousin? What problems might it cause?

# Little Girl,
# Be Careful What You Say

CARL SANDBURG

Little girl, be careful what you say
when you make talk with words, words—
for words are made of syllables
and syllables, child, are made of air—
and air is so thin—air is the breath of God—
air is finer than fire or mist,
finer than water or moonlight,
finer than spider-webs in the moon,
finer than water-flowers in the morning:
    and words are strong, too,
    stronger than rocks or steel
stronger than potatoes, corn, fish, cattle,
and soft, too, soft as little pigeon-eggs,
soft as the music of hummingbird wings.
    So, little girl, when you speak greetings,
when you tell jokes, make wishes or prayers,
    be careful, be careless, be careful,
    be what you wish to be.

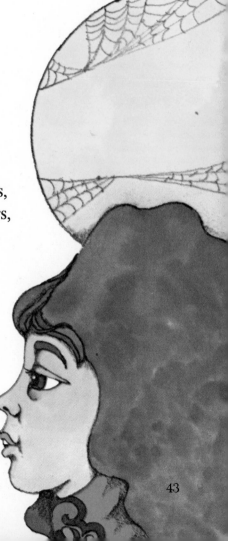

# The Boy Who Changed His Mind

NELLIE BURCHARDT

### *That Awful Reggie Thompson*

The three o'clock bell clanged inside the school on First Avenue. Almost at once the boys of Mrs. Sullivan's fourth grade, which was nearest the door, burst out onto the sidewalk. As usual, Reggie Thompson was in the lead. He blinked and shaded his eyes with his hand as he came out into the June sunlight.

"Hey, Reggie," yelled a boy behind him. Reggie turned his head just in time to be hit in the face with a baseball cap.

"I'll get you for that, Joey," he yelled.

He snatched the cap from the ground and flung it back at Joey. Joey ducked when he saw it coming, and the cap hit a girl behind him.

"It's that awful Reggie Thompson," said one of the girls.

"He's the worst pest in the whole school," another added.

The boys tore off at top speed along the crowded sidewalk.

In the next block they slowed down. They started to take a shortcut through the playground.

Beyond the playground was Reggie's building, and there the housing project trees began—the only trees within blocks. In one of them was a nestful of blue jay fledglings. Two of them had just pulled themselves up to the edge of the nest, where they teetered and clutched the rim with their still-weak claws. They stretched their half-grown wings. It would still be some time before they were strong enough to fly.

"I'll bet I can hit that no-good old blue jay there," said Reggie. As no stone was handy, he picked up a crushed tin can lying beside a wastebasket and threw it at the birds.

"Missed," shrieked Joey. "Is your aim rotten today!"

One baby jay fluttered unsteadily back into the nest. The other one flapped its wings wildly, then lost its balance, and fell to the ground.

Several girls were walking behind them. "It's a baby bird," one cried.

"Ha!" said Reggie. "I did not miss. I got him, all right, all right." The bird lay on the ground, its eyes closed. "I got him. I got him," bragged Reggie. He did a dance around the trunk of the tree.

"Reggie Thompson, you're the meanest boy in the whole school," said Diane, one of the girls.

He stopped prancing around the tree. "I sure am," he said, grinning proudly. "And I've got the best aim in the whole school, too," he boasted.

"Is the bird dead?" asked Diane.

Reggie shrugged. "I guess so," he said.

"Why don't you find out?" asked Diane.

Reggie looked at her. "How?" he asked.

"Why don't you pick it up?"

Reggie didn't move. He had never touched anything dead before.

"You're scared to touch it," said Diane.

"I am not."

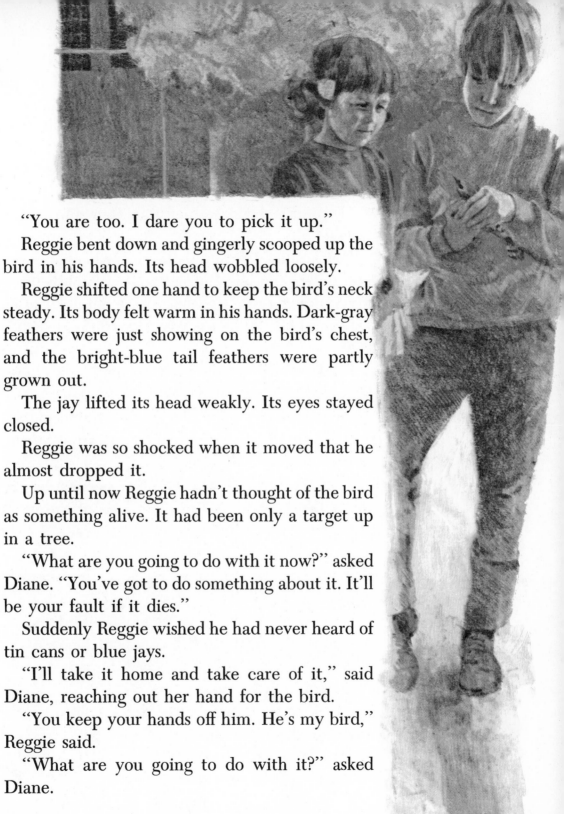

"You are too. I dare you to pick it up."

Reggie bent down and gingerly scooped up the bird in his hands. Its head wobbled loosely.

Reggie shifted one hand to keep the bird's neck steady. Its body felt warm in his hands. Dark-gray feathers were just showing on the bird's chest, and the bright-blue tail feathers were partly grown out.

The jay lifted its head weakly. Its eyes stayed closed.

Reggie was so shocked when it moved that he almost dropped it.

Up until now Reggie hadn't thought of the bird as something alive. It had been only a target up in a tree.

"What are you going to do with it now?" asked Diane. "You've got to do something about it. It'll be your fault if it dies."

Suddenly Reggie wished he had never heard of tin cans or blue jays.

"I'll take it home and take care of it," said Diane, reaching out her hand for the bird.

"You keep your hands off him. He's my bird," Reggie said.

"What are you going to do with it?" asked Diane.

"Mind your own business," said Reggie. He turned and went up the walk toward his own building. He felt the bird stir inside his shirt. Now why on earth had he taken the bird, and what was he going to do with it? He really didn't know.

### Nice for a Change

The next day the children in Reggie's class were talking about his blue jay. It wasn't surprising that Mrs. Sullivan, Reggie's teacher, heard them.

"So you have a blue jay, Reginald," she said. "How interesting! Where did you get it?"

"I—I found him. He fell out of his nest in one of the trees on the project," said Reggie, shifting from one foot to the other.

"Blue jays aren't very common around here," said Mrs. Sullivan. "They must have flown over from the park. What did you name your bird, Reginald?"

"Charley."

"And how old is he?"

"I'm not sure. But I know he can't fly yet. All he does is flap his wings."

"And what does your bird eat?" asked Mrs. Sullivan.

"Caterpillars and stuff like that."

Then Reggie listened in amazement as Mrs. Sullivan said, "I do hope you'll bring Charley to school. Few of us have seen a baby blue jay."

She smiled at him as he sat down. Reggie couldn't remember when a teacher had last smiled at him. Bringing Charley in to school might even help on his report card, he thought, and he sure could use a little help.

That afternoon Reggie and Joey asked Mr. Santino, Reggie's neighbor, to help them build a cage for Charley. Mr. Santino had been a carpenter, but since he spent most of his time at home now, he was happy to help the boys.

In a week they had finished the cage, and Reggie took Charley to school in it. The whole class crowded around to see him, and he was a big hit.

"Can I hold him?" almost everyone asked.

"Let me pat him," said Diane.

Finally Mrs. Sullivan had to tell Reggie to set Charley's cage on the ledge at the back of the room so that the class could get some work done.

When Reggie got home that afternoon, he was feeling very happy. He went straight to his room and took Charley out of his cage. As he held him, Reggie noticed something was different about Charley. He was beginning to look just like the adult jays Reggie saw now and then outside. Only the smoky dark feathers on his face and throat and his lighter-colored beak marked Charley as a young bird. Reggie supposed he'd have to let him go soon. The only question was, would Charley know how to feed himself? Up until now he would not eat unless Reggie fed him.

All at once, the jays in the tree outside started shrieking. Both Reggie and Charley looked up at the open window. When Charley heard "Ja-ay!" from outside the window, he went wild. Sometime, long ago, that sound had meant something to him. Angrily he struck out at the hands that held him, and all at once the hands were gone. Charley hurled himself through the open window and toward the screeching "Ja-ay!" He beat his full-grown wings wildly, suddenly found his balance in the air, and was flying.

"Charley!" shrieked Reggie. "Come back here!" But he could do nothing but watch helplessly as Charley flew toward the tree where the other jays were calling. The leaves hid him as he landed somewhere among the lower branches. As long as there was any daylight left, Reggie kept watching the tree, but he saw nothing. Finally, when it grew dark, Reggie went to bed. Charley was gone.

### All the Pets in the World

The next day was Saturday, and Reggie got up very early. He left some bread crumbs on the windowsill, just in case Charley did come back, and then he went outside to the playground. It was empty, and Reggie walked slowly in the direction of some cement barrels that were placed on their sides and painted with bright colors. When he was smaller, he used to crawl inside one of them to hide. He crawled inside one now.

After a while he saw a small black and white dog trotting along, sniffing at each barrel. When he got to Reggie's barrel, he began wagging his tail so hard, it almost knocked Reggie over.

"Go on! Go on home!" Reggie said. The dog gave a little bark, as if to say, "You can't fool me. I know you're only joking."

"I said, go on home! Go on! Get out of here!" shouted Reggie. He picked up a pebble and pretended to throw it at the dog. The dog walked

away slowly. Reggie put the pebble down. The dog looked so unhappy. "He's a nice little mutt," Reggie told himself. "And anyway, even if Charley is gone, it isn't the dog's fault."

"Hey!" called Reggie. "Come on back! Here, boy! Come on, boy! Good boy!"

The dog came back with joyful leaps and flung himself into the barrel and onto Reggie. Reggie covered up his face with his arms as the dog tried to lick it all over. He rubbed the dog's ears for a while. Then he said, "You'd better go now." He gave the dog a little pat, and it ran off.

Reggie started back home and met Joey on the way. He told him about Charley, and then, without saying another word, the two boys walked slowly back to Reggie's house.

In Reggie's room they went straight to the window to see if any of the food Reggie had left for Charley was gone.

"One bread crumb is gone!" Reggie cried. "Do you suppose Charley ate it?" He leaned out the window. "Charley!" he called. "Come, Charley!"

There was a great squawking in the tree. Suddenly two blue jays burst out of the thick leaves. One of the birds headed for Reggie's window.

"Charley? Charley?" called Reggie. He held out his hand as he used to for Charley to make a landing. The bird flew almost to Reggie's window, then turned and started back toward the tree. "Charley, come back!" called Reggie.

The bird circled again and started back towards
Reggie's window. "It *is* Charley! It is!" Reggie
cried. "Did you see how he turned back when
I called his name? Come on, Charley!"

The blue jay landed on Reggie's hand, teetering
only a moment to get his balance. Then he
opened his beak wide and gave his baby cry for
food. Reggie's heart sank. Hadn't Charley learned
to feed himself yet? Reggie picked up the bread
crumb from the windowsill and held it a few
inches away from Charley's beak.

"Peep—peep—peep!" cried Charley, opening
his beak even wider and begging to be fed.

"No, you great big spoiled baby!" said Reggie. "I'm not going to give it to you. You'll have to get it for yourself this time. You have to grow up sometime."

Charley stopped peeping and cocked his head on one side to look at the crumb. Then he turned his head to the other side to get a look from that eye. Suddenly the crest on top of his head shot up, and he squawked angrily. Then, faster than Reggie's eye could follow, Charley struck out and grabbed the crumb with his beak.

"You did it! You did it!" cried Reggie. "Good boy, Charley!"

When the crumb was gone, Charley looked up at Reggie for more.

"That's all," said Reggie. Charley looked at him with his head on one side. Suddenly a Japanese beetle flew past the window. Charley's head shot out, and the beetle was in his beak. Then the beetle disappeared down his throat.

"That's the boy, Charley!"said Reggie. "Now you've got the idea!"

"Ja-ay! Ja-ay!" came a call from the tree. Charley turned his head in the direction of the sound.

"Ja-ay! Ja-ay!" he answered. He took off and headed straight for the tree.

Reggie watched Charley as he went. He sighed. Charley had been a lot of trouble to feed, but he'd miss him. He remembered that first day, when he had thought Charley was going to die. He had thought then that if only he could save Charley, he would be a doctor when he grew up. Maybe he'd do better than that—maybe he'd be an animal doctor. Then, in a way, all the pets in the whole world would be his. All the dogs and cats and horses and parakeets. And, of course, there'd be all the no-good birds he could find.

### Reflections

1. At the beginning Reggie is called "the meanest boy in school." Do you think this is a good description of him? Why or why not?
2. Why do you think he was proud to be called this?
3. How did Mrs. Sullivan treat Reggie after she learned about the blue jay? How had she been treating him before that?
4. Why do you think Reggie acted toward the little dog the way he did?
5. How did Reggie feel when he discovered Charley could feed himself? Why did he feel that way?
6. Do you think that Reggie would make a good veterinarian (animal doctor) when he grows up? Why or why not?
7. Reread the title of this story. What did Reggie change his mind about?

# The Quarrel

ELEANOR FARJEON

I quarreled with my brother,
I don't know what about,
One thing led to another
And somehow we fell out.
The start of it was slight,
The end of it was strong,
He said he was right,
I knew he was wrong!

56

We hated one another.
The afternoon turned black.
Then suddenly my brother
Thumped me on the back,
And said, "Oh, *come* along!
We can't go on all night—
*I* was in the wrong."
So he was in the right.

# The Fun They Had

ISAAC ASIMOV

Margie even wrote about it that night in her diary. On the page headed May 17, 2157, she wrote, "Today Tommy found a real book!"

It was a very old book. Margie's grandfather once said that when he was a little boy, *his* grandfather told him that there was a time when all stories were printed on paper.

They turned the pages, which were yellow and crinkly, and it was awfully funny to read words that stood still instead of moving the way they were supposed to—on a screen, you know. And then, when they turned back to the page before, it had the same words on it that it had had when they read it the first time.

"Gee," said Tommy, "what a waste. When you're through with the book, you just throw it away, I guess. Our television screen must have had a million books on it, and it's good for plenty more. I wouldn't throw the screen away."

"Same with mine," said Margie. She was eleven and hadn't seen as many telebooks as Tommy had. He was thirteen.

She said, "Where did you find it?"

"In my house." He pointed without looking, because he was busy reading. "In the attic."

"What's it about?"

"School."

Margie was scornful. "School? What's there to write about school? I hate school."

Margie always hated school, but now she hated it more than ever. The mechanical teacher had been giving her test after test in geography. She had been doing worse and worse until finally her mother had sent for the County Inspector.

He was a round little man with a red face and a whole box of tools with dials and wires. He smiled at Margie and gave her an apple, then took the teacher apart. Margie had hoped he wouldn't know how to put it together again, but he knew how all right. After an hour or so, there it was again, large and gray and ugly, with a big screen on which all the lessons were shown and the questions were asked. That wasn't so bad. The part Margie hated most was the slot where she

was to put homework and test papers. She always had to write them out in a punch code, which she had learned when she was six years old. The mechanical teacher calculated her mark in no time.

The Inspector had smiled after he was finished and patted Margie's head. He said to her mother, "It's not the little girl's fault, Mrs. Jones. I think the geography sector was geared a little too quick. Those things happen sometimes. I've slowed it up to an average ten-year level. Actually, her progress is quite satisfactory." And he patted Margie's head again.

Margie was disappointed. She had been hoping that they would take the teacher away altogether. They had once taken Tommy's teacher away for nearly a month because the history sector had blanked out completely.

So she said to Tommy, "Why would anyone write about school?"

Tommy looked at her with very superior eyes. "Because it's not our kind of school. This is the old kind of school that they had hundreds and hundreds of years ago." He added, proudly pronouncing the word, "*Centuries* ago."

Margie was hurt. "Well, I don't know what kind of school they had all that time ago." She read the book over his shoulder for a while, then said, "Anyway, they had a teacher."

"Sure they had a teacher, but it wasn't a *regular* teacher. It was a man."

"A man? How could a man be a teacher?"

"Well, he just told the boys and girls things and gave them homework and also asked them questions."

"A man isn't smart enough."

"Sure he is. My father knows as much as my teacher."

"He can't. A man can't know as much as a teacher."

"He knows almost as much, I betcha."

Margie wasn't prepared to dispute that. She said, "I wouldn't want a strange man in my house to teach me."

Tommy screamed with laughter. "You don't know much, Margie. The teachers didn't live in the house. They had a special building, and all of the kids went there."

"And all the kids learned the same thing?"

"Sure, if they were the same age."

"But my mother says a teacher has to be adjusted to fit the mind of each boy and girl it teaches, and that each kid has to be taught differently."

"Just the same, they didn't do it that way then. If you don't like it, you don't have to read the book."

"I didn't say I didn't like it," Margie said quickly. She wanted to read about those funny schools.

They weren't even half finished when Margie's mother called, "Margie! School!"

Margie looked up. "Not yet, Mama."

"Now!" said Mrs. Jones. "And it's probably time for Tommy, too."

Margie said to Tommy, "May I read the book some more with you after school?"

"Maybe," he said. He walked away whistling, the dusty old book tucked beneath his arm.

Margie went into the schoolroom. It was right next to her bedroom, and the mechanical teacher was on and waiting for her. It was always on at the same time every day except Saturday and Sunday, because her mother said little girls learned better if they learned at regular hours.

The screen was lit up, and it said: "Today's arithmetic lesson is on the addition of fractions. Please insert yesterday's homework in the proper slot."

Margie did so with a sigh. She was thinking about the old schools they had when her grandfather's grandfather was a little boy. All the kids from the whole neighborhood came, laughing and shouting in the school yard, going home together at the end of the day. They learned the same things, so they could help one another on the homework and talk about it.

And the teachers were people....

The mechanical teacher was flashing on the screen: "When we add the fractions $\frac{1}{2}$ and $\frac{1}{4}$—"

Margie was thinking about how the kids must have loved it in the old days. She was thinking about the fun they had.

$$\frac{1}{2} + \frac{1}{4}$$

## Reflections

1. What did Tommy find, and why did it interest him so much?
2. Compare Margie's way of "going to school" with your own. Which way do you prefer? Tell why.
3. How did Margie "write" her homework?
4. How would you explain to Margie and Tommy what your school is like?
5. If you could create your own school, what would it be like?

# ? What Will They Be?

Do people ever ask you what you would like to be when you grow up? Do you wonder yourself? Maybe something you enjoy doing now will someday be part of your job.

What about the characters you have read about so far in this unit? Each one has different interests. Each one has different likes and dislikes. What kinds of work do you think each one might like to do?

*(top)* This man is a **veterinarian,** or animal doctor. He takes care of all kinds of animals. Here he is treating a seal that has been hurt. What kinds of things would a veterinarian need to learn in order to care for animals? Which story character do you think might want to do this kind of work? Why?

*(bottom)* Hunting for pirates might lead one character to become a **detective.** Part of her job is to hunt for lawbreakers. Why do you think a detective might not wear a uniform? Which character would be likely to want to be a detective?

(left) A **chef** might work for a hotel or restaurant, planning menus and cooking food. Other chefs may work with him. Perhaps he once "concocted" recipes. Perhaps he cooked so much food, he didn't know what to do with all the garbage.

(top right) This **scientist** is working in a laboratory where she conducts tests on air and water. Which character might one day work to help clean up pollution?

(bottom right) A **librarian** organizes a library and helps people pick out books to read. Might someone who lived in a time when books were no longer printed want to be a librarian?

# Miss Kirby's Room

JEAN HORTON BERG

## Red Handlebars

It was the last inning. The score was fifteen to fourteen in favor of Miss Kirby's room. Mrs. Otto's room was up at bat. They had one out, and the bases were loaded. Hank Yurchenko, the hardest hitter in Mrs. Otto's room, came up to the plate.

*Crack!* Hank slammed Nick's first pitch on the ground to Scott Boles, the third baseman. Scott scooped up the ball and fired it to Jamie, the catcher, in time to force the man at home plate. That was the second out.

Swinging around in a complete circle, and without seeming to take aim, Jamie let the ball fly. Like an arrow, it flew straight to the target and caught Hank by a half step at first. The game was over.

Miss Kirby's room went wild. They had won!

Susan was waiting for Jamie at the edge of the playground. They were going to walk home together as usual. "You really were great," Nick was saying to Jamie as the team came to the gate. "And don't forget," he said to Scott, "you made as many funny jokes as anybody when I picked Jamie to be our catcher."

"I know," Scott said, "but you've got to admit, it looks pretty funny to be the only baseball team in the whole school with a girl for a catcher!"

Jamie's face got red, and she ducked her head the funny way she always did when she felt embarrassed. But Susan could tell she was pleased with what the boys were saying. In fact, Jamie was very popular with the boys in school. But except for Susan, she didn't have any really close friends among the girls.

As Susan stopped to tie her shoelace, she thought to herself, "I don't know why I keep Jamie for my practically best friend. She doesn't act like the other girls. And it isn't just playing baseball. It's other things, like—well, like that rabbit's foot."

She looked up. The boys had run on ahead. Jamie was walking along slowly, waiting for her. Susan could see the back of Jamie's head. The red hair, parted unevenly, was pulled to either side and fastened in "handlebars," with a green rubber band on the right. Caught on the left handlebar by a little key chain was a white rabbit's foot. Jamie always wore it for luck. Susan could remember the time she had tried to get Jamie to take it off.

Jamie had answered her, "You wear a ribbon in your hair; I wear a rabbit's foot in mine. What's the difference?"

"There's a whole lot of difference, if you want to know so much!" Susan had yelled back. But the rabbit's foot had stayed.

She pulled the shoelace tight and got to her feet. "I don't know why I keep her for my practically best friend," she sighed and ran to catch up.

The next day, when the bell rang announcing the end of the lunch period, Susan had already started in from the playground.

"Come on, Pam; come on, Peggy," she called. "The sooner we get in, the sooner Miss Kirby will start to read *Treasure Island*." She ran lightly up the stairs to the room.

"Miss Kirby, are we going to—" Susan stopped short and drew back in confusion. Miss Kirby stood right inside the coatroom door, a frown on her usually gently smiling face. Beside her, fists scrubbing hard at his eyes, stood Nick.

Just then the last bell rang. When everyone was seated, Miss Kirby said, "Boys and girls, we have a problem to solve. Nick brought a dollar to school this morning, and now it's gone. Has anyone seen Nick's dollar?"

Everyone looked at everybody else.

"What is it, Tim? Have you seen Nick's money?" asked Miss Kirby.

"No ma'am," said Tim. "But maybe he only thought he brought it. Maybe he left it at home on his desk, like you forget your homework sometimes."

"No. I brought it with me. My mother gave it to me when I went out the door this morning. She wanted me to get some things for her at the store on my way home from school."

"Maybe it fell out of your pocket," said Scott.

"No, it didn't drop out of my pocket!" Nick was excited now. "It was right in my pocket till I got to school, and I put it in my cubbyhole as soon as I got in the room. I never touched it again, and I never saw it again."

"Maybe you stuck it so far back in your cubbyhole, you didn't see it when you looked," said Susan.

"I took every single thing out of that cubbyhole about a million times," Nick said. "It isn't there. It's gone. And what am I going to tell my mother?"

"Miss Kirby," said Jamie, "why don't we all look in our cubbyholes and see if Nick's money is in one of them? Maybe he made a mistake and put his money in the wrong one."

It seemed like a good idea. A lot of the boys and girls did find things they hadn't thought about in months. But no one found Nick's money.

Finally Susan said loudly, "If everyone doesn't hurry up and sit down, there won't be any time left for reading."

But even when everyone was seated, Miss Kirby only looked sadly around the room. "We won't have our reading today," she said. "We'll sit quietly in our seats and think. Whenever the person who took Nick's money decides to return it, we'll go back to reading *Treasure Island.*"

For twenty minutes the class sat still. Feet shuffled, throats were cleared, a pencil or two dropped, and several sneezes were heard. But there wasn't any talking. Then, as though everything were normal, Miss Kirby said, "Take out your spelling books."

Everyone was glad to be doing something. Probably no spelling lesson had ever seemed so interesting.

At the end of school, Miss Kirby lent Nick a dollar. Now he could buy the things his mother wanted at the store. Everything seemed to be all right again.

### Not Fair

The next morning Susan waited and waited for Jamie to walk to school with her. Finally at a quarter after eight, she gave up and ran down the street to meet Pam. By running almost the whole way, the two girls got to school on time. Jamie wasn't there. But then just as the last bell rang, Jamie rushed into the room and slid into her seat. It wasn't until recess that Susan had a chance to ask Jamie why she had been so late.

"I forgot my baseball glove," Jamie said, "and I had to go all the way back home to get it. We only have four more days to practice before our big game with Mr. Shock's room."

Pam joined them. "Why did you have to go home for your glove, Jamie? Why couldn't you borrow somebody else's when it's your turn to catch?"

"I'm the only one on the team that's left-handed," Jamie said. "I have to have my own glove. But it's getting so worn out, it isn't much good anymore. I wish I could get a new one."

After lunch Miss Kirby sat down quietly at the desk and began marking papers. Susan raised her hand, but Miss Kirby didn't see it. Then she cleared her throat, shuffled her feet, and waved her hand wildly. Miss Kirby looked up. "Yes, Susan, what is it?" she said.

"Miss Kirby, aren't you going to read?" Susan asked.

"No, Susan, I'm not," she said slowly. "I told you yesterday, there would be no extra reading until Nick's money was returned. There were lots of chances for whoever took it to put it on my desk or in Nick's cubbyhole without anyone seeing. You all understand, I'm sure."

"It's not fair to make everybody miss the story because one person is a thief," Pam whispered.

"That's not fair, Miss Kirby," Jamie said right out loud.

"Jamie's right," several others said loud enough for the whole room to hear.

Miss Kirby looked upset, but when she spoke, her voice was her regular calm, quiet voice. "I'll tell you what isn't fair," she said. "It isn't fair for one person to rob everybody. And that's what is happening. Our room is like a family. We should be able to trust one another. Now I am trusting whoever made the mistake of taking Nick's money to put it back. I'm going to go on without reading until the money is returned, because it's wrong to pretend that everything is all right when it isn't." Miss Kirby began marking papers again.

The rest of the day nothing was right in the room. You could practically see anger and suspicion walking up and down the aisles like an invisible imp touching this one and that one, making people treat each other differently.

"It's like nobody in our whole room is nice anymore," Susan thought. "It's bad enough having Miss Kirby be so mean and stop reading to us, but it's even worse to know that somebody in our own room is a thief!"

That night Susan made up her mind. "I'll try to stay by myself tomorrow," she thought before she went to sleep. "Then I won't have to hear anything about 'Maybe it was so-and-so' or 'Whoozis has got a guilty look if I ever saw one.' I'll leave home early, before Jamie comes and before Pam is out on the corner. I'll walk to school by myself and stay by myself."

That's what she did. Susan felt happier than she had for days as she ran up the steps and started to go in the first door to Miss Kirby's room.

"Well! It's nice to be the first one here," she thought.

But she wasn't the first one. There, just across the room from her, putting her hand in Nick's cubbyhole, was the last person in the world Susan would ever have expected to see. She covered her mouth to keep from crying out.

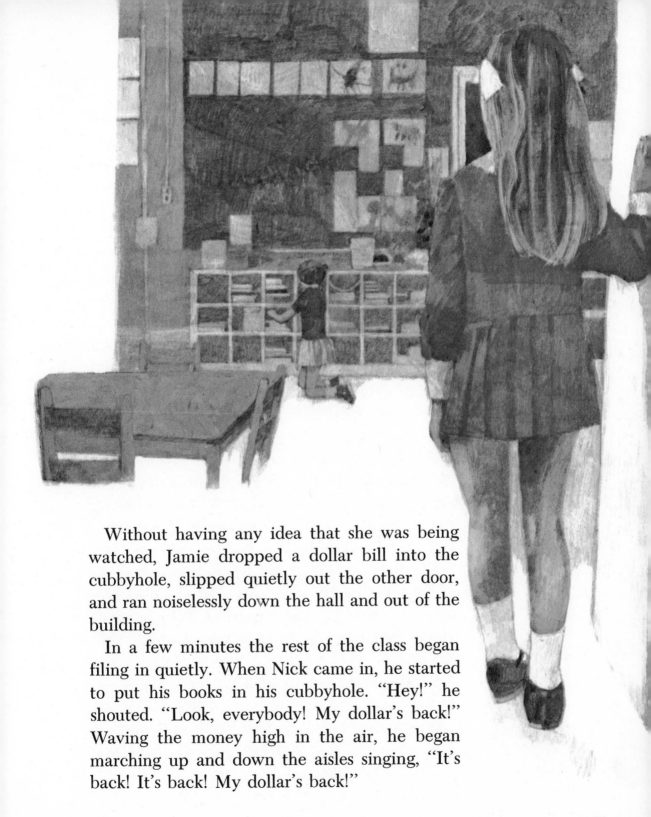

Without having any idea that she was being watched, Jamie dropped a dollar bill into the cubbyhole, slipped quietly out the other door, and ran noiselessly down the hall and out of the building.

In a few minutes the rest of the class began filing in quietly. When Nick came in, he started to put his books in his cubbyhole. "Hey!" he shouted. "Look, everybody! My dollar's back!" Waving the money high in the air, he began marching up and down the aisles singing, "It's back! It's back! My dollar's back!"

The rest of the boys and girls happily fell into step with him. Just before the bell rang, Pam and Jamie hurried into the noisy room. As soon as she saw what was going on, Pam grabbed Jamie and pulled her into line with the others.

Miss Kirby was as excited as anybody. She didn't say a word about the noise or the marching until the bell rang. After everyone had quieted down, Nick went up to the desk and handed Miss Kirby the money.

"Thank you for lending me the dollar until I got mine back," he said. Miss Kirby took it with a smile, and for the first time in days, everything in the room seemed to be right again.

But it wasn't all right for Susan. As the class stood for the pledge, she looked at Jamie standing straight and tall in front of her, her right hand over her heart, the rabbit's foot in her hair.

" . . . with liberty and justice for all." Jamie's voice rang out loud and clear as she finished pledging allegiance to the flag.

"How can she stand there like that?" Susan thought. "How can she even come to school?"

After lunch Jamie said, "Miss Kirby, couldn't you read two chapters of *Treasure Island* today? Then we could get caught up on what we've missed."

Miss Kirby looked at the clock and said, "I think we can do that today, Jamie. Thank you for the suggestion."

## The Secret

Susan was spending Friday night at Pam's house. After everything that had happened that day, Susan wished she didn't have to go anywhere. She was afraid she might say something about seeing Jamie that morning. And she had made up her mind never to tell anyone that Jamie was a thief. After all, Jamie had returned the money. So that proved she wanted to do what was right, and there was no sense in thinking about it anymore. No one seemed to care who took the money, as long as it had been returned to its owner.

"I was mad at you this morning. I waited and waited for you on the corner," Pam said as they snuggled under the covers. "I was ready to go on by myself when Jamie came along. You know what, Susan? That was the first time I was ever alone with Jamie. I never really liked her. But now I do. She always seemed so different. But once you get to know her, she's nice. I like her next best to you, I guess."

Susan felt a nasty little stab of jealousy. To have Pam admire Jamie so much was almost more than Susan could bear.

"Hey!" Pam nudged Susan. "Don't go to sleep yet. I'm not finished. Jamie and I had a good talk about school and Miss Kirby and all the trouble over Nick's money. I bet Jamie's the only kid that wasn't good and mad at whoever took it.

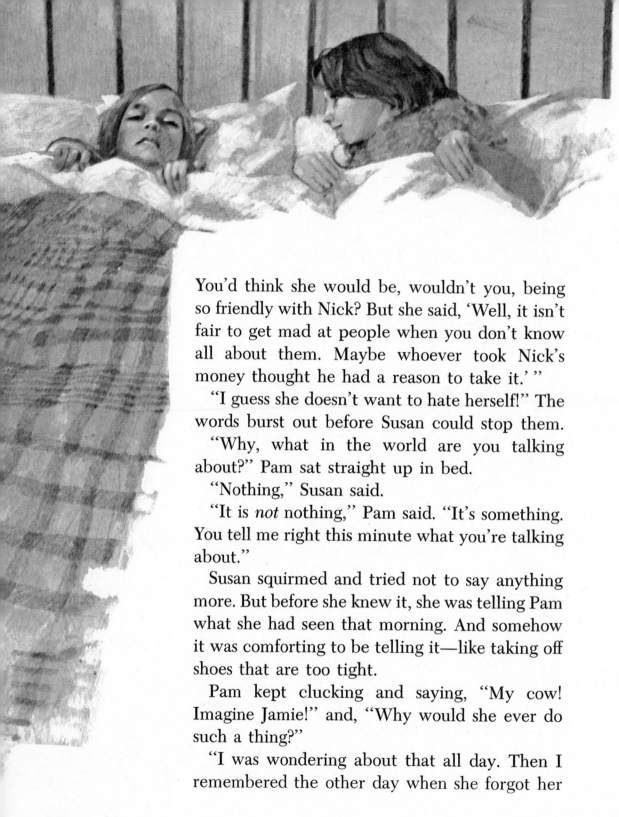

You'd think she would be, wouldn't you, being so friendly with Nick? But she said, 'Well, it isn't fair to get mad at people when you don't know all about them. Maybe whoever took Nick's money thought he had a reason to take it.'"

"I guess she doesn't want to hate herself!" The words burst out before Susan could stop them.

"Why, what in the world are you talking about?" Pam sat straight up in bed.

"Nothing," Susan said.

"It is *not* nothing," Pam said. "It's something. You tell me right this minute what you're talking about."

Susan squirmed and tried not to say anything more. But before she knew it, she was telling Pam what she had seen that morning. And somehow it was comforting to be telling it—like taking off shoes that are too tight.

Pam kept clucking and saying, "My cow! Imagine Jamie!" and, "Why would she ever do such a thing?"

"I was wondering about that all day. Then I remembered the other day when she forgot her catcher's mitt. And she said it was almost worn out, and she wished she could get a new one."

"Yes!" Pam's voice cracked like a trap snapping. "Why didn't we think of that before?"

"Well, it doesn't make any difference now," Susan said. "She put the dollar back, and Nick gave it to Miss Kirby. Everything is just like it was before."

"Oh, sure," Pam said.

There was a long silence. Then Susan said sleepily, "Don't say anything to anybody else, will you, Pam? Because after all, Jamie's my practically best friend."

"I won't," Pam said. "Except maybe I ought to tell Chrissie. Sometimes she asks Jamie over after school. She ought to know about this. I'd better tell her."

"I guess you can tell Chrissie," Susan said. "But tell her not to tell anybody else."

Susan was glad she had told Pam about Jamie. It was even kind of fun at school on Monday for Susan to be able to give Pam a special smile and have Pam wink back at her.

Later in the afternoon, though, Susan began to feel funny. At lunch she had looked across the lunchroom and seen Jamie sitting alone in a corner. When Jamie looked up at her, Susan dropped her eyes quickly and pretended she was looking at Chrissie's new shoes. And at afternoon recess, Chrissie, whose cubbyhole was beside

Jamie's, took everything out of her cubbyhole except her school books. Susan heard her say to Pam, "My sister's going to keep my stuff for me. The kids in her room have desks. Hey, maybe I ought to say something to Myra. Her cubbyhole is right underneath Jamie's."

"Good idea," Pam said.

Susan realized that quite a few of the boys and girls had made it plain to Jamie that day that they didn't want her around. "I guess Pam told Chrissie, and Chrissie told those other kids," she thought as she walked home slowly. "I guess that's why they've started to be mean to her. I guess it's all my fault."

"Well, it's not!" she said out loud. "It isn't my fault if Jamie took the money. I didn't make her do it, and I'm not going to feel funny because I told Pam."

She did, though. No matter what Jamie had done, Susan didn't want to be the one who hurt her.

### Falling Apart

On Wednesday the weather was perfect for a baseball game. And it was the day of the most important game of the season, the game between Miss Kirby's room and Mr. Shock's room. The class was too excited to work. Everyone wanted Nick to talk about the team's chances of winning.

"We have a pretty good chance," he said. "Mr. Shock's room has better batters, but we have a good outfield. And Jamie's the best catcher in the whole school. Nothing gets past her. I think we have a pretty good chance of winning, all right."

Nobody asked Jamie anything. Nobody paid any attention to her.

Susan tried to put out the guilty feeling that was growing bigger and bigger inside her. She twisted in her seat so she couldn't see Jamie out of the corner of her eye.

After lunch Susan realized with a start that Jamie wasn't in her seat. No red-hair handlebars fastened with rubber bands stuck out in front of her. No silly white rabbit's foot bobbed up and down.

"Where's Jamie, Miss Kirby?" Nick sounded worried.

"She had to take care of something downstairs," Miss Kirby answered carefully.

"Oh, boy! She's not sick, is she?" Nick sounded sick himself. "That's all we need! If Jamie can't play today, we're sunk!"

The buzzer on the wall telephone sounded. It was Mr. Blair, the principal.

"Oh, my," Miss Kirby said after a moment, "we can't have anything like that."

Everybody was looking at Miss Kirby. There wasn't a sound in the room. As Miss Kirby put the receiver back on the hook, she said, "Susan, it's time for afternoon recess. I have to go down to the office for a few minutes. If I'm not back when recess is over, you take charge of the class. Maybe you'd like to go ahead with reading *Treasure Island*. We're already up to the next to the last chapter."

During recess the boys were at the back of the playground, practicing. They were very noisy. Pee-Wee Brewster was acting as catcher since Jamie wasn't there, and the whole team seemed to be yelling at him.

"The team's falling apart," Nick said gloomily to Susan as they went back to the room. "If

Pee-Wee has to be the catcher, we're sunk. He'll be the greatest player for the other side you ever saw."

Miss Kirby wasn't back yet, so Susan sat at the big desk at the front of the room and began to read. A tap sounded on the door nearest the cubbyholes, and Chrissie's sister, Alice, poked her head in. Chrissie went up to the door, and the two girls stood whispering excitedly. Then Alice left.

"Guess what!" Chrissie called out in a loud voice. "Jamie got caught!"

The whole room was in an uproar. A few hadn't heard the ugly rumors. "Keep quiet!" Chrissie yelled. "If you keep quiet, I'll tell you what happened." When everyone quieted down, she began. "My sister had to take the absence slips from her room to the office," she said. "People were talking in Mr. Blair's office. His door was open a teensy bit, so she peeked in. *Jamie* was in there with Mr. Blair and Miss Kirby. Mr. Blair kept saying, 'Jamie, we want to help you. You must answer me.'

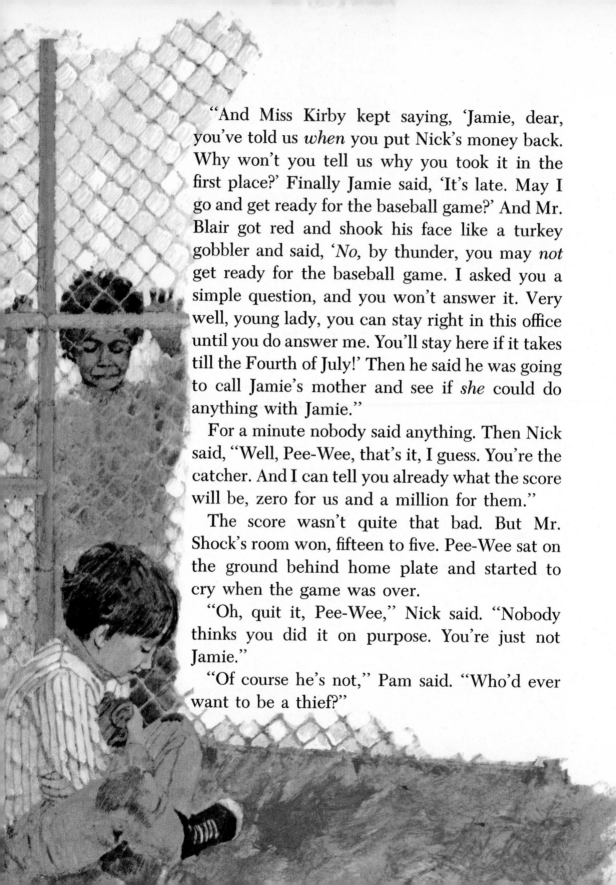

"And Miss Kirby kept saying, 'Jamie, dear, you've told us *when* you put Nick's money back. Why won't you tell us why you took it in the first place?' Finally Jamie said, 'It's late. May I go and get ready for the baseball game?' And Mr. Blair got red and shook his face like a turkey gobbler and said, '*No*, by thunder, you may *not* get ready for the baseball game. I asked you a simple question, and you won't answer it. Very well, young lady, you can stay right in this office until you do answer me. You'll stay here if it takes till the Fourth of July!' Then he said he was going to call Jamie's mother and see if *she* could do anything with Jamie."

For a minute nobody said anything. Then Nick said, "Well, Pee-Wee, that's it, I guess. You're the catcher. And I can tell you already what the score will be, zero for us and a million for them."

The score wasn't quite that bad. But Mr. Shock's room won, fifteen to five. Pee-Wee sat on the ground behind home plate and started to cry when the game was over.

"Oh, quit it, Pee-Wee," Nick said. "Nobody thinks you did it on purpose. You're just not Jamie."

"Of course he's not," Pam said. "Who'd ever want to be a thief?"

### *The Last Chapter*

Jamie wasn't in school the next morning.

After lunch Miss Kirby settled herself comfortably in her chair with *Treasure Island*. She had just started to read when the telephone buzzer sounded.

When Miss Kirby came back from the telephone, she looked around the room. "I'm going to ask you all to do something that won't be easy," she said. "Mr. Blair called to tell me that Jamie is on her way up to the room. When she comes in, I'd like you to act as if she had left the room for a few minutes to go on an errand. Is that clear?"

The children nodded, and some said, "Yes, Miss Kirby."

In a moment the door opened quietly, and Jamie slipped into the room. Miss Kirby looked up from the book. "Oh, Jamie," she said, "it's a bit chilly. Would you mind getting me my sweater from the hanger in the coatroom before you sit down?

"Thank you, dear." Miss Kirby slipped her sweater on as Jamie walked to her seat. She went on with the reading. As she read, Miss Kirby slipped one hand into her sweater pocket. She went on reading as she took her hand out of the pocket and laid something on her desk.

"Why, what's this?" she exclaimed.

The class watched as she unfolded a little paper-wrapped package. A dollar bill fluttered to the floor. Tim rushed to pick it up. Miss Kirby said, "Thank you, Tim," absentmindedly. She was busy reading the note that had been wrapped around the folded dollar.

In a minute she looked up. "Girls and boys," she said, "I've found something very interesting. Listen."

She read from the smudged paper:

"Here is Nick's dollar back. I don't want this old dollar, and I wish I'd never seen it. When I found out Jamie put the money back, I felt bad. She never took the money, cause I did. And we lost the game, too. I don't know if you can fix it up, but anyway I don't want the money. I'm not telling who I am. I don't want to be treated like Jamie."

A buzzing started in the room. Some of the girls and boys laughed, and some looked solemn. Susan didn't know what to do. She wanted Jamie to know she was glad everything was cleared up and that they could be friends as they always had been before. She leaned forward and poked Jamie. Jamie turned her head slowly.

"How about stopping at the drugstore with me on the way home?" Susan said, trying to return to the old friendly way.

Jamie looked right through her. Susan shivered, and all the warm, friendly words that had been ready to pop out froze on her tongue as Jamie turned back to face the front of the room.

Chrissie and Pam were whispering. Then Chrissie called out, "How do we know Jamie didn't take it anyway? How do we know that she didn't write the letter for a trick to get everybody on her side? Why would she give Nick a whole dollar if she didn't take it in the first place?"

Miss Kirby looked at Jamie. "Jamie," she said, "I think it's time you told everyone why you put the dollar in Nick's cubbyhole and where it came from."

Jamie ducked her head, and Susan could see the back of her neck getting red. "Well," she said in a hoarse voice, "it was awful. We couldn't have our reading, and the kids were all getting suspicious of each other and mean. I had all these nickels and dimes saved for a new catcher's mitt. So I asked my father to give me a paper dollar for it, and, well, I came in early one day and stuck it in Nick's cubbyhole. I thought that would fix everything. But it didn't." She shook her head sadly. "I'll never try a thing like that again."

"But, Miss Kirby," Chrissie broke the silence that followed Jamie's stumbling speech. "It's not fair that everybody got mad at Jamie on account of what this other—person—did. Don't you think we should know who it is? In case that—person—should try something bad again, I mean."

Susan couldn't stand it any longer. "Well, I don't!" she said. "I don't want to know who did it. If the rest of you feel the way I do, you don't even want to hear about anybody taking anything that doesn't belong to him for the next million years! I'm sick of the whole thing! I just want our room back the way it was!" And to her own surprise, she burst into tears.

"Me, too!" echoed from every side.

"Well, if that's the way everybody feels," Chrissie said, not very happily.

"That's the way we all feel," Nick said.

"Then I guess me, too," Chrissie said in a small voice.

Miss Kirby picked up *Treasure Island*. "Don't anybody dare look at the clock," she said. "I think we'll finish *Treasure Island* today, no matter how long it takes."

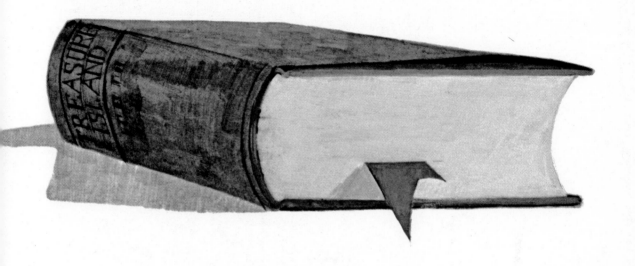

**Reflections**

1. Is this story mainly about a baseball game, about a theft, or about friendship? Give reasons for your answer.

2. Why did the children think Miss Kirby was unfair when she refused to read any more from *Treasure Island?* What did Miss Kirby think was unfair?

3. If you had been one of the children, would you have believed Jamie was a thief? What was the "evidence" against her?

4. From what you know about Jamie, do you think that she would forgive Susan for what she had done? Give reasons for your opinion.

5. Do you think this story could really have happened?

6. How do you feel about the ending of this story? Give reasons for your opinion.

7. Did you ever suspect that Jamie hadn't taken the money? If so, tell at what point in the story and why.

# Pad and Pencil

DAVID McCORD

I drew a rabbit. John erased him
and not the dog I said had chased him.

I drew a bear on another page,
but John said, "Put him in a cage."

I drew some mice. John drew the cat
with nasty claws. The mice saw that.

I got them off the page real fast:
the things I draw don't *ever* last.

We drew a bird with one big wing:
he couldn't fly worth anything,

but sat there crumpled on a limb.
John's pencil did a job on *him*.

Three bats were next. I made them fly.
John smudged one out against the sky

above an owl he said could hoot.
He helped me with my wolf. The brute

had lots too long a tail, but we
concealed it all behind a tree.

By then I couldn't think of much
except to draw a rabbit hutch;

but since we had no rabbit now
I drew what must have been a cow,

with curvy horns stuck through the slats—
they both looked something like the bats.

And feeling sad about the bear
inside his cage, I saw just where

I'd draw the door to let him out.
And that's just all of it, about.

# Until I Was Ten

DAVID McCORD

   This is really a letter from me to you. All I ask is that you read it slowly and *don't* skip the lines of verse. I ask that you do this because my boyhood somehow edged me into poetry, and though the poems I am quoting from were written long after, they almost always talk about the boy who was once somewhere near your age. For all his faults, he was a boy who wanted desperately to learn all he could about the world he lived in. He would teach himself if necessary, and he often did. You can do the same.

From the very beginning I was fascinated by the sight and sound and shape of everything that moved with rhythm—and everything that had a special motion or made a special noise. For rhythm, not rhyme, is the basis of poetry. I was living a kind of poetry and did not know it.

Of course, there is rhythm in your world today. But today we live, or seem to live, for speed alone, as I most happily did not. We live in a crowded world, as I did not. We youngsters had fewer things to be excited about, but we had time to enjoy and savor our excitements one by one.

I was born in New York City on East Tenth Street and lived near Washington Square until I was three. Then, after trying a small town on southern Long Island, we moved out into the country, into a farmhouse, and stayed there until I was almost ten.

I was two, however, and still in New York when I became very ill with malaria. The fever recurred now and then over the next six years and kept me pretty steadily out of school.

I had no brothers or sisters and saw very few people my own age. But freedom and solitude gave me two very precious things: the chance to read all sorts of books (beginning with *The Wizard of Oz*) and endless hours in which to learn something about life in the fields and in the woods which were close at hand. Mine was a green world, and I loved the color green.

So, in spite of spells of illness, it was a joyful time, a lucky time, and I am grateful beyond words for every minute of it. Our place looked big to me, but it was really small, with a barn, a tiny orchard, an outdoor well, a toolshed-playhouse, and a white picket fence all around it. To walk along that fence, with a stick dragging against it, made music. Seventeen years later I wrote "The Pickety Fence," now in a lot of different books. Perhaps you know it?

> The pickety fence
> The pickety fence
> Give it a lick it's
> The pickety fence
> Give it a lick it's
> A clickety fence
> Give it a lick it's
> A lickety fence
> Give it a lick
> Give it a lick
> Give it a lick
> With a rickety stick
> Pickety
> Pickety
> Pickety
> Pick

You have to say that *slowly* with the accent on the *pick* in *pickety*.

Summers seemed to last forever, like the sea wind passing over grasses in great waves with sunlight on them. There was tall yellow wheat in a neighboring field, and I would lose myself making tunnels through it. And there were walks in the woods on Sunday with my father.

> "Walk,"
> My Father used to say,
> "Don't talk."

> "Words,"
> My Father used to say,
> "Scare birds."

The roads in every direction were dirt—not paved—and we rarely saw more than two or three noisy, backfiring automobiles in a single day. Often the driver was busy changing a tire. If we didn't own a horse, we rented one, and my mother (who had ridden the plains around Denver as a little girl) drove me about the countryside in a high-wheeled Hempstead cart.

I remember those drives (as she did) mostly for the strong sea-smell of the marshlands and the sight of soaring gulls and the swifter flight of thin-winged terns as we neared the beaches and the sea. There were bicycle trips with my parents when I was old enough to ride. We had no boat, but we used to spend uncrowded hours at the seashore, often by the empty dunes. And on the hard sand, with my father—a man of great patience—we would fly a marvelous big box kite.

Above everything, in those Long Island days, there was that endless rhythm in the clouds. All my life I have loved the sky: it is my daily and nightly inspiration. I can remember lying on my back, the world forgotten, watching the serried progress of the summer cloud-fleets sailing out to sea. Why, I am always asking, don't more people ever watch the sky except at sunset for the colors? *Why?* No theater, no movie, no TV western ever equals the best of it for splendor and for drama.

The cool grey clouds at dawn devise the sea
in perfect stillness: just the beach and me.

Those thunderheads that pile above the sun,
so white before they blacken and I run,

are more than castles, mountains, what you will—
they're all my windows opening, opening still.

Several times each year I went up to New York with my mother. There were as yet no tunnels under the East River or the Hudson, so we took the ferry over from Long Island City. The ferryboats were brave and brassy, with real shiny brass. They were very fat and wide, like giant water bugs in action. They steamed out boldly from their slips (a kind of dock all made with wooden piles) and zigzagged through a thick cross-traffic of great ocean liners, tugs, all sorts of barges, freighters, small boats, flatboats with a lot of freight cars on them. And they went fast—no speedboats then—faster than anything afloat except the larger tugs. They often seemed to miss collision just by inches. On lucky days I saw the last of the old sailing ships standing into—which means "sailing into"—the harbor east of the Statue of Liberty, or tied up to the dock, with their huge bowsprits sticking straight out over the streets. You didn't just ride under or fly over all this movement and confusion: you were part of it.

I listened always for the sound of harbor whistles, but being aboard that agile ferry somewhat lessened their effect. I think we heard them best on other days down by the old aquarium at Battery Park. So many whistles talking to and answering each other! Sixteen years later I wrote about it in "The Conning Tower" in the *New York World*. The poem began like this:

On a windy day, for a lark, a lark,
They took me down to Battery Park;
On a windy day when the harbor boats
Whistled their long and lovely notes. . . .

I wish that Aaron Copland, the composer, would write a symphony about those whistles. He must have heard them as I did.

Today you hear the sirens, catch a flash or two of red, and know that somewhere there's a fire. But walking down a New York street when I was a boy, we might well hear the sudden clang of bells, the thundering hoofs of great white horses at the gallop, till they and the old fire engine hurtled by. There was time enough to see the big fat polished upright boiler streaming sparks out through the chimney at the top.

Or then—while I am talking of stupendous rhythms—to stand one chilly morning in the country at the edge of that long, bumpy, new-mown field not thirty feet from one of the first Wright biplanes taking off, the first real plane I

ever saw! Was it going down that farmer's field on bicycle wheels and up into the sky? "Look at it," I thought, "a double kite made out of struts and ribs and wire and canvas, and one noisy stuttering engine and propeller." But up it rose, all wobbly, steadied itself, and *flew*.

And did we cheer! We were seeing a new sight and hearing a new rhythm. We were *in* on the beginning of a new age.

Just beyond our house there was a chicken farm with thousands of white leghorn pullets, moving in white flocks quite like the drifting clouds across the landscape. When I was eight, I began to raise chickens myself, hatching the eggs in an incubator.

> I've broken lots of eggs, I guess.
> The ones in pockets make a mess,
> The ones on floors don't clean up well,
> The older ones may leave a smell.
> Eggs in a bag when dropped won't splash;
> The thrown egg will—a yellow smash.

All this time I was falling deeper and deeper in love with words. My mother, of strong will, courage, laughter, and imagination, was original in speech. She could always find the surprising word to express the surprising idea. She knew that happiness has to be earned or won: it is *never* given for free. She was a rare and lovely human being; and whenever she laughed or sang or smiled or read to me aloud, there was music for a long time.

My grandmother (my mother's mother) had an even finer speaking and singing voice. She played the piano until she was nearly ninety. She read most of the Bible through to me—parts of it twice—before I was ten. And if you don't know the sound of the fall of syllables in the King James Version of the Psalms, you will never understand the true range and power of the English language. Far better than this letter would be a recording of my grandmother reading *you* the Bible. I don't know why, but her untroubled voice comes back to me at night sometimes when I am looking at the stars.

But don't let me forget Uncle Robert, my mother's brother. He was a Westinghouse electrical engineer and had spent two years in Japan in the 1890's, installing generators to light the city of Tokyo. He was full of Japan, full to the brim of the love of books and reading, full of the quaint, queer songs he taught me, full of poems he had got by heart, full of imagination, charm, and gaiety, but fullest of all of bantering good humor. He taught me the value of ideas, for he was an inventor. He made me feel that I was not alone in loving the sound of words and the rhythm of words put together in the right order.

So there I was—raising chickens, fooling around with electricity, learning the Morse code, and building apparatus on the way to becoming an early licensed wireless telegraph operator; working at carpentry with my father on weekends, feeding a twelve-inch alligator, finding turtles and cocoons, climbing trees, catching crabs, getting stung by bees, and digging in a garden of my own. What school ever equaled *that*? And what school would ever have taught me a love of nonsense and nonsense words?

> One mouse adds up to many mice,
> One louse adds up to lots of lice,
> One chickenhouse to chickenhice.

At five I learned "The Owl and the Pussy-Cat" by heart, and sometimes I sang it. Do you know it? Do you know that Edward Lear wrote it? If you don't, then get *The Complete Nonsense Book* (Dodd, Mead, 1956) from the library today.

Last of all, a word about the Pocono Mountains in Pennsylvania, where we spent a month each summer for six or seven years. It was there I learned to find red newts in the woods. After rain at five or six in the morning is the best time, for then they walk abroad, though not for long. Spotting these tiny dots of brilliant color in among the leaves sharpened my eyes. If you have never held a newt in your hand and watched his delicate, dry (not slimy) way of walking, you have missed something.

> The little newt
> Is not a brute,
> A fish or fowl,
> A kind of owl:
> He doesn't prowl
> Or run or dig
> Or grow too big.
> He doesn't fly
> Or laugh or cry—
> He doesn't try.

In spite of my instinctive love of nature and the woods, until I was eight I had never read many nature stories. But in the Poconos I read nine or ten books by the New Brunswick writer, Charles G. D. Roberts. He wrote *Red Fox*—one of the two greatest animal stories in the world. If I have told you nothing else, let me urge you to search for it. Ask your librarian. *Red Fox* was the *one* book that somehow *made* me want to become a writer. Of course, I was far from being ready. I had simply entered the world of books.

But I was nearly ready for three more schoolless years on a ranch in the south of Oregon just two miles from the wild Rogue River. A life on the real frontier! And what an exciting life it was to be! Well, you are right this very minute on the frontier of the greatest and most flexible language in the world. Learn to use it well. Learn to listen to the sound of your words as you put them together and speak them. Read everything you can that is good and *well written*. Learn—but learn above all to teach yourself. *Be proud of your ability to be exact.* Learn to love words, especially those words that *sound* the way they mean:

> Like wind upon the mouth
> Sad, summer, rain, and south.
> Amen. Put not asunder
> Man's *first* word: wonder . . . wonder . . .

## Reflections

1. Why would an older person want to tell young people about himself?

2. David McCord says that he was greatly attracted to things that moved with rhythm. Look back through the "letter" and name some of these things. What are some things that move with rhythm that you especially like?

3. David McCord loves words. He is always searching for the right words to describe what he has seen or felt. What vivid ways of saying things and of painting pictures with words can be found in this selection?

4. David McCord remembers favorite sounds from his childhood. What are some of *your* favorite sounds? What makes each of them one of your favorites?

5. David McCord is a poet. Why is the love of rhythm and of words especially important to a poet?

6. Why is the ability to wonder important to a poet?

# SPOKEN AND WRITTEN LANGUAGE

Suppose you were walking by a cool lake on a hot day and wanted to go swimming. But you saw a sign that had these words on it:

PRIVATE NO
SWIMMING
ALLOWED

Suppose someone came along and added some punctuation marks to the sign. He put a question mark after the word *private;* he added an exclamation point after the word *no;* he put a period after *allowed.* Could you go swimming then?

Try changing the meaning of the sign below with punctuation marks.

QUIET NO TALKING ALLOWED

Now discuss the following pairs of sentences, telling how the words are alike but how punctuation, capitals, and the space that separates words make a difference in meaning.

1. What's up the road ahead?
   What's up the road, a head?
2. John Henry is here.
   John, Henry is here.
3. We visited the White House in Washington.
   We visited the white house in Washington.

## Twelve Ways to Spell a Sound

Listen as your teacher reads the following words. Notice especially the underscored letters.

| | | | |
|---|---|---|---|
| b<u>e</u> | p<u>eo</u>ple | bel<u>ie</u>ve | <u>ea</u>ch |
| sw<u>ee</u>t | am<u>oe</u>ba | mach<u>i</u>ne | k<u>ey</u> |
| C<u>ae</u>sar | rec<u>ei</u>ve | <u>Y</u>vonne | qua<u>y</u> |

What sound is alike in all of these words? How many different ways is this sound spelled? With what letter or letters is it spelled? What letter in our alphabet has the name of this sound? Do letters make sounds?

Suppose you were making a new alphabet and you decided that you would design a new letter which would stand for the twelve spellings seen above. Use your new letter and respell each of the twelve words above.

The sooner you learn to match the sounds of spoken language with the letters of written language, the sooner you will master reading. You already know the sounds of English. As you continue to read, you will learn more and more about matching spoken sounds to written letters.

# English

As gardens grow with flowers
English grows with words,
Words that have secret powers,
Words that give joy like birds.

Some of the words you say,
Both in and out of school,
Are brighter than the day,
And deeper than a pool.

Some words there are that dance,
Some words there are that sigh,
The fool's words come by chance,
The poet's to heaven fly.

When you are grown, your tongue
Should give the joys of birds;
Get while you are young
The gift of English words.

*Eleanor Farjeon*

# The Gift of Language

# The Loudest Noise
# in the World

BENJAMIN ELKIN

Once upon a time the noisiest place in the world was a city called Hub-Bub. The people of Hub-Bub never talked; they yelled. They were very proud that their ducks were the quackiest, their doors the slammiest, and their policemen's whistles the shrillest in the whole world.

Their favorite song was the following:

"Slam the door,
Bang the floor.
Days we roar,
Nights we snore.
Hub-Bub!"

Of all the noisy people in Hub-Bub, the noisiest was a young prince named Hulla-Baloo. He could make more noise than the grown-ups. Hulla-Baloo loved to yell, bang pots and pans together, and blow a whistle, all at the same time.

His favorite game was to climb up a ladder, piling up trash cans and tin pails as high as he could. Then he would knock over the whole pile with a loud crash. He would make the piles higher and higher. And they made louder and louder crashes. But still he wasn't satisfied. Prince Hulla-Baloo wanted to hear the loudest noise in the world.

A few weeks before Hulla-Baloo's birthday, his father, the King of Hub-Bub, asked him what he wanted for a present. "I want to hear the loudest noise in the world," said Prince Hulla-Baloo.

"Fine," said the king. "I'll order the royal drummers to get out the special super-loud drums for the whole day."

"But I've heard them before," complained the prince. "That wouldn't be the loudest noise in the world."

"All right," promised the king. "I'll also order all policemen to blow their special super-loud whistles."

"I've already heard those, too," said Hulla-Baloo. "They wouldn't be loud enough."

"Tell you what," said the king. "At the same time I'll close the schools. The children will stay home all day and slam the super-slammy doors. How's that?"

"That would help," agreed the prince. "But it still wouldn't be the loudest noise in the world."

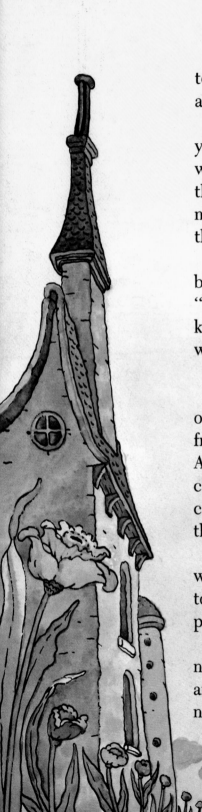

The king was a very kind father, but he began to lose his patience. "What's on your mind?" he asked. "What great idea do you have?"

"Well," answered Prince Hulla-Baloo, "I'll tell you what I've been wanting for a long time. I want to hear every person in the world yell at the same minute. If millions and millions and millions of people all yelled together, I'm sure that would be the loudest noise in the world."

The more the king thought about this idea, the better he liked it. "It might be fun," he thought. "And besides, I'll go down in history as the first king who ever got all the people in the whole world to do the same thing at the same time."

"Yes, I'll try it," he said.

Then the King of Hub-Bub got busy. He sent out hundreds of messengers to visit every country, from the hottest jungles to the coldest icelands. And every day thousands of messages were carried—by telegraph and tom-tom, by car and carrier pigeon, by airplane and dog sled. And soon the answers began to pour in.

Everybody was delighted with the idea. All would be glad to help. The whole world seemed to be thrilled by the thought that every living person would be yelling at the very same time.

The weeks passed. As the birthday date grew nearer and nearer, the excitement grew greater and greater. In every country people talked of nothing but Prince Hulla-Baloo's birthday. There wasn't a village in this world that didn't have a poster in its own language giving the exact minute of local time at which to yell, "Happy Birthday!"

One day, in a city far away, a lady was talking to her husband about Prince Hulla-Baloo's birthday. "Something bothers me," she said. "How am I going to hear everyone else yelling when I'm making so much noise myself? All I'll hear is my own voice."

"You're right," said her husband. "When the time comes, let's open our mouths with the rest of the crowd. But let's not make a sound. While the others are shouting their heads off, we'll be quiet and really hear the noise." That seemed to be a wonderful idea.

Without meaning any harm, the lady told her neighbors about her plan.

113

Without meaning any harm, her husband told his friends at the office. Still without meaning any harm, the friends told their friends. And those friends told other friends.

Before long, people all over the world, even in the city of Hub-Bub, were privately telling one another, "Open your mouths at the right time but don't yell. Then you will be able to hear all the noise made by everyone else."

No one was trying to spoil the prince's birthday celebration. It was just that each person thought, "My voice won't be missed among so many millions. All the others will be yelling and screaming. It won't hurt if I stay quiet so I can really listen."

And so the important moment came closer and closer. In all corners of the earth, crowds of people began gathering in their public meeting

places. All over the world, eyes stared at large clocks ticking away the seconds. It seemed that a shock of excitement, like electricity, swept around the entire globe. In Hub-Bub, of course, the excitement was especially great.

Thousands of people jammed the palace grounds. They cheered and shouted. And high on the balcony the young prince waited happily for what would be the loudest noise in the world.

Fifteen seconds to go . . . ten seconds . . . five seconds . . . NOW!

Two billion people strained their ears to catch the loudest noise in the world. Two billion people heard nothing but absolute silence. All the people had kept quiet so they could hear the others yell. All the people had expected the others to do the work, while they sat back and enjoyed it.

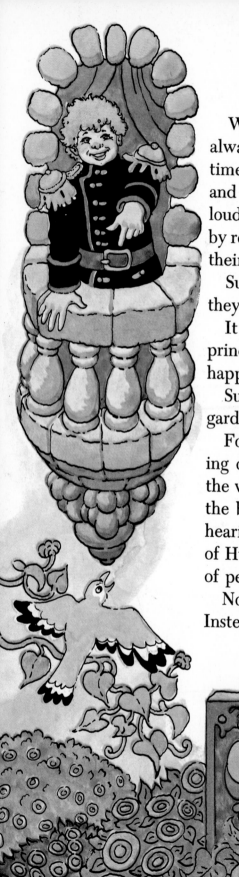

What about the city of Hub-Bub, which had always been so proud of its noise? For the first time in a hundred years, Hub-Bub, too, was silent and still. Instead of honoring their prince by the loudest noise in the world, they had belittled him by remaining absolutely quiet. The people bowed their heads in shame and started to creep away.

Suddenly they stopped. What was that sound they heard up in the balcony?

It couldn't be true! And yet, there was the prince, clapping his hands in glee and laughing happily!

Sure enough, the prince was pointing to the garden with great delight.

For the first time in his life, he heard the singing of a little bird. He heard the whispering of the wind in the leaves and the ripple of water in the brook. For the first time in his life, he was hearing the sounds of nature instead of the noise of Hub-Bub. The prince had been given the gift of peace and quiet. And he loved it!

Now the city of Hub-Bub is noisy no more. Instead, visitors see this sign.

WELCOME TO HUB-BUB THE CITY OF QUIET

The people of Hub-Bub speak gently. They are proud that their ducks are the quietest, their doors the lightest, and their policemen's whistles the softest in the whole world.

### Reflections

1. Read the first and last paragraphs of the story. When would you have preferred to live in Hub-Bub?

2. Did the king succeed in getting all the people in the world to do the same thing at the same time? Explain your answer.

3. In what way were the man and woman who wanted to keep silent sensible? In what way were they foolish?

4. This story could easily have had a different ending. Look back to where the people bow their heads in shame. Starting there, make up a different happy ending. What sad ending can you think of?

5. Which parts of the story do you think are especially funny? What funny words can you find?

6. People often make noises that are not words but that have special meanings. What might each of the following noises mean?
   a. a sigh
   b. a giggle
   c. a moan
   d. a yawn
   e. a hiss
   f. a cough
   g. a clapping of hands
   h. a snap of the fingers
   i. a stamp of the foot

# The Boy Who Wouldn't Talk

LOIS KALB BOUCHARD

*One day Carlos stopped talking. It was not exactly a sudden decision. When his family had moved from Puerto Rico to New York City, all at once he couldn't read his school books or understand what people said—he couldn't even ask directions. Then Carlos had begun to think about this matter of talking. And he had decided he was just fed up with words—with Spanish names for things and English names for things. He, Carlos Vega, did not need to talk; he could point, nod, make faces, or draw pictures instead.*

*No one was happy with the situation, least of all Carlos. He didn't like worrying his parents. He was sad that his younger brother, Angel, felt hurt and lonely, and he was sorry he couldn't join his school friends' games. But Carlos still didn't want to talk—until a new friend, Ricky, forced him to think about how words might, after all, be more than just names for things.*

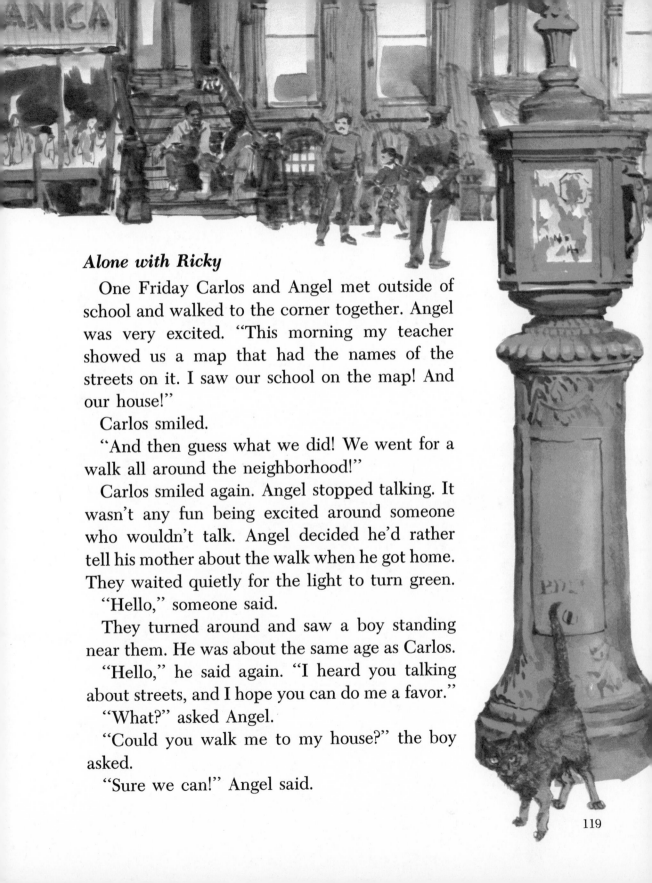

### Alone with Ricky

One Friday Carlos and Angel met outside of school and walked to the corner together. Angel was very excited. "This morning my teacher showed us a map that had the names of the streets on it. I saw our school on the map! And our house!"

Carlos smiled.

"And then guess what we did! We went for a walk all around the neighborhood!"

Carlos smiled again. Angel stopped talking. It wasn't any fun being excited around someone who wouldn't talk. Angel decided he'd rather tell his mother about the walk when he got home. They waited quietly for the light to turn green.

"Hello," someone said.

They turned around and saw a boy standing near them. He was about the same age as Carlos.

"Hello," he said again. "I heard you talking about streets, and I hope you can do me a favor."

"What?" asked Angel.

"Could you walk me to my house?" the boy asked.

"Sure we can!" Angel said.

Carlos nodded his head to the boy and smiled. But he wondered why the boy wanted someone to walk him home. Carlos had been going home by himself for a long time.

"Do you go to this school?" Angel asked.

"I go to a school six blocks from here," the boy said. "My mother meets me at my school and takes me home. And if she's late, I'm supposed to wait for her. But today I didn't want to wait. A boy walked me to this corner, but then he had to meet his sister."

"What's your name?" Angel asked.

"Ricky Hernández."

"I'm Angel Vega. And this is my brother Carlos."

Ricky smiled and put out his hand. "I'm glad to meet you," he said. Angel shook Ricky's hand. Then Carlos shook Ricky's hand. "Why don't you say anything?" Ricky asked Carlos. "Why doesn't your brother say anything?"

"He doesn't like to talk," said Angel. "He can talk when he wants to, but he doesn't want to any more." Suddenly Angel shouted "Oh!"

"What's the matter?" Ricky asked.

"I forgot the hamster! It's my turn to take it home for the weekend. And I left the cage on my desk!"

"Will it be all right there?" Ricky asked.

Carlos shook his head. He didn't think a hamster should stay in school all weekend. His class had a hamster, too, and Anna had taken it home with her.

"No," Angel answered. "It won't be all right in school. It's just a baby, and it has to get food every day. I have to go back in the school and get it."

"We can wait for you," said Ricky.

"No, you better not wait," Angel said, "because my teacher went home, and I'll have to look for Mr. Davis so he can open the door of my classroom. He has all the keys because he's the cus—, cust—"

"Custodian," Ricky said.

"That's right. But Carlos will take you home." Then Angel looked sad. "I wish I had the hamster now so I could go home with you . . . Well. 'By, Carlos. I'll tell Mommy you're taking Ricky home." Angel ran back into the school, and Carlos was left alone with Ricky.

"Say, Carlos, you don't know where I live yet, do you?" Ricky asked.

Carlos shook his head.

"I wish you'd talk. Will you *listen* if I tell you how to get to my house?"

Carlos nodded his head.

"Listen, Carlos. If you're not going to talk to me at all, I'm going to wait for Angel to come out."

Carlos opened his eyes wide in surprise. "My other friends don't get so angry," he thought.

"Why won't he tell me where he lives? Why wait for Angel?"

"Say—what if Angel comes out another door?" Ricky asked. "And doesn't come this way? Maybe I'll go home with you and wait for Angel there. Okay? Where do you live?"

Carlos pointed around the corner.

"Do you live far from here?" Ricky asked.

### Just This Once

Carlos didn't know what to do. All his other friends understood him when he pointed some-where. Then Carlos thought of something. He took a piece of chalk from his pocket, bent down, and drew a map of the streets. He drew one building to show where his school was and another building to show where his house was. Then he stood up and smiled at Ricky.

"I know you don't like to talk much," Ricky said. "Your brother told me you don't like to talk much. But I wish just this once you'd talk to me."

Carlos threw his chalk down on the sidewalk. It broke in three pieces. He was so angry, he thought of walking away.

"I can't see what you wrote on the sidewalk, you know," Ricky said. "I know you wrote something because I heard the chalk rub against the sidewalk. But I can't see it. I can't see you or anything else. So will you please just take me to your house to wait for Angel?"

Carlos stood very still. This was the first boy he had ever met who could not see. He was very curious to know why. But he knew he'd have to ask Ricky to find out why. For a minute Carlos didn't know what he wanted to do. Then he said, "Why can't you see?" It felt strange to talk again.

"My eyes don't work," Ricky said. "Boy, I'm glad you talked to me!"

"I draw pictures a lot," Carlos told him. "Like I drew on the sidewalk. I wish you could see it."

"You could tell me about it," Ricky answered.

"But if you make something out of clay, you don't have to tell me about it. I can tell by myself."

"How?"

"By touching it." Ricky thought a second. "But I'd still want you to tell me about a clay thing. It's easier that way. And I like talking."

Carlos thought for a minute. He didn't want to start talking to Ricky and then change his mind again later. But Ricky couldn't see him nod his head or draw pictures. "Okay," Carlos said. "I'm going to talk to you. Not to everybody. Just to you. Where do you live?"

"We go down two blocks and right two blocks, and it's the fifth house."

"I live three blocks the other way. That's what I drew on the sidewalk." Carlos took Ricky's hand. He waited for the traffic light to change and made sure there were no cars coming. Then he took Ricky across the street.

"If you *can* talk," Ricky said, "why don't you talk to everybody?"

"I don't know. There are too many words. And I don't like every word there is."

"What do you mean," asked Ricky, "you don't like every word?"

"Well," said Carlos, "some words I like in Spanish better than English."

"Like what?" asked Ricky, very interested. "I like Spanish, too. I can't speak it, though, because

my father and my mother talk in English at home. They only talk Spanish when they visit my aunt and uncle or when they don't want me to know what they're saying."

"I like *libro* better than *book*," said Carlos, "and *muchacho* better than *boy*. And I think I like *casa* better than *house*."

"They sound nice in Spanish," said Ricky. "You teach those words to me some day, and I'll say them in Spanish, too."

They came to the next corner. The light was green, so Carlos told Ricky to step down off the curb, and they crossed the street. Carlos walked very slowly with Ricky, holding his hand all the time.

"Wait a second." Ricky stopped walking, put his hand into his pocket, and took out some money. "My father gave me two dimes this morning. So now we can buy something."

"*Bueno*—good," Carlos said. "I see an ice-cream man. Let's go and get some ice cream." They walked over and waited while the man handed an ice-cream cone to a girl. "Hey, Ricky," Carlos whispered. "Could you tell the man we want some? I want chocolate."

"Okay," Ricky said. "I'll tell him if you want me to."

Carlos took the ice-cream cones from the man and gave one of them to Ricky. Then they went on their way again to Ricky's house.

## Spelling with Blocks

When the boys got to Ricky's apartment house, Ricky's mother was walking out of the door. "Ricky! What are you doing here? You know you're supposed to wait for me at school even if I'm late!"

"Yes, I know," said Ricky. "And I thought you'd be angry. But just this once I didn't want to wait for you."

Ricky's mother looked sad. "I know what you mean," she said quietly. "It's hard on a boy as old as you to have to be taken home from school. But please," she said louder, "wait for me next time."

"Okay," Ricky said. "This is Carlos. This is my mother."

"Hi, Carlos. Thank you for walking Ricky home. Did you meet him at his school?"

Carlos shook his head.

"One boy walked me part way. And then I met Carlos and his brother, and I asked them to walk me the rest of the way. But his brother had to go back to school."

"Come on up for a while, Carlos," said Mrs. Hernández. "Does your mother know you'll be late from school?"

Carlos nodded. He looked at her smile and then at her eyes. He tried to figure out if she could see him. Carlos hoped she could understand him if he didn't talk.

"I wish you'd talk to my mother," Ricky said. "But you don't have to. She can see you if you move your head yes or no. Carlos doesn't like to talk," Ricky explained to his mother. "He decided to talk to me, but that's all." They went upstairs to Ricky's apartment.

In Ricky's room Carlos saw a big book open on the desk. The book had no letters on the page. It had lots of bumps instead. "What's this book?" Carlos asked Ricky. "With bumps on it."

"That's how I read," Ricky said. "The bumps are letters. I read by touching the bumps with my fingers."

Carlos touched the bumps on the page. "*Es bueno*—that's good," he said. "I like touching letters. I wish I could touch the letters I read."

"Of course you can," Ricky said. "I learned your letters, too, by touching them." He went over to a closet, opened it, and felt all the toys on the bottom. "Here they are." He pulled out a bag of blocks and emptied the blocks onto the floor.

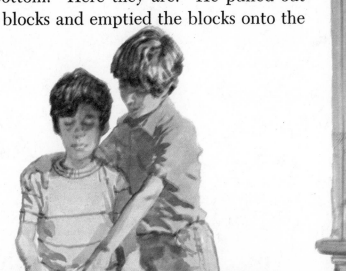

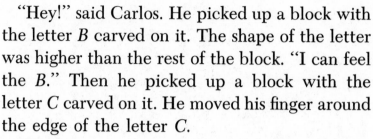

"Hey!" said Carlos. He picked up a block with the letter *B* carved on it. The shape of the letter was higher than the rest of the block. "I can feel the *B*." Then he picked up a block with the letter *C* carved on it. He moved his finger around the edge of the letter *C*.

"Can you spell my name with the blocks?" Ricky asked.

"No. That's *difícil*—that's hard."

"I'll show you how," Ricky said, smiling. "It would be fun to show you how."

Carlos thought to himself, "But I don't like spelling. I don't even like names." He almost said, "Don't show me."

"I said I'll show you how," Ricky told him. He stopped smiling. "Don't you want me to?"

Carlos looked at Ricky's serious face. Then he moved his finger around the edge of the letter *C* again. "Okay. Show me," he said.

Ricky felt all the blocks and picked out the letters that spelled his name. "See? *R–i–c–k–y*. That's how you spell *Ricky*." He was smiling again. "Can you spell your name?"

"Yes," said Carlos. He picked out the letters. "Here's my name." He put Ricky's hand on the blocks that spelled *Carlos*.

"I'll learn it," said Ricky, and he felt each letter slowly. "*C–a–r–l–o–s*."

"I can spell the Spanish word for *yes*," said Carlos. He picked out the letters *S* and *I* and put Ricky's hand on the blocks. "That word is *sí*," he told Ricky.

They played a game with the blocks. Carlos spelled words, and Ricky tried to read them. And Ricky spelled words, and Carlos tried to read them. Carlos did not know as many words as Ricky knew, but he didn't care. He liked spelling with blocks.

After a while Ricky's mother brought in two glasses of milk and a plate of cookies. "Why don't you lend your blocks to Carlos for a while?" she asked Ricky. "Then he can play with them at home."

"Okay," Ricky said.

"*Bueno!*" said Carlos. He smiled at Ricky's mother. "And I can show them to my brother." Then he stopped smiling. He was thinking that he had just talked to Ricky's mother. "I guess I'll talk to your mother, too," he said to Ricky.

"Good," Ricky said.

"Thank you," said Ricky's mother. "Let me know if you want more milk." And Ricky's mother smiled as she left the room.

"I have a great idea, Carlos. Sometimes on Saturdays my father takes me to a park that has lots of flowers. And he lets me take a friend along."

"Flowers?" asked Carlos.

"You know," said Ricky. "They smell good."

"Oh, I know," said Carlos. "*Flores*—flowers."

He said the word *flowers* to himself so he would remember it.

"We have to take a train there," said Ricky. "How would you like to go with us?"

"*Bueno.* I want to."

"We can't touch the flowers much," Ricky said. "But there's a special part for blind people where they let you touch the plants all you want. And they have plants there that feel great."

"Can I touch the plants, too?" Carlos asked.

"Sure. My father can sit on a bench and read his newspaper. And you can show me where to walk. Okay?"

"Okay," said Carlos. "I could tell you when we get to a tree. Or the water. Does this park have water?"

"Oh yes."

"Great," said Carlos. "I like water."

"So do I," said Ricky. "And we can make believe we're firemen putting out a forest fire."

"Make believe?" asked Carlos. "What does that mean?"

"We play that *we're* the firemen," Ricky said. "Or anything else we want to be."

"Oh. I know how to play make-believe. I used to play it with my brother." Carlos remembered how much fun that game was. "Let's do that now," he said to Ricky.

"Sure!" Ricky went over to his desk. "This is the fire engine." He pretended to pull something from the fire engine.

"I see!" said Carlos. "You're pulling the—"

"The hose," said Ricky. "Turn on the water!" he shouted.

Carlos ran to the desk and turned his hand in the air. "Okay! I put the water on! Now I'll show you where the fire is."

"When we make believe," Ricky said softly, "I know where the fire is." He went over to the bed. "The fire's in this tree, okay?"

"Sure," said Carlos very low. He suddenly felt bad that Ricky couldn't see. "Sure. The fire's in this tree."

They carried the hose over to the fire and made noises like water. They thought the noises were so funny that they started laughing. And then Carlos didn't feel so bad that Ricky couldn't see. "He has a lot of fun," Carlos thought. "He can play make-believe and have a good time."

Soon Ricky said, "Whew! The fire's out."

"Whew!" said Carlos. "Let's put the hose back on the truck."

### *Things to Tell*

Then they made believe they were chopping down trees in the forest. Carlos was having such fun that he didn't hear Ricky's mother come into the room.

"Carlos," she said, "it's five thirty. Don't you think you should go home for supper now so your parents won't worry? But I hope you come again soon."

"Oh. I guess I have to go now," Carlos told Ricky. He took a long time putting on his sweater.

Ricky put the blocks in the bag and gave the bag to Carlos. "Can you come with us to that park on Saturday?" Ricky asked.

"Sure," said Carlos. "Well, I guess I'll have to ask my father and mother first. But I think they'll say yes."

"You mean you're going to talk to them?" asked Ricky.

Carlos shrugged his shoulders. "I don't know yet."

"I hope you ask them," Ricky said.

When Carlos got to his house, he climbed the stairs very slowly. He didn't know if he wanted to talk to everybody or if he didn't. He knocked softly on the door.

Angel opened the door. "Hi, Carlos!"

Carlos didn't smile. He walked into the room and stood near the door. Everyone was at the table eating supper, and they all said hello. The whole family was watching him.

Carlos was afraid to start talking again. It would be such a big change. And he was afraid his family might laugh at him. He ran into his room and closed the door and started to cry. He didn't hear Angel come into the room.

"What's in the bag?" Angel asked.

Carlos looked down at the bag. He had forgotten he still had the bag of blocks in his hand. He kept his eyes down on the bag and took a deep breath. "Blocks," Carlos whispered.

"What?" Angel asked.

Carlos looked at his brother and saw that Angel wasn't laughing. "Blocks," Carlos said louder. "Blocks with letters on them. Why are your fingers crossed?"

"I was wishing you would talk tonight," Angel said. He still wasn't laughing. "Let's go and eat."

Carlos looked at the door, but he didn't move.

"Come on," Angel said. "Bring the blocks with you and show me." Carlos took another deep breath. Then he went with Angel to the table.

Carlos slowly took two blocks out of the bag and put them on the table. Everyone was quiet. "These are blocks with letters on them," Carlos said. He looked at his family. No one laughed.

"Where did you get them?" his sister asked.

"Ricky let me have them for a while," Carlos said. He sat down in his chair. He felt funny talking to everyone again. But he felt good, too. He smiled at his family. "I have a whole lot of things to tell you about Ricky. I can't just draw pictures to tell you. It would take far too many pictures."

"That's good," everyone said. They were all smiling.

"First there's the blocks. And then Ricky's book. And me walking Ricky home. And the park. Can I go with him to the park?"

"Wow!" said Mr. Vega. "One thing at a time!"

### Reflections

1. Why did Angel leave Carlos alone with Ricky? How is this fact important to the outcome of the story?
2. How does Ricky usually read? How was he able to learn the shape of the letters Carlos uses to read and write?
3. Suppose you had to describe a tree to someone who did not know the word for it. What would you tell him?
4. Pretend that you are spending an afternoon alone with Ricky. Make up a game that you could both play equally well.
5. Why was Carlos afraid to start talking again to his family? What do you think made him start talking?

# What Is Your Name?

CLARENCE WACHNER

What is your name? Why do you have it? Where did it come from? Of course, you can answer the first question, but can you answer the other two? Perhaps your parents will be able to help you. Dictionaries, encyclopedias, and books about names will also be useful.

People have probably had names almost since language began. The very first words may have been the names or sounds people used to identify themselves. It is likely that long ago each person had only one name. Much later, people began to have more than one name.

Today everyone usually has a given and a family name. A family name is called a surname. A person may have one or more middle names, or a middle initial, in addition to his given name and surname.

### Given Names and Nicknames

At one time a given name described a person in some way. *Bernard* means "bold as a bear," and *Bonita* means "pretty." An Indian boy with the name *Morning Cloud* might later earn the name *Deer Slayer* because of his hunting skill. Today people have names that may not describe them at all, but their nicknames might. *Lefty* and *Smiley* are such nicknames.

Other nicknames are short ways to say a name. *Bill, Will,* and *Willie* are nicknames for *William. Pat* and *Patty* (or *Pattie*) are short for *Patrick* or *Patricia. Rob* or *Bob* may be used instead of *Robert.* Some nicknames have endings that mean "little." *Annie* means "little Ann." Other nicknames come from the way young children mispronounce names. *Lilibet* comes from *Elizabeth.* Sometimes a name that started as a nickname will be the given name of another person.

Your own given name probably has a special story behind it. Do you know what language it comes from? Does your parents' choice of a name for you show that they hoped you would be strong, smart, good, joyful, pretty, or handsome? Did they name you for a jewel, a flower, a place, or something that happened when you were born? Did they like the sound or spelling of your

name? Does your name come from the Bible, a story, a play, or a poem? Were you named after a parent, a relative, or a movie star? Was your name made from another name? Was your name made from two or more names put together? Or was it just made up?

---

### SOME GIVEN NAMES

If your name is not in this short list, you can probably find it in a reference book in your library.

| Name | Source | Meaning |
|------|--------|---------|
| John | Hebrew | God is gracious |
| Dorothy | Greek | the gift of God |
| Daisy | Anglo-Saxon | the day's eye |
| Norman | Scandinavian | a Northman |
| Lewis | German | famous warrior |
| Celeste | French | celestial, heavenly |

---

### Reflections

1. Is a nickname always a shorter way to say a name? Can it sometimes be longer? Why do you think people often call each other by nicknames?
2. What four nicknames can you think of that are short forms of given names? What four nicknames can you think of that describe the people or tell something about them?
3. If you could pick a different name for yourself, what would it be? Why would you pick that name?

# Names for Twins

ALASTAIR REID

Each pair of twins,
rabbits or dogs,
children or frogs,
has to have names
that are almost the same
(to show that they're twins)
but are different too;
so here's what you do.
Find double words,
like Higgledy-Piggledy
(good names for pigs)
or Shilly and Shally
or Dilly and Dally
or Knick and Knack.
Namby and Pamby
are better for poodles;
Whing-Ding for swallows;
Misty and Moisty
and Wishy and Washy
especially for fish.
Call twin kittens
Inky and Pinky
or Helter and Skelter,
or Pell and Mell.
(It's easy to tell
they are twins if their names
have a humdrum sound.)

Crinkum and Crankum
are perfect for squirrels,
like Hanky and Panky
or Fiddle and Faddle;
but Mumbo and Jumbo
are mainly for elephants.
(Airy and Fairy
would never suit *them*.)
Willy and Nilly
will fit almost any twins.
Hubble and Bubble
or Hodge and Podge
or Roly and Poly
are mainly for fat twins.
Chitter and Chatter
or Jingle and Jangle
or Pitter and Patter,
of course, are for noisy twins.
Further than that,
there's Harum and Scarum,
or Hocus and Pocus,
or Heebie and Jeebie,
but these are peculiar,
and have to be used,
like Mixty and Maxty,
for very *odd* pairs....
You see what begins
when you have to name twins.

# Talk

HAROLD COURLANDER and GEORGE HERZOG

Once, not far from the city of Accra on the Gulf
of Guinea, a country man went out to his garden
to dig up some yams to take to market. While
he was digging, one of the yams said to him:

"Well, at last you're here. You never weeded
me, but now you come around with your digging
stick. Go away and leave me alone!"

The farmer turned around and looked at his
cow in amazement. The cow was chewing her
cud and looking at him.

"Did you say something?" he asked.

The cow kept on chewing and said nothing, but
the man's dog spoke up.

"It wasn't the cow who spoke to you," the dog
said. "It was the yam. The yam says leave him
alone."

140

The man became angry, because his dog had never talked before, and he didn't like his tone besides. So he took his knife and cut a branch from a palm tree to whip his dog. Just then the palm tree said:

"Put that branch down!"

The man was getting very upset about the way things were going, and he started to throw the palm branch away, but the palm branch said:

"Man, put me down softly!"

He put the branch down gently on a stone, and the stone said:

"Hey, take that thing off me!"

This was enough, and the frightened farmer started to run for his village. On the way he met a fisherman going the other way with a fish trap on his head.

"What's the hurry?" the fisherman asked.

"My yam said, 'Leave me alone!' Then the dog said, 'Listen to what the yam says!' When I went to whip the dog with a palm branch, the tree said, 'Put that branch down!' Then the palm branch said, 'Do it softly!' Then the stone said, 'Take that thing off me!'"

"Is that all?" the man with the fish trap asked. "Is that so frightening?"

"Well," the man's fish trap said, "did he take it off the stone?"

"Wah!" the fisherman shouted. He threw the fish trap on the ground and began to run with the farmer, and on the trail they met a weaver with a bundle of cloth on his head.

"Where are you going in such a rush?" he asked them.

"My yam said, 'Leave me alone!' " the farmer said. "The dog said, 'Listen to what the yam says!' The tree said, 'Put that branch down!' The branch said 'Do it softly!' And the stone said, 'Take that thing off me!' "

"And then," the fisherman continued, "the fish trap said, 'Did he take it off?' "

"That's nothing to get excited about," the weaver said, "no reason at all."

"Oh yes it is," his bundle of cloth said. "If it happened to you, you'd run too!"

"Wah!" the weaver shouted. He threw his bundle on the trail and started running with the other men.

They came panting to the ford in the river and found a man bathing.

"Are you chasing a gazelle?" he asked them.

The first man said breathlessly:

"My yam talked at me, and it said, 'Leave me alone!' And my dog said, 'Listen to your yam!'

And when I cut myself a branch, the tree said, 'Put that branch down!' And the branch said, 'Do it softly!' And the stone said, 'Take that thing off me!'"

The fisherman panted:

"And my trap said, 'Did he?'"

The weaver wheezed:

"And my bundle of cloth said, 'You'd run too!'"

"Is that why you're running?" the man in the river asked.

"Well, wouldn't you run if you were in their position?" the river said.

The man jumped out of the water and began to run with the others. They ran down the main street of the village to the house of the chief. The chief's servants brought his stool out, and he came and sat on it to listen to their complaints.

"I went out to my garden to dig yams," the farmer said, waving his arms. "Then everything began to talk! My yam said, 'Leave me alone!' My dog said, 'Pay attention to your yam!' The tree said, 'Put that branch down!' The branch said, 'Do it softly!' and the stone said, 'Take it off me!'"

"And my fish trap said, 'Well, did he take it off?'" the fisherman said.

"And my cloth said, 'You'd run too!'" the weaver said.

"And the river said the same," the bather said hoarsely, his eyes bulging.

The chief listened to them patiently, but he couldn't refrain from scowling.

"Now this is really a wild story," he said at last. "You'd better all go back to your work before I punish you for disturbing the peace."

So the men went away, and the chief shook his head and mumbled to himself, "Nonsense like that upsets the community."

"Fantastic, isn't it?" his stool said. "Imagine, a talking yam!"

## Reflections

1. What unusual things happened to the farmer, the fisherman, the weaver, and the bather?

2. If you had been the chief, what would you have said when the four men told you their story? Would you have done anything?

3. What sort of man was the chief? Be ready to show the class how he probably walked and sat and spoke.

4. The setting of this story is near Accra, a city in Africa. Although the story is written in English, the farmer and all the other men speak the language of their tribe. What language do you think the yam, the dog, the palm tree, and the other things speak? Give the reasons for your answer.

5. What is meant when we talk of a tree "whispering in the wind"? Do you think trees really can talk or whisper? Explain.

# Ululation
EVE MERRIAM

With a bray, with a yap,
with a grunt, snort, neigh,
with a growl, bark, yelp,
with a buzz, hiss, howl,
with a chirrup, mew, moo,
with a snarl, baa, wail,
with a blatter, hoot, bay,
with a screech, drone, yowl,
with a cackle, gaggle, guggle,
with a chuck, cluck, clack,
with a hum, gobble, quack,
with a roar, blare, bellow,
with a yip, croak, crow,
with a whinny, caw, low,
with a bleat, with a cheep,
    with a squawk, with a squeak:

animals
      —and sometimes humans—
           speak!

146

# Radio

RICARDA DANIELS

From the time people first walked the earth, they have looked for ways to send messages to friends who were out of sight. First, they shouted. Then they probably discovered that if they cupped their hands around their mouths, the sound would travel farther. They found that they could send messages by beating on a hollow log. Drums were then made that could send greetings or warnings to friends in another part of their small world. But the sounds they made could not travel far.

Hundreds of years later steamships used horns and trains used whistles but even these signals couldn't be heard more than a few miles away.

Then electricity was discovered! This led to the invention of the telegraph and telephone. Sounds could then be sent along wires for great distances. But it was not until radio waves were understood, that messages could be sent all over the earth without wires. And today we can build such powerful transmitters that we can communicate with astronauts on the moon.

By turning a switch on your radio, you can

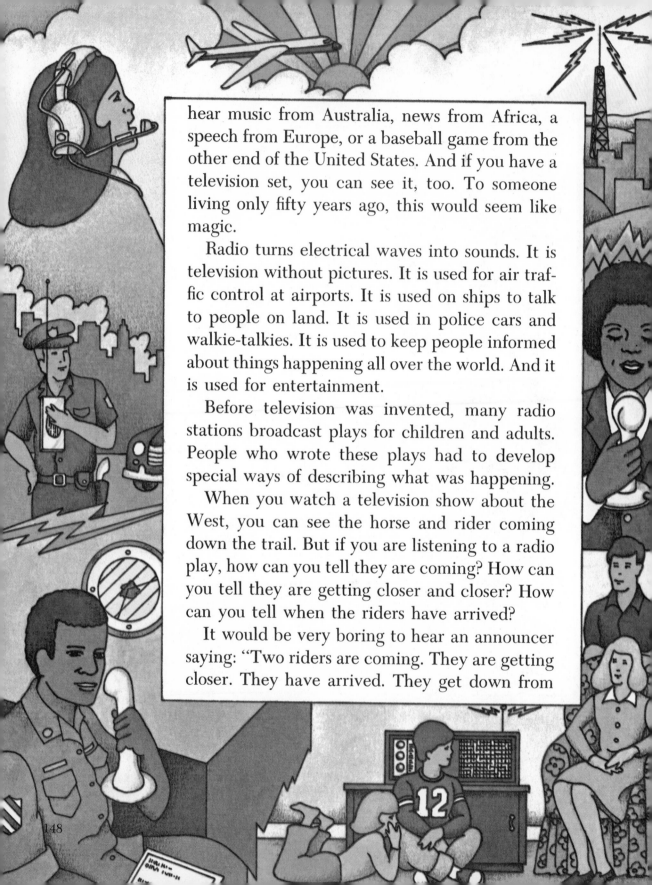

hear music from Australia, news from Africa, a speech from Europe, or a baseball game from the other end of the United States. And if you have a television set, you can see it, too. To someone living only fifty years ago, this would seem like magic.

Radio turns electrical waves into sounds. It is television without pictures. It is used for air traffic control at airports. It is used on ships to talk to people on land. It is used in police cars and walkie-talkies. It is used to keep people informed about things happening all over the world. And it is used for entertainment.

Before television was invented, many radio stations broadcast plays for children and adults. People who wrote these plays had to develop special ways of describing what was happening.

When you watch a television show about the West, you can see the horse and rider coming down the trail. But if you are listening to a radio play, how can you tell they are coming? How can you tell they are getting closer and closer? How can you tell when the riders have arrived?

It would be very boring to hear an announcer saying: "Two riders are coming. They are getting closer. They have arrived. They get down from their horses. They come up to a building. They open the door. Now they are closing it."

One of the ways radio writers make the audience hear what and when something is happening is to use *sound effects*.

Sound effects take the place of scenery. They take the place of seeing the action on a stage. We hear tires screeching, automobile horns, a police whistle, and we know the setting is a busy city street. The radio writer paints pictures with sounds.

As you read the radio script, "The Queen Who Couldn't Make Spice Nuts," notice the words at the left in italics. They tell the person who does the effects what sounds to make and when to make them. They tell the engineer when to make the sounds and voices louder or lower. They tell the actors what feelings their voices should show.

The actors stand in front of a microphone and read their lines. It doesn't matter what they look like or what they wear; the audience can think that the princess is beautiful or ugly, tall or short, wearing a crown or not as they choose. The words, the music, the sound effects, together with the imagination of the listener, make a radio play.

# The Queen Who Couldn't Make Spice Nuts

## A RADIO PLAY

### Characters

| | | |
|---|---|---|
| *Stacia* | ESTRELLITA | *a young princess* |
| *Ben* | KING LINDSAY | *her father* |
| *Todd* | KING FEODOR | *a young king* |
| *Dougie* | DORFEL | *Feodor's servant* |
| *Capers* | GRANNY FLINDERS | *Feodor's old nurse* |

*King Feodor is looking for the perfect queen. And in order to be perfect, she has to be able to make his favorite cookie, spice nuts. Feodor visits his neighbor, King Lindsay, who has three daughters. He meets the eldest princess, and he meets the middle one. Both are lovely and clever—perfect in every way but one. Alas, they cannot make spice nuts. Then. . . .*

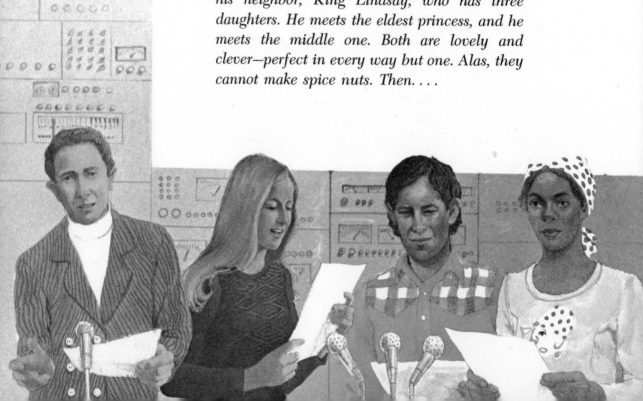

LINDSAY (*fading in*). King Feodor, I have brought back my youngest daughter, Estrellita.

FEODOR (*really hit*). Estrellita . . .

ESTRELLITA. How do you do, King Feodor?

FEODOR. I am enchanted to meet you.

ESTRELLITA. You are kind to say so. However, before King Feodor continues, I think I should tell him frankly . . . *I shall marry no man unless he can play the harmonica.*

FEODOR (*pause*). What?

ESTRELLITA. The harmonica. It's my favorite instrument.

FEODOR. You mean that . . . that comb-sized wheeze pipe?

ESTRELLITA. It takes real talent to play the harmonica well. Can you, Feodor?

LINDSAY (*suddenly*). Yes, how about it, Feodor? Can you play the harmonica?

DORFEL (*suddenly starts to laugh*). Oh, my stars and garters . . .

FEODOR (*angrily*). What's so funny, Dorfel?

151

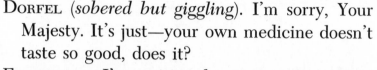

DORFEL (*sobered but giggling*). I'm sorry, Your Majesty. It's just—your own medicine doesn't taste so good, does it?

ESTRELLITA. I'm waiting for your answer, Feodor. Can you play the harmonica?

FEODOR. Well, frankly . . . no. But I'm sure I could learn.

ESTRELLITA (*firm*). I'm sorry, Feodor. It is most unfortunate, but realizing perfection is a matter of standing firm, I vowed I would never marry a man who couldn't play the harmonica. And so. . . . you do understand, don't you? (*Laughs.*) So sorry. Excuse me, gentlemen. (*Fading.*) Goodbye, King Feodor.

SOUND. *Footsteps over fade. Door closes.*

LINDSAY (*quietly*). King Feodor, you look somewhat taken aback.

FEODOR. Why . . . why . . . did you hear what she said? She'll stand firm! She'll refuse even to consider marrying me because I don't play the harmonica! Did you ever *hear* of such a thing?

DORFEL (*brief beat*). Well, now that you mention it, sire—yes.

FEODOR. Yes? But it's absurd. Preposterous! Ridiculous! How dare she? How—(*Up. Almost pitiful.*) Dorfel, how do *I* stand firm now? What do I do now? I'm going to see Granny Flinders.

MUSIC. *Out.*

SOUND. *Footsteps fading in. Rap on door.*

FEODOR (*through door*). Granny? Granny Flinders, it's Feodor.

GRANNY (*up*). Come right in, Feodor.

SOUND. *Door opens. Steps in.*

FEODOR (*fading in. Very embarrassed*). Hello, Granny dear . . .

GRANNY. Well, Feodor, it's a long time since you've been to see your old Granny Flinders.

FEODOR. Yes, I guess so. I . . . I've been out looking for a princess to marry.

GRANNY. Dorfel told me about it. He said you couldn't find a one that was perfect.

FEODOR. Oh, but I did. The Princess Estrellita is beautiful—lovely—she is *perfect*.

GRANNY. But I thought none of 'em could make spice nuts.

FEODOR. Oh . . . Oh, yes. The thing is, Granny, I . . . I've been sort of wondering . . . if that is really such an . . . an important condition after all.

GRANNY. Why, Feodor—first time in all your life I ever heard you back down on what you consider perfect.

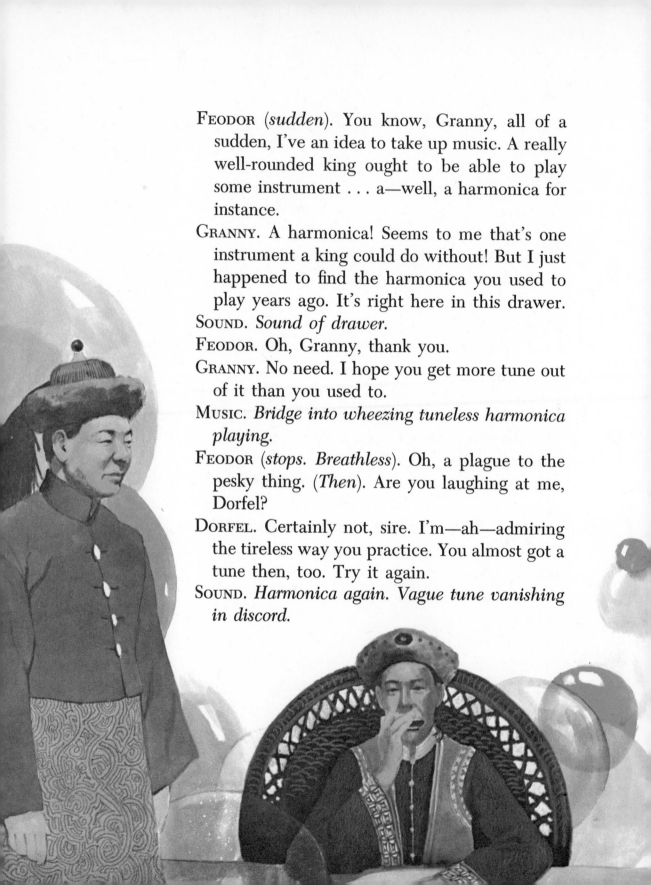

FEODOR (*sudden*). You know, Granny, all of a sudden, I've an idea to take up music. A really well-rounded king ought to be able to play some instrument . . . a—well, a harmonica for instance.

GRANNY. A harmonica! Seems to me that's one instrument a king could do without! But I just happened to find the harmonica you used to play years ago. It's right here in this drawer.

SOUND. *Sound of drawer.*

FEODOR. Oh, Granny, thank you.

GRANNY. No need. I hope you get more tune out of it than you used to.

MUSIC. *Bridge into wheezing tuneless harmonica playing.*

FEODOR (*stops. Breathless*). Oh, a plague to the pesky thing. (*Then*). Are you laughing at me, Dorfel?

DORFEL. Certainly not, sire. I'm—ah—admiring the tireless way you practice. You almost got a tune then, too. Try it again.

SOUND. *Harmonica again. Vague tune vanishing in discord.*

FEODOR. Oh, it's no good. Dorfel, are you sure you sent that letter to Princess Estrellita?

DORFEL. Positive, sire. Weeks ago.

FEODOR. Then why do you suppose she doesn't answer?

SOUND. *Wheezing on harmonica.*

DORFEL. I can't imagine, sire. But may I ask what you said in it?

SOUND. *Wheezing stops.*

FEODOR. Well,—confidentially—I told her that . . . perhaps my ideas of perfection had been a little exaggerated.

DORFEL. Your majesty!

FEODOR. That making spice nuts wasn't really so important. Then I said *I* really agreed that playing the harmonica *was* important, that I was practicing on it, and would do all I could to meet her idea of a perfect husband . . .

SOUND. *Knock on door.*

FEODOR (*up*). Enter!

SOUND. *Door opens.*

FEODOR. Oh—a page. Take care of whatever it is, Dorfel.

SOUND. *Harmonica again, sad and wheezing.*

FEODOR. Oh, how do you play the thing?

SOUND. *Door closes.*

DORFEL (*fading in*). Your majesty! A letter from King Lindsay's court!

SOUND. *Paper tears . . . rattles . . .*

DORFEL. What does she say, sire?

FEODOR. To His Majesty, King Feodor—greetings! In answer to your letter, I too—(*rising excitement*) have decided one cannot place too much importance on absolute perfection. And because I believe you and I can be happy, I have reconsidered my decision and will become your queen. The Princess Estrellita! . . . Dorfel!

DORFEL. I'm so glad for you, sire.

FEODOR. She loves me—she'll marry me.

MUSIC. *Sting.*\*

FEODOR. Tell the decorators—tell the cooks!

MUSIC. *Sting.*

FEODOR. Get the tailors—order the cakes!

MUSIC. *Sting.*

FEODOR. Clean up the castle—shine the wedding bells! She loves me! Everything's perfect now!

MUSIC. *Wild wheeze on harmonica.*

## Reflections

1. Do you think Feodor would make a good king? Why or why not?
2. Dorfel said, ". . . your own medicine doesn't taste so good, does it?" What did he mean?
3. How important was the harmonica to Estrellita?
4. How is a script for a radio play different from a TV play script? What would you have to add? What would you leave out?

\* STING: Loud, short blast of music.

# The Story of Lengthwise

ERNESTINE COBERN BEYER

### From A to B

Lengthwise was a bookworm who made his home in a dictionary. He began life among the A's and started nibbling right away. A-words were very tasty. They were flavored with printer's ink. And the paper had a crispy, crunchy crackle like cornflakes. As he swallowed each A-word, Lengthwise digested its meaning. It wasn't long before he had tunneled his way from *an* to *at*. And he grew smarter and stronger with every bite.

Then one day Lengthwise reached the end of the A's. He decided that he was now strong enough and smart enough to leave his bookshelf. So he left his dictionary home and crawled along the bookshelf until he came to an open window. Then over the sill and down the outside wall he went. It was a long, hard trip, but he made it.

When he reached the outside, Lengthwise looked around. The day was cold and drizzly, but since he had never been outdoors before, he felt satisfied and cheerful. He ambled along the damp,

green grass until his path was blocked by a plant. He knew its name at once, for it began with the letter *A*, an amaryllis.

Lengthwise climbed the amaryllis and sat down in its topmost blossom, which swayed like a tiny rocking chair in the breeze. From this dizzy height, he looked down at the garden. His eyes were round and darkly rimmed as if he wore black spectacles. They grew wider with all that he saw. What did he see? He saw a sparrow on a bough, a butterfly hovering over a tulip, and an ant bringing a crumb to her family.

He didn't know what a sparrow or a butterfly was. But when he saw the ant, he recognized her. He had come across her name among the *A*'s. The ant, who was a friendly little creature, put down her crumb and stared at Lengthwise. "Hi!" she said. "You're new around here, aren't you?"

"An accurate assumption!" replied Lengthwise, using *A*-words, which were all he had so far digested.

"Horrible weather we're having!" the ant continued.

"Aye, aye," Lengthwise replied. "Absolutely awful!"

"How funny you talk!" the ant exclaimed.

Lengthwise gazed at her wistfully. He wanted very much to be her friend. He wanted, in fact, to ask her to go walking with him and share the many marvels in the garden. But how could he do this when all he knew were *A*-words? Once more Lengthwise did his little best.

"Advance, amiable ant!" he began. "Amazing adventures await!"

"Goodness gracious!" said the ant. "What a show-off!" Then she picked up a crumb and scurried away.

"Adieu!" said Lengthwise sadly.

Feeling puzzled and hurt, Lengthwise crawled up the wall and over the sill. He returned to his dictionary, thinking that perhaps *A*'s were not quite enough to have under his belt. He would most certainly have to have a few *B*'s before he could visit the garden again. Many weeks passed as he tunneled his way through the pages. *B*-words were delightful. Lengthwise enjoyed them so much that he nibbled steadily from *baa* to *buzz*. By the time he had digested *Byzantine*, he felt strong enough and smart enough to go again into the wide, wide world. So once more he sought the open window and crawled down the outside wall.

Back in the garden, the little bookworm found to his amazement that everything looked different. This was because the sun was shining. Grass and moss were astir with busy bugs, all talking excitedly together. How he wished he knew what they were saying! At last he spied a bug whom he recognized at once. It was a beetle. He had come across the word *beetle* not long ago. "Beautiful big black beetle," he burst out in a flurry of lately digested *B*-words, "behold a backward bookworm!"

"Huh?" gasped the beetle. "Why all the big words, pal?"

Lengthwise took a deep breath and tried again. "Beautiful big black beetle, befriend a befuddled bookworm baffled by bewildering bug-babble!"

Like the ant, the beetle thought Lengthwise was a show-off. Disgusted, he dived into a rose and pulled its petals over him.

Poor Lengthwise wondered what he should do now. He had just about decided to return to the dictionary when a boy entered the garden. Under his arm he carried a book. The boy sat down under a tree. He opened the book to study his lesson. Lengthwise crawled close. "Boy!" he said. "Brave bright boy bearing beautiful big book, befriend a bewildered bookworm." The boy did not hear him. He went on reading. Lengthwise saw that he did not swallow the words on the page. He seemed to nibble them with his eyes. "Bye-bye, boy," said Lengthwise.

### Back to the Book

Since neither beetle nor boy paid any attention to him, Lengthwise returned to his bookshelf and started chewing again. Many days passed as he went from the *C*-section to the *M*'s. He liked *M*-words immensely. "Mmmmm!" he murmured happily. He nibbled *M*-words until he could hold no more. Then he went again for another adventure in the garden. But what was wrong? Where *was* the garden? He thought it had disappeared, but it was nighttime, and the garden was lost in shadows. Suddenly something round and silvery peeped from behind a cloud.

"Moon!" Lengthwise whispered. "Marvelous mellow moon!" Awed, he continued to stare up at the sky. He had never seen the stars before. He didn't even know they *were* stars, for he had not yet come to the *S*-section in the dictionary. Then a tiny light twinkled in the bushes. Lengthwise thought at first that one of the lights in the

sky must have fallen to earth. But it was not a falling star. It was only a firefly. "Miraculous midget meteor!" exclaimed Lengthwise.

The firefly's light blinked nervously. "Big words frighten me," he said.

"Mortification makes me miserable," apologized Lengthwise.

The light in the bushes went out. It was obvious that the firefly did not want to be his friend.

Poor Lengthwise didn't know how he had failed. He sat himself down on a stone and thought about it. It must be that he had not eaten *enough* words. Yes, that was it. He must go back to the dictionary and eat more. In fact, he would not stop eating words until he had eaten the very last one. And so he returned to his dictionary and ate his way right through to the Z's.

It was then that the trouble began. Z-words did not agree with Lengthwise. They had sharp corners which scratched as they went down. He turned white when he swallowed *zigzag;* it was almost more than he could bear. Hoping to take the taste from his mouth, he hastily gobbled *zucchini,* and that was his final mistake. His eyes grew cloudy, his skin became damp, and his body began to tremble. He lost his grip on the page and tumbled out of the dictionary and onto the shelf.

"Now I will surely die," he thought. But he didn't die. He slowly regained his strength and crawled weakly to the garden to get some air, and there he lay curled up in pain.

Not far off, an elf sat on a moss-covered stone doing a crossword puzzle. Hearing the bookworm's groans, he glanced up. "What's the matter?" he asked. "Are you sick?"

"Zounds!" exclaimed Lengthwise. "I've lost my zest. My zip has come unzipped." But even with unzipped zip, Lengthwise was not able to use all the words he had digested.

"How funny you talk," said the elf. "You sound as though you've swallowed a dictionary."

"I have," said Lengthwise. "That's the trouble with me."

"Hmmmm!" said the elf. "If you've swallowed a dictionary, perhaps you can help me with my crossword puzzle."

"I know lots of cross words," Lengthwise replied. "*Don't* is a cross word, and *won't* is a cross word, too—especially if you say it in a cross tone of voice."

"That's not what I mean," said the elf. "I've been working on this puzzle all day, and I can't go any further. I can't find the word that fits into this space. See?"

Lengthwise studied the puzzle. "The word is *knowledge,*" he said, and he spelled it out for the elf.

The elf was very grateful. "You've helped me a lot," he said. "Now, how may I help *you?* You were unhappy being a bookworm. How would you like to be a lion?"

"No, thanks," said Lengthwise. "I'd be afraid of myself."

"What about an elephant?" suggested the elf. "Or a zebra, maybe?"

"No." Lengthwise shook his head sadly.

"Wait a minute," said the elf. "I have an idea. You helped me with a word I needed; maybe you can do the same for someone else. We wouldn't have to change you into anything. Would you like that?"

"Oh, yes, more than anything," replied Lengthwise. "What is your idea?"

"I know a man who is an author. Sometimes when he is writing a story, he has a very hard time thinking of just the right word he needs in a certain place. You could live with him and help him."

Lengthwise was very happy. "Let's do it right away," he said.

And that is exactly what happened. Lengthwise, the bookworm, went to live with Mr. Wright, the author, who also loved words. He was a bespectacled man, the bookworm type. They became friends immediately. And that very day they set to work on a story. From that time on, Mr. Wright dedicated every book he wrote: "To my friend L." And nobody but Mr. Wright knew that the *L* was for Lengthwise.

## Reflections

1. Lengthwise had a serious problem in this story. What was it?

2. Instead of using just *B*-words the second time he went out, how could Lengthwise have increased his vocabulary?

3. Why couldn't the ant understand Lengthwise?

4. Do you think *Lengthwise* is a good name for a bookworm?

5. A pun is a joke based on the fact that some words sound the same but have different meanings. Find the pun that Lengthwise made when he met the elf. Did Lengthwise know it was a pun? What pun was made with the author's name?

6. Alliteration is the repetition of the same beginning sound or letter in two or more words in a row. Find an example of alliteration in the fourth sentence of this story. Then find other examples in things Lengthwise said. Now make up several examples of your own.

# Teacher

## ANNE SULLIVAN
## (1866–1936)

Helen Keller, blind and deaf, gave hope to millions who shared her handicaps. But it was Anne Sullivan who gave Helen the gift of new life.

Nearly blind, and an orphan at ten, Anne Sullivan spent four years in a Massachusetts poorhouse. But then she was sent to the Perkins Institution for the Blind in Boston. Graduating first in her class, Anne was chosen to teach Helen. Because of her own sad childhood, Anne brought understanding and sympathy to Helen. But "Teacher," as Helen called Anne, found that her pupil had never known discipline of any kind. And she needed discipline as well as sympathy if she was to become more than a wild, unhappy creature.

The rest is history. Anne Sullivan's patience, kindness, and skill helped Helen to understand and use language. Anne Sullivan held the key that let Helen Keller out of her dark and silent prison into a new world.

# No Schools for the Deaf Ones

ETTA DeGERING

## *Something Different*

Thomas Hopkins Gallaudet sat on the porch steps of his family home in the July sun. He was thinking about what he might do after his graduation from school.

His thoughts were interrupted by his younger brothers and sisters and their playmates. They all came trooping around the corner of the house, laughing and panting. The children sat down in a circle on the grass. As they rested, they played a guessing game. Thomas noticed one girl sitting apart from the group. There was something different about this girl. It wasn't her pink ruffled dress nor her blond curls. It wasn't her pretty face—but wait, it *was* her face. Her face was the face of a four-year-old child, but her size showed she must be twice that age.

Thomas called Theodore, his nine-year-old brother, from the circle. "Who is the little girl sitting over there by herself?" he asked.

Teddy looked at the little girl. "Her? Why, don't you know? She's Alice Cogswell. Doc Cogswell's girl. She lives next door."

"Why doesn't she play with the group?" asked Thomas.

Teddy shrugged. "She can't. She's deaf and dumb."

Deaf and dumb. So that was it. "Bring her to me.
Maybe I can think of a game she can play. She
looks lonesome."

Teddy ran over to Alice, made a sweeping motion to come, left her with Thomas, and hurried
back to the circle. Thomas smiled and patted the
step beside him. Alice sat on the very edge like a
pink butterfly—if there are pink butterflies—
ready to take flight. Thomas wanted to give her

a way to speak to other children. He picked up his hat and gave it to Alice. Then he stooped down and wrote *hat* in the sand of the path.

Alice looked at him blankly. The marks in the sand meant nothing to her. Again and again Thomas handed her the hat and wrote *hat* in the sand. He pointed to the writing. Then he pointed to other things and shook his head. He pointed to the hat and nodded vigorously.

Alice's forehead puckered. She was trying to understand. She looked from the hat to the writing. What did those marks in the sand have to do with the thing she held in her hand?

Thomas breathed a prayer.

Finally a glimmer of light shone in Alice's eyes. Her forehead smoothed. She smiled and nodded. For the first time in her life, Alice understood that things had names. They had names that could be written in the sand. She showed that she wanted to write. Thomas helped her until she could write *hat* from memory.

He turned the writing into a game. When Alice wrote *hat,* he offered his handkerchief, a twig, a stone. She laughed and shook her head until he held out the hat.

Suddenly Alice pointed to herself and then to the sand. She wanted to write the word that meant herself. When Thomas wrote *Alice,* she again pointed to herself and looked at him, asking. He nodded. Satisfied, she began practicing her name.

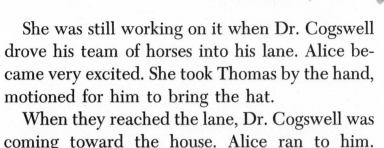

She was still working on it when Dr. Cogswell drove his team of horses into his lane. Alice became very excited. She took Thomas by the hand, motioned for him to bring the hat.

When they reached the lane, Dr. Cogswell was coming toward the house. Alice ran to him. Thomas saw by their actions how close this father and daughter were. Alice tugged at her father to come. Thinking Alice wanted him to meet her friend, he smiled and shook hands with Thomas.

But Thomas knew what Alice wanted. He handed her his hat. She passed it to her father and dropped to her knees. In the roadway she wrote *hat* in the dust.

Thomas would never forget the look in Dr. Cogswell's eyes. It was a look of astonishment, joy, and love—all mixed up with tears that wouldn't stay back. He tried to hug his little daughter, but she would have none of it. She hadn't finished. She pointed to herself and began to write. She wrote *Ali* but could not go on. She held up her hand to Thomas for help. Together they completed her name. Now she was ready for the hug and the "well-done" pat.

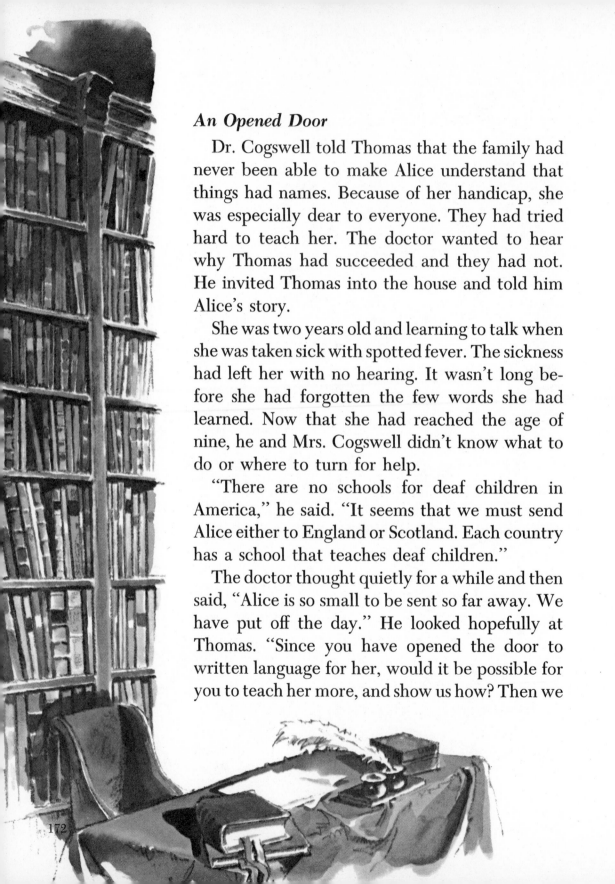

## An Opened Door

Dr. Cogswell told Thomas that the family had never been able to make Alice understand that things had names. Because of her handicap, she was especially dear to everyone. They had tried hard to teach her. The doctor wanted to hear why Thomas had succeeded and they had not. He invited Thomas into the house and told him Alice's story.

She was two years old and learning to talk when she was taken sick with spotted fever. The sickness had left her with no hearing. It wasn't long before she had forgotten the few words she had learned. Now that she had reached the age of nine, he and Mrs. Cogswell didn't know what to do or where to turn for help.

"There are no schools for deaf children in America," he said. "It seems that we must send Alice either to England or Scotland. Each country has a school that teaches deaf children."

The doctor thought quietly for a while and then said, "Alice is so small to be sent so far away. We have put off the day." He looked hopefully at Thomas. "Since you have opened the door to written language for her, would it be possible for you to teach her more, and show us how? Then we could wait until she is older to send her away to school."

"I will be glad to do what I can, but I have no training," Thomas answered.

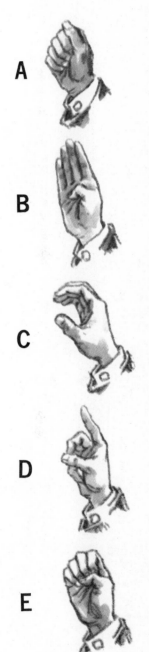

Dr. Cogswell went to his library and took down a book called *Theory of Signs*. He turned the pages of the book and said, "Most of this book lists signs and words for deaf-mutes to use. There is a sign for each word. The back of the book has the manual alphabet. You will see that the letters of the alphabet are made by different positions of the fingers on only one hand. The book is like a dictionary, except that it lists signs instead of definitions." Dr. Cogswell stopped speaking and passed the book to Thomas.

Thomas thought it was very interesting that the deaf could talk with their hands and also spell words with their fingers. "Have you tried to teach Alice finger spelling?" he asked.

"With no more success than our efforts at teaching her writing," answered the doctor. "She imitates our motions as a sort of game, but they mean nothing to her. Would you care to take the book home and see if you can use it?"

Thomas said he would be glad to. He set a time for Alice to come the next day.

He thought of Alice's happiness on learning just two words. What would it be if she could read a book! If only there were a school for her in America . . . for all those other deaf ones, too.

Thomas walked until late. Before returning home, he had outlined a plan of work for himself. When he finished college, he would search out the deaf. He would try to help them help themselves.

Before Alice came for class the next day, Thomas made out a list of words to teach her, and then he tore it up. He would let Alice lead the way. As she needed a word, he would teach her to write and finger-spell it. She had already learned to write *hat*. Today she would spell it on her fingers.

Thomas was astonished at how fast Alice learned. Sometimes she learned more than twenty words at a lesson, and the next day she remembered them. Thomas's brothers and sisters also wanted to learn the new way of talking. Alice was delighted to be in a class. They talked to each other by spelling words on their fingers and by signs.

Signs were fun. They were like drawing pictures in the air. Sometimes they were shortcuts to spelling words. To sign *elephant,* one just swooped his hand down as if along an elephant's trunk. By learning signs, Alice learned many new words.

Thomas kept the children laughing as he acted out the meaning of *sad, angry, fast, slow, tumble,* and *fly.* He gave the children stories to read. Alice was very excited when she could read a whole story.

Thomas Gallaudet's interest in helping the deaf never stopped. With the support of citizens in Hartford, Connecticut, he founded the first school for the deaf.

### Reflections

1. Why did Thomas Gallaudet decide to help Alice?
2. How did Thomas teach Alice the word *hat*?
3. When Thomas saw Alice with her father, what did he learn from their actions?
4. When Thomas began teaching Alice, how were new words chosen? Why was this a good method?
5. In what ways, do you think, did the settlers communicate with the Indians? How many of these ways resemble methods used today to communicate with the deaf?
6. What signs do ordinary people often use to
   a. hitch a ride?
   b. say good-by?
   c. tell someone not to speak?
   d. say that something doesn't matter?

# School for Deaf Ones

Today, many deaf children go to regular schools. But others go to special schools for the deaf. People work in these schools taking care of the building and the lunchroom and the library. And schools for the deaf have teachers who teach math, science, and reading just as your teachers do. But the teachers have special training so that they can help the children with their hearing and speech.

*(top)* This **classroom teacher** is helping her pupil learn to say a word. She must show the girl how to shape her mouth. Here she is showing her how to feel the breath as it comes from her mouth. With practice, she too will soon be able to say the word.

*(bottom)* This **gym teacher** and his helper show the class a wrestling hold. As they do this, the teacher talks to the pupils. This helps them learn to read lips. He also uses his hand to *sign* some of the words he is speaking.

*(top)* The **audiologist** tests hearing. Here a pupil is wearing earphones plugged into a machine. By sign language, the audiologist asks her to tell him when she hears even a tiny bit of sound. The machine tells him how much hearing loss she has. This helps him decide what kind of hearing aid she needs. The audiologist also fixes the hearing aids when they need it.

*(center)* Deaf children need special help to learn how to form words even when they can hear a little. This **speech teacher** is saying a word into a microphone. The boy tries to hear the sounds through his headset. Then he will try to repeat back the word.

*(bottom)* The **guidance counselor** helps students decide about their future. Here a student, using sign language, speaks to his guidance counselor.

177

# KNOWING WORDS

Our English language has many words. Most of us will never master all these words. But we can master a large number of them by knowing some ways that words came into our language and how these words are put together.

English, like you, has parents and grandparents. The English we use today is in many ways like Anglo-Saxon, or Old English. Old English was written and spoken in England hundreds of years ago.

Our English language has borrowed many words from Greek, a language over three thousand years old. We have also borrowed many words from Latin. Latin was used in parts of Europe for over two thousand years, and much of it is based on Greek.

Because today's English has borrowed from these three older languages to make its words, we have many ways of saying things. Let's see how this works by studying the word *foot.*

## A Word from Old English

From the time you were very young, you have used the word *foot.* This word is descended from the Old English word *fot.* The plural of *foot* is *feet.* *Foot* may be added at the beginning of six of the following words to make compound words. Which words do you think they are?

| | | |
|---|---|---|
| ball | apple | step |
| stool | lights | pen |
| book | wear | print |

How does knowing the meaning of *foot* help you define the six compound words you have made?

## A Word from Latin

As Old English grew and changed, it borrowed words from many languages including Latin. In Latin the word for *foot* is *pedes* (pronounced ped′ āz). Knowing that *pedes* means "foot," see if you can explain the meanings of the underlined words in these sentences.

1. She put her foot on the bicycle pedal.
2. The pedestrian hurried across the street.
3. Who led this expedition through the jungle?
4. People and other two-footed animals are bipeds.
5. The peddler pushed his cart of goods into town.

How does knowing that *pedes* means "foot" help you understand the sentences above?

## A Word from Greek

The Greek word for *foot* is *pous*. In English *pous* is often -*pod*- or -*pus*-. The Greek word for *foot* is in these words:

tripod      octopus      podiatrist

Discuss the meaning of these words. Here are some clues:

- How many wheels does a tricycle have?
- If eight people make an octet for singing, how many "feet," or tentacles, does an octopus have?
- If your feet hurt, you may visit a special kind of doctor.

Check your definitions with those in a dictionary. One of the secrets of good reading is to know word parts and what they mean. By learning a few new words each week, you can increase your reading power.

# In Time of Silver Rain

In time of silver rain
The earth
Puts forth new life again,
Green grasses grow
And flowers lift their heads,
And over all the plain
The wonder spreads
Of life, of life, of life!

In time of silver rain
The butterflies lift silken wings
To catch a rainbow cry,
And trees put forth
New leaves to sing
In joy beneath the sky
As down the roadway passing boys
And girls go singing, too,
In time of silver rain
When spring
And life are new.

*Langston Hughes*

# The Wonder of Life

# James Henry Trotter and the Fantastic Peach

ROALD DAHL

*James Henry Trotter lived in a house on the top of a hill in England. One day he met a little old man who gave him a strange mixture in a paper bag. The mixture was magic and contained tiny green things that moved. The old man told James that he would have wonderful adventures if he put the mixture in water and drank it. Then the man disappeared.*

*Very excited, James rushed home to get water. But, just as he was passing the old peach tree in the garden on the top of the hill, he slipped and fell. The paper bag burst, and the tiny green things in the magic mixture sank into the soil. When James got up, he was startled to see a huge peach growing on a branch of the peach tree. The peach grew and grew until its weight bent the branch down and the peach lay on the ground.*

*That evening James stood in the garden and stared at the huge peach.*

## The Giant Peach

"Something else," he told himself, "something stranger than ever this time, is about to happen to me again soon." He was sure of it. He could feel it coming.

He looked around him, wondering what on earth it was going to be. The garden lay soft and

silver in the moonlight. The grass was wet with dew, and a million dewdrops were sparkling and twinkling like diamonds around his feet. And now suddenly the whole place, the whole garden seemed to be *alive* with magic.

Almost without knowing what he was doing, as though drawn by some powerful magnet, James Henry Trotter started walking slowly toward the giant peach. He climbed over the fence that surrounded it and stood directly beneath it, staring up at its great bulging sides. He put out a hand and touched it gently with the tip of his finger. It felt soft and warm and slightly furry, like the skin of a baby mouse. He moved a step closer and rubbed his cheek lightly against the soft skin. And then suddenly, while he was doing this, he happened to notice that right beside him and below him, close to the ground, there was a hole in the side of the peach.

It was quite a large hole, the sort of thing an animal about the size of a fox might have made.

James knelt down in front of it and poked his head and shoulders inside.

He crawled in.

He kept on crawling.

"This isn't just a hole," he thought excitedly. "It's a tunnel!"

The tunnel was damp and murky, and all around him there was the curious bittersweet smell of fresh peach. The floor was soggy under

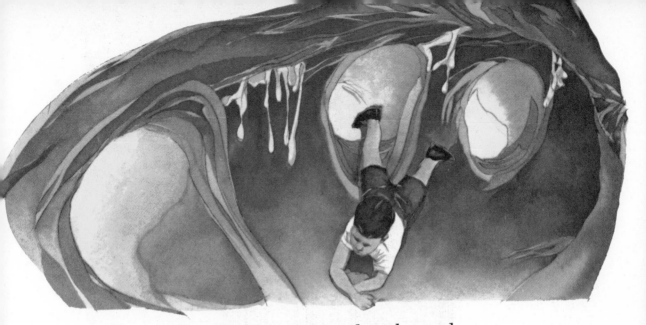

his knees, the walls were wet and sticky, and peach juice was dripping from the ceiling. James opened his mouth and caught some of it on his tongue. It tasted delicious.

He was crawling uphill now, as though the tunnel were leading straight toward the very center of the gigantic fruit. Every few seconds he paused and took a bite out of the wall. The peach flesh was sweet and juicy and marvelously refreshing.

He crawled on for several more yards, and then suddenly—*bang*—the top of his head bumped into something extremely hard blocking his way. He glanced up. In front of him there was a solid wall that seemed at first as though it were made of wood. He touched it with his fingers. It certainly felt like wood, except that it was very jagged and full of deep grooves.

"Good heavens!" he said. "I know what this is! I've come to the stone in the middle of the peach!"

Then he noticed that there was a small door cut into the face of the peach stone. He gave a push. It swung open. He crawled through it, and before he had time to glance up and see where he was, he heard a voice saying, "*Look* who's here!"

Another said, "We've been *waiting* for you!"

James stopped and stared at the speakers, his face white with horror.

He started to stand up, but his knees were shaking so much, he had to sit down again on the floor. He glanced behind him, thinking he could bolt back into the tunnel the way he had come, but the doorway had disappeared. There was now only a solid brown wall behind him.

James's large frightened eyes traveled slowly around the room.

The creatures, some sitting on chairs, others reclining on a sofa, were all watching him quite intently.

Creatures?

Or were they insects?

An insect is usually something rather small, is it not? A grasshopper, for example, is an insect.

So what would you call it if you saw a grasshopper as large as a dog? as large as a *large* dog? You could hardly call *that* an insect, could you?

There was an Old-Green-Grasshopper as large as a large dog, sitting on a chair directly across the room from James now.

And next to the Old-Green-Grasshopper, there was an enormous Spider.

And next to the Spider, there was a giant Ladybug with nine black spots on her scarlet shell.

Each of these three was squatting upon a magnificent chair.

On a sofa nearby, reclining comfortably in curled-up positions, there were a Centipede and an Earthworm.

On the floor over in the far corner, there was something thick and white that looked as though it might be a Silkworm. But it was sleeping soundly, and nobody was paying any attention to it.

Every one of these "creatures" was at least as big as James himself, and in the strange greenish light that shone down on them from somewhere in the ceiling, they were absolutely terrifying to behold.

"I'm hungry!" the Spider announced suddenly, staring hard at James.

"*I'm* famished!" the Old-Green-Grasshopper said.

"So am *I!*" the Ladybug cried.

The Centipede sat up a little straighter on the sofa. "*Everyone's* famished!" he said. "We need food!"

Four pairs of round, black, glassy eyes were all fixed upon James.

The Centipede made a wriggling movement with his body as though he were about to glide off the sofa—but he didn't.

There was a long pause—and a long silence.

The Spider (who happened to be a female spider) opened her mouth and ran a long black tongue delicately over her lips. "Aren't *you* hungry?" she asked suddenly, leaning forward and addressing herself to James.

Poor James was backed up against the far wall, shivering with fright and much too terrified to answer.

### Very, Very Peculiar

"What's the matter with you?" the Old-Green-Grasshopper asked. "You look positively ill!"

"He looks as though he's going to faint any second," the Centipede said.

"Oh, my goodness, the poor thing!" the Ladybug cried. "I do believe he thinks it's *him* that we are wanting to eat!"

There was laughter from all sides.

"Oh dear, oh dear!" they said. "What an awful thought!"

"You mustn't be frightened," the Ladybug said kindly. "We wouldn't *dream* of hurting you. You are one of *us* now, didn't you know that? You are one of the crew. We're all in the same boat."

"We've been waiting for you all day long," the Old-Green-Grasshopper said. "We thought you were never going to turn up. I'm ever so glad you made it."

"So cheer up, my boy, cheer up!" the Centipede said. "And meanwhile I wish you'd come over here and give me a hand with these boots. It takes me *hours* to get them all off by myself."

James decided that this was most certainly not a time to be disagreeable, so he crossed the room to where the Centipede was sitting and knelt down beside him.

"Thank you so much," the Centipede said. "You are very kind."

"You have a lot of boots," James murmured.

"I have a lot of legs," the Centipede answered proudly. "And a lot of feet. One hundred, to be exact."

"*There* he goes again!" the Earthworm cried, speaking for the first time. "He simply cannot stop telling lies about his legs! He doesn't have anything *like* a hundred of them! He's only got forty-two! The trouble is that most people don't bother to count them. They just take his word. And anyway, there is nothing *marvelous*, you know, Centipede, about having a lot of legs."

"Poor fellow," the Centipede said, whispering in James's ear. "He's blind. He can't see how splendid I look."

"In my opinion," the Earthworm said, "the *really* marvelous thing is to have no legs at all and to be able to walk just the same."

"You call that *walking!*" cried the Centipede. "You're a *slitherer,* that's all you are! You just *slither* along!"

"I glide," said the Earthworm primly.

"You are a slimy beast," answered the Centipede firmly.

"I am *not* a slimy beast," the Earthworm said. "I am a useful and much-loved creature. Ask any gardener you like. And as for you . . ."

"I am a pest!" the Centipede announced, grinning broadly and looking round the room for approval.

"He is *so* proud of that," the Ladybug said, smiling at James. "Though for the life of me, I cannot understand why."

"I am the only pest in this room!" cried the Centipede, still grinning away. "Unless you count Old-Green-Grasshopper over there. But he is long past it now. He is too old to be a pest any more."

The Old-Green-Grasshopper turned his huge black eyes upon the Centipede and gave him a withering look. "Young fellow," he said, speaking in a deep, slow, scornful voice, "I have never been a pest in my life. I am a musician."

"Hear, hear!" said the Ladybug.

"James," the Centipede said. "Your name *is* James, isn't it?"

"Yes."

"Well, James, have you ever in your life seen such a marvelous, colossal Centipede as me?"

"I certainly haven't," James answered. "How on earth did you get to be like that?"

"*Very* peculiar," the Centipede said. "*Very, very* peculiar indeed. Let me tell you what happened. I was messing about the garden under the old peach tree, and suddenly a funny little green thing came wriggling past my nose. Quite a bright green it was, and extraordinarily beautiful, and it looked like some kind of a tiny stone or crystal . . ."

"Oh, but I know what it was!" cried James.

"It happened to me, too!" said the Ladybug.

"I swallowed three!" the Centipede cried. "But who's telling this story anyway? Don't interrupt!"

"It's too late to tell stories now," the Old-Green-Grasshopper announced. "It's time to go to sleep. We've got a tough day ahead of us tomorrow. . . ."

*Down . . . Down . . . Down . . . Down . . .*

"We're off!" someone was shouting. "We're off at last!"

James woke up with a jump and looked about him. The creatures were all out of their hammocks and moving excitedly around the room. Suddenly the floor gave a great heave, as though an earthquake were taking place.

"Here we go!" the Old-Green-Grasshopper shouted, hopping up and down with excitement. "Hold on tight!"

"What's happening?" cried James, leaping out of his hammock. "What's going on?"

"In case you didn't know it," the Ladybug said, "we are about to depart forever from the top of this ghastly hill that we've all been on for so long." . . .

And now the peach had broken out of the garden and was over the edge of the hill, rolling and bouncing down the steep slope at a terrific pace. Faster and faster and faster it went, and the crowds of people who were climbing up the hill suddenly caught sight of this terrible monster plunging down upon them, and they screamed and scattered to right and left as it hurtled by.

At the bottom of the hill, it charged across the road, knocking over a telegraph pole and flattening two parked automobiles as it went by.

Then it rushed madly across about twenty fields, breaking down all the fences and hedges in its path. It went right through the middle of a herd of fine Jersey cows and then through a flock of sheep and then through a paddock full of horses and then through a yard full of pigs, and soon the whole countryside was a seething mass of panic-stricken animals stampeding in all directions.

The peach was still going at a tremendous speed, with no sign of slowing down, and about a mile farther on it came to a village.

Down the main street of the village it rolled, with people leaping frantically out of its path right and left. At the end of the street, it went crashing right through the wall of an enormous building and out the other side, leaving two gaping round holes in the brickwork.

This building happened to be a famous factory where they made chocolate, and almost at once a great river of warm, melted chocolate came pouring out of the holes in the factory wall. A minute later this brown sticky mess was flowing through every street in the village, oozing under the doors of houses and into people's shops and gardens. Children were wading in it up to their knees, and some were even trying to swim in it, and all of them were sucking it into their mouths in great greedy gulps and shrieking with joy.

But the peach rushed on across the country-side—on and on and on, leaving a trail of destruction in its wake. . . .

Then it began to fall . . .

Down . . .

Down . . .

Down . . .

Down . . .

Down . . .

*SMACK!* It hit the water with a colossal splash and sank like a stone.

But a few seconds later, up it came again, and this time, up it stayed, floating serenely upon the surface of the water. . . .

"Pardon me," murmured the Ladybug, turning a trifle pale, "but am I wrong in thinking that we seem to be bobbing up and down?"

"*Bobbing* up and down!" they cried. "What on earth do you mean?"

"You're still giddy from the journey," the Old-Green-Grasshopper told her. "You'll get over it in a minute. Is everybody ready to go upstairs now and take a look around?"

"Yes, yes!" they chorused. "Come on! Let's go!"

"I *refuse* to show myself out of doors in my bare feet," the Centipede said. "I simply *must* get my boots on again first."

"For heaven's sake, let's not go through all that nonsense again," the Earthworm said.

"Let's *all* lend the Centipede a hand and get it over with," the Ladybug said. "Come on."

So they did, all except Miss Spider, who set about weaving a long rope ladder that would reach from the floor up to a hole in the ceiling. The Old-Green-Grasshopper had wisely said that they must not risk going out of the side entrance when they didn't know where they were, but must first of all go up onto the top of the peach and have a look around.

So half an hour later, when the rope ladder had been finished and hung and the forty-second boot had been laced neatly onto the Centipede's forty-second foot, they were all ready to go out. Amid mounting excitement and shouts of "Here we go, boys! The Promised Land! I can't wait to see it!" the whole company climbed up the ladder one by one and disappeared into a dark, soggy tunnel in the ceiling that went steeply, almost vertically, upward.

### A Rather Awkward Situation

A minute later they were out in the open, standing on the very top of the peach near the stem, blinking their eyes in the strong sunlight and peering nervously around.

"What happened?"

"Where are we?"

"But this is *impossible!*"

"Unbelievable!"

"Terrible!"

"I *told* you we were bobbing up and down," the Ladybug said.

"We're in the middle of the sea!" cried James.

And indeed they were. A strong current and a high wind had carried the peach so quickly away from the shore that already the land was out of sight. All around them lay the vast black ocean, deep and hungry. Little waves were lapping against the sides of the peach.

"But how did it happen?" they cried. "Where are the fields? Where are the woods? Where is England?" Nobody, not even James, could understand how in the world a thing like this could have come about.

"Ladies and gentlemen," the Old-Green-Grasshopper said, trying very hard to keep the fear and disappointment out of his voice, "I am afraid that we find ourselves in a rather awkward situation."

"Awkward!" cried the Earthworm. "My dear Old Grasshopper, we are finished! Every one of us is about to perish! I may be blind, you know, but that much I can see quite clearly!"

"Off with my boots!" shouted the Centipede. "I cannot swim with my boots on!"

"I can't swim at all!" cried the Ladybug.

"Nor I!" said Miss Spider. . . .

"But you won't *have* to swim," said James calmly. "We are floating beautifully. And sooner or later a ship is bound to come along and pick us up."

They all stared at him in amazement.

"Are you quite sure that we are not sinking?" the Ladybug asked.

"Of course, I'm sure," answered James. "Go and look for yourselves."

They all ran over to the side of the peach and peered down at the water below.

"The boy is quite right," said the Old-Green-Grasshopper. "We are floating beautifully. Now we must all sit down and keep perfectly calm. Everything will be all right in the end."

"What absolute nonsense!" cried the Earthworm. "Nothing is ever all right in the end, and well you know it!"

"Poor Earthworm," the Ladybug said, whispering in James's ear. "He loves to make everything into a disaster. He hates to be happy. He is only happy when he is gloomy. Now isn't that odd? But then, I suppose just *being* an Earthworm is enough to make a person pretty gloomy, don't you agree?"

### Strange and Scrumptious Dishes

"If this peach is not going to sink," the Earthworm was saying, "and if we are not going to be drowned, then every one of us is going to *starve* to death instead. Do you realize that we haven't had a thing to eat since yesterday morning?"

"By golly, he's right!" cried the Centipede. "For once Earthworm is right!"

"Of course, I'm right," the Earthworm said. "And we're not likely to find anything around here either. We shall get thinner and thinner and thirstier and thirstier, and we shall all die a slow and grisly death from starvation. I am dying already. I am slowly shriveling up for want of food. Personally, I would rather drown."

"But good heavens, you must be *blind!*" said James.

"You know very well I'm blind," snapped the Earthworm. "There's no need to rub it in."

"I didn't mean that," said James quickly. "I'm sorry. But can't you *see* that—"

"See?" shouted the poor Earthworm. "How can I see if I am blind?"

James took a deep, slow breath, "Can't you *realize,*" he said patiently, "that we have enough food here to last us for weeks and weeks?"

"Where?" they said. "Where?"

"Why, the peach, of course! Our whole ship is made of food!"

"Jumping Jehoshaphat!" they cried. "We never thought of that!"

"My dear James," started the Old-Green-Grasshopper, laying a front leg affectionately on James's shoulder, "I don't know *what* we'd do without you. You are so clever. Ladies and gentlemen—we are saved again!"

"We are most certainly not!" said the Earth-worm. "You must be crazy! You can't eat the ship! It's the only thing that is keeping us up!"

"We shall starve if we don't!" the Centi-pede said.

"And we shall drown if we do!" the Earth-worm said.

"Oh dear, oh dear," said the Old-Green-Grasshopper. "Now we seem to be worse off than before!"

"Couldn't we just eat a *little* bit of it?" asked Miss Spider. "I am so dreadfully hungry."

"You can eat all you want," James answered. "It would take us weeks and weeks to make any sort of dent in this enormous peach. Surely you can see that?"

"Good heavens, he's right again!" cried the Old-Green-Grasshopper, clapping his hands. "It would take weeks and weeks! Of course, it would! But let's not go making a lot of holes all over the deck. I think we'd better simply scoop it out of that tunnel over there—the one that we've just come up by."

"An excellent idea," said the Ladybug.

"What are you looking so worried about, Earthworm?" the Centipede asked. "What's the problem?"

"The problem is . . ." the Earthworm said, "the problem is . . . well, the problem is that there is no problem!"

Everyone burst out laughing. "Cheer up, Earthworm!" they said. "Come and eat!" And they all went over to the tunnel entrance and began scooping out great chunks of juicy, golden-colored peach flesh.

"Oh, marvelous!" said the Centipede, stuffing it into his mouth.

"*Dee*-licious!" said the Old-Green-Grasshopper.

"Oh, my!" said the Ladybug primly. "What a heavenly taste!" She looked up at James, and she smiled, and James smiled back at her. They sat down on the deck together, both of them chewing away happily. "You know, James," said the Ladybug, "up until this moment, I have never in my life tasted anything except those tiny little green flies that live on rosebushes. They have a perfectly delightful flavor. But this peach is even better."

"Isn't it glorious!" Miss Spider said, coming over to join them. "Personally, I had always thought that a big, juicy, caught-in-the-web blue-bottle was the finest dinner in the world—until I tasted *this*."

"*What* a flavor!" the Centipede cried. "It's terrific! There's nothing like it! There never has been! And I should know because I personally have tasted all the finest foods in the world!" Whereupon, the Centipede, with his mouth full of peach and with juice running down all over his chin, suddenly burst into song.

"I've eaten many strange and scrumptious dishes
in my time,
Like jellied gnats and dandiprats and earwigs
cooked in slime,
And mice with rice—they're really nice
When roasted in their prime.
(But don't forget to sprinkle them with just a
pinch of grime.)

"I've eaten fresh mudburgers by the greatest
cooks there are,
And scrambled dregs and stinkbugs' eggs and
hornets stewed in tar,
And pails of snails and lizards' tails,
And beetles by the jar.
(A beetle is improved by just a splash of
vinegar.)

"I often eat boiled slobbages. They're grand
when served beside
Minced doodlebugs and curried slugs. And have
you ever tried
Mosquitoes' toes and wampfish roes
Most delicately fried?
(The only trouble is they disagree with my
inside.)

"I'm mad for crispy wasp stings on a piece of
buttered toast.
And pickled spines of porcupines. And then a
gorgeous roast
Of dragon's flesh, well hung, not fresh—
It costs a buck at most.
(And comes to you in barrels if you order it
by post.)

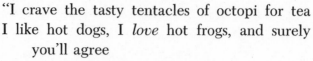

"I crave the tasty tentacles of octopi for tea
I like hot dogs, I *love* hot frogs, and surely
    you'll agree
A plate of soil with engine oil's
A super recipe.
(I hardly need to mention that it's practically
    free.)

"For dinner on my birthday, shall I tell you
    what I chose:
Hot noodles made from poodles on a slice of
    garden hose—
And rather smelly jelly
Made of armadillo's toes.
(The jelly is delicious, but you have to hold
    your nose.)

"Now comes," the Centipede declared, "the
    burden of my speech:
These foods are rare beyond compare—some
    are right out of reach;
But there's no doubt I'd go without
A million plates of each
For one small mite,
One tiny bite,
Of this *FANTASTIC PEACH!*"

Everybody was feeling happy now. The sun was shining brightly out of a soft blue sky, and the day was calm. The giant peach, with the sunlight glinting on its side, was like a massive golden ball sailing upon a silver sea.

**Reflections**

1. The old man told James to *drink* the mixture. What do you think might have happened to James if he had?

2. Why did the garden seem magical to James? Reread the lines that describe how it looked.

3. Inside the peach stone James met a number of "creatures." Compare what the story says about these creatures with facts you know about them or, if necessary, with what an encyclopedia says about them.

4. What kind of personality did the Centipede have? How do you know? What kind of personality did the Ladybug have? the Earthworm?

5. This selection is only a small part of a much longer story. How do you think that James and the others were rescued from their plight? Make up your own ending for this wonderful adventure with the fantastic peach.

# Señor Billy Goat
PURA BELPRÉ

Once there was and was not, up in the High-
lands in Puerto Rico, a little old woman and a
little old man. They were very happy. They lived
in their peasant hut thatched with straw. Together they shared a vegetable garden. There
they grew peppers, tomatoes, radishes, turnips,
pumpkins, potatoes, beans, and corn. They spent
hours talking about their garden. They talked
about the tasty dishes they would prepare with

some of the vegetables. And they made plans for what they would do with the money they would get from the vegetables they would sell at the market.

In the morning while his wife was busy brewing the coffee, the husband would rush to the window, and say, "Ay, María, my darling. What beauty! Look at my lettuce. There is nothing in the garden like it."

That would bring María running to the window, and she would say, "Ay, Ramón! Put on your glasses and see for yourself, for it is blind, blind as a bat you must be. Look at my corn and my radishes! Such glowing colors! What gold! What red! Fit for a king's mantle!"

And then both would laugh and turn back to enjoy the hot coffee which María had left on the table.

Now, one morning, when Ramón went to the window to look at the garden, he saw, moving about among his choice lettuce heads, something big and strange—nipping, yes, nipping, the young green leaves! He looked and looked. He thought the strange beast had the shape of a billy goat, yet he was not sure.

"María! María!" he called. "Come, quick, something big and strange is eating up our garden. Look," he said, pointing to the shape which, having finished with some lettuce, had now turned to some turnips. "Do you see what I see?"

"Ay, Ramón," cried María. "A billy goat came to eat our garden. What shall I do?"

"Do not worry," cried Ramón. "I will go to him and make him go away."

So he went down to the field, and patting the billy goat on its back, he said, "*Buenos días*, Señor Billy Goat. Please do not eat up the garden. You are so young and strong and can find food somewhere else, but we are weak and old. Please go away."

But Señor Billy Goat turned and made for him with horns all set.

"Ay, María! María!" cried the old man, running up the hill as fast as he could. "Open the door, please! The billy goat is after me." Puffing and panting, poor Ramón dropped on a chair and began to cry.

"Do not cry," said María. "A little tact is what he needs. I will go to him and make him go away." So she went down to the field.

She tiptoed to where the billy goat was, and bowing low, said, "*Buenos días*, Señor Billy Goat. That is a fine breakfast you are having. I wonder if you know how long it takes to till the soil, how long to plant the seeds, and how long to pull the weeds. So I came to ask you . . ."

That was as far as she got. The billy goat, tired of her chatter, turned upon her, his legs up in the air and head low for butting the better.

Up the hill went the little old woman, crying

"Ay, Ramón! The billy goat is after me. Open the door, please!" And she, too, tumbled inside the hut.

"*Ay de mí!*" she cried. "Gone are the radishes and the turnips."

"Ruined are the lettuce and the beans," cried the old man.

They cried and cried. Then suddenly something stung Ramón's ears. He shook his head to get rid of it, and as he did so, down dropped a little black ant right in the very palm of his hand.

"María, look—la Hormiguita!" he cried.

"I have come to help you," the ant whispered softly. "What will you give me if I do so?"

"How can you help us, Hormiguita?" asked María.

"You are so small, what can you do?" asked Ramón.

"I can make Señor Billy Goat go away," said la Hormiguita.

"You!" cried María.

"Yes, what will you give me if I do so?"

"Anything you want," said Ramón.

"*Sí, sí,* anything," said María.

La Hormiguita thought for a while and then asked for a little sack of flour and one of sugar for her family.

Ramón and María promised, and the little black ant crawled down, and disappeared through a crack in the floor. Out into the open

she went, crawling on and on until she reached the field. There was the billy goat, head bent—eating, eating. La Hormiguita crawled up his hind legs and up his back, straight to his ear and stung him.

"Ouch!" cried the billy goat. And he raised one leg to scratch himself. But la Hormiguita had now crawled to the other ear and was stinging him with all its might. "Ouch!" cried the billy goat again. He raised his other leg to scratch his other ear. But by that time la Hormiguita was crawling up and down his back, stinging as she crawled along.

"Ouch! Ouch! An ant hill! I have stepped on an ant hill," the billy goat cried.

Quickly he jumped out of the vegetable patch. He thought he was all covered with ants, and he rolled on the ground to shake them off. So he rolled and rolled. Faster and faster he went—rolling . . . rolling . . . rolling. He forgot that he was on a hill, and so he found himself going down the hill and out of sight. For all I know, he is still rolling.

But Ramón and María gave la Hormiguita one little sack of flour, and one little sack of sugar, and since then have continued to live happy and contented in their hut.

### Reflections

1. Why couldn't María and Ramón make Señor Billy Goat leave their garden?
2. María said of Señor Billy Goat, "A little tact is what he needs." Was she right?
3. Why did la Hormiguita ask for so little in return for her favor? What does this tell about her?
4. Señor Billy Goat was bigger and stronger than la Hormiguita. But la Hormiguita was more clever. How did she show this cleverness? Which is it better to be—strong or clever? Why?

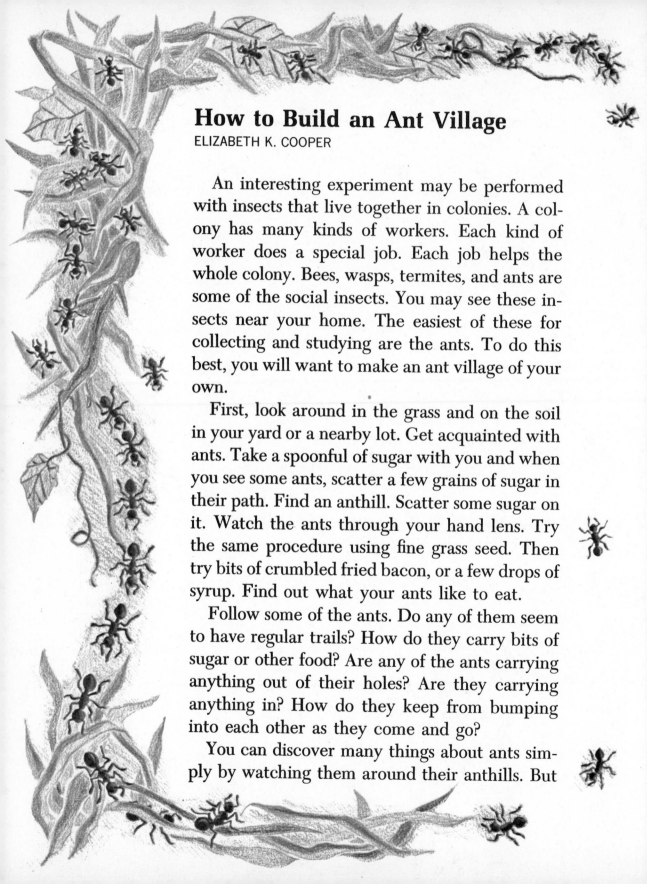

# How to Build an Ant Village

ELIZABETH K. COOPER

An interesting experiment may be performed with insects that live together in colonies. A colony has many kinds of workers. Each kind of worker does a special job. Each job helps the whole colony. Bees, wasps, termites, and ants are some of the social insects. You may see these insects near your home. The easiest of these for collecting and studying are the ants. To do this best, you will want to make an ant village of your own.

First, look around in the grass and on the soil in your yard or a nearby lot. Get acquainted with ants. Take a spoonful of sugar with you and when you see some ants, scatter a few grains of sugar in their path. Find an anthill. Scatter some sugar on it. Watch the ants through your hand lens. Try the same procedure using fine grass seed. Then try bits of crumbled fried bacon, or a few drops of syrup. Find out what your ants like to eat.

Follow some of the ants. Do any of them seem to have regular trails? How do they carry bits of sugar or other food? Are any of the ants carrying anything out of their holes? Are they carrying anything in? How do they keep from bumping into each other as they come and go?

You can discover many things about ants simply by watching them around their anthills. But

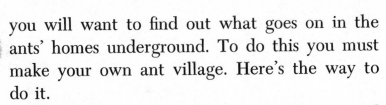

you will want to find out what goes on in the ants' homes underground. To do this you must make your own ant village. Here's the way to do it.

Take a quart glass Mason jar with a metal screw top. Remove the sealer lid. In place of the sealer, cut two circles of fine window screen just the size of the sealer. Find an anthill. With a large spoon carefully fill the jar about three-fourths full of earth from the anthill. Add as many extra ants as you can find from the same hill. These will probably all be ants from the same colony. You can move ants from the ground to your jar by letting the ants climb onto a small twig. Then shake them off into the jar. Another

jar
top
sealer

large spoon
anthill

extra ants

top
screen
screen

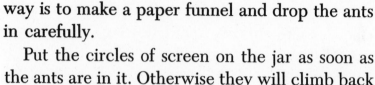

way is to make a paper funnel and drop the ants in carefully.

Put the circles of screen on the jar as soon as the ants are in it. Otherwise they will climb back out. Sprinkle a few drops of water on the top of the soil in your jar. Scatter some grass seed and a bit of sugar on the top. A small piece (about one inch square) of plastic sponge that is kept wet will give your ants all the water they need. Finally, screw the jar ring on over the circles of screen. Then wrap the glass sides of the jar with a layer of black construction paper.

The ants now have a new home. They will not be able to climb through the double layer of screen. They have a place to build their underground homes and some food to eat. Leave the paper around the jar. Take it off only when you want to find out what is happening inside the jar.

Once the ants feel at home, they will go about their regular lives, building rooms and tunnels. Watch how they carry bits of earth to the surface as they dig. Notice where they store their food. How do they keep their homes tidy? How do they clean their own bodies? Try different kinds of food and find out what your ants like best.

From time to time, add a few ants from different anthills. What happens to these strangers? How do your ants behave when ants of different size or color are added to their village? How do the newcomers behave?

black paper

You will think of other ways of finding out about ants as you watch them for a while each day. Whole books have been written just about ants. You may want to find out what some of the scientists know about life in an ant colony. There are many books in the library that will tell you.

### Reflections

1. What does the word *colony* mean in this article?
2. Why is the ant an easy insect to study close at hand?
3. Why do you think you must replace the jar cover with screening?
4. Why do you think you need to put black paper around the glass jar containing your ant village?
5. What kind of things can you learn about ants from observing them? What are some things about ants you could only find out in a book?

# Charlotte's Web

E. B. WHITE

From the very beginning Fern was Wilbur's best friend. When Wilbur was born, everyone thought he was too small to live. It was Fern who saved him. She fed him from a bottle until he was ready to eat scraps. She took him for walks and even after Wilbur had been sold to Uncle Homer Zuckerman, Fern visited him at his pen in the barn. No doubt about it, Fern was Wilbur's best friend.

Still, Wilbur was lonely at the Zuckerman's. The other animals were not too friendly. And Fern did not come to visit on rainy days. Wilbur needed another friend—if possible, one near at hand. Then one day he met Charlotte.

"Salutations!" said the voice.

Wilbur jumped to his feet. "Salu–*what?*" he cried.

"Salutations!" repeated the voice.

"What are *they*, and where are *you?*" screamed Wilbur. "Please, *please*, tell me where you are. And what are salutations?"

"Salutations are greetings," said the voice. "When I say 'salutations,' it's just my fancy way of saying hello or good morning. Actually, it's a silly expression, and I am surprised that I used it at all. As for my whereabouts, that's easy. Look up here in the corner of the doorway! Here I am. Look, I'm waving!"

At last Wilbur saw the creature that had spoken to him in such a kindly way. Stretched across the upper part of the doorway was a big spiderweb, and hanging from the top of the web, head down, was a large grey spider. She was about the size of a gumdrop. She had eight legs, and she was waving one of them at Wilbur in friendly greeting. "See me now?" she asked.

"Oh, yes indeed," said Wilbur. "Yes indeed! How are you? Good morning! Salutations! Very pleased to meet you. What is your name, please? May I have your name?"

"My name,' said the spider, "is Charlotte."

"Charlotte what?" asked Wilbur, eagerly.

"Charlotte A. Cavatica. But just call me Charlotte."

"I think you're beautiful," said Wilbur.

"Well, I *am* pretty," replied Charlotte. "There's no denying that. Almost all spiders are rather nice-looking. I'm not as flashy as some, but I'll do. I wish I could see you, Wilbur, as clearly as you see me."

"Why can't you?" asked the pig. "I'm right here."

"Yes, but I'm near-sighted," replied Charlotte. "I've always been dreadfully near-sighted. It's good in some ways, not so good in others. Watch me wrap up this fly."

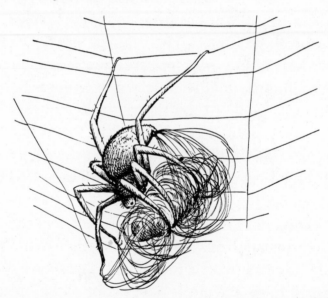

A fly that had been crawling along Wilbur's trough had flown up and blundered into the lower part of Charlotte's web and was tangled in the sticky threads. The fly was beating its wings furiously, trying to break loose and free itself.

"First," said Charlotte, "I dive at him." She plunged headfirst toward the fly. As she dropped, a tiny silken thread unwound from her rear end.

"Next, I wrap him up." She grabbed the fly, threw a few jets of silk around it, and rolled it over and over, wrapping it so that it couldn't move. Wilbur watched in horror. He could hardly believe what he was seeing, and although he detested flies, he was sorry for this one.

"There!" said Charlotte. "Now I knock him out, so he'll be more comfortable." She bit the fly. "He can't feel a thing now," she remarked. "He'll make a perfect breakfast for me."

"You mean you *eat* flies?" gasped Wilbur.

"Certainly. Flies, bugs, grasshoppers, choice beetles, moths, butterflies, tasty cockroaches, gnats, midges, daddy longlegs, centipedes, mosquitoes, crickets—anything that is careless enough to get caught in my web. I have to live, don't I?"

"Why, yes, of course," said Wilbur. "Do they taste good?"

"Delicious. Of course, I don't really eat them. I drink them—drink their blood. I love blood," said Charlotte, and her pleasant, thin voice grew even thinner and more pleasant.

"Don't say that!" groaned Wilbur. "Please don't say things like that!"

"Why not? It's true, and I have to say what is true. I am not entirely happy about my diet of flies and bugs, but it's the way I'm made. A spider has to pick up a living somehow or other, and I happen to be a trapper. I just naturally build a web and trap flies and other insects. My mother was a trapper before me. Her mother was a trapper before her. All our family have been trappers. Way back for thousands and thousands of years we spiders have been laying for flies and bugs."

"It's a miserable inheritance," said Wilbur, gloomily. He was sad because his new friend was so bloodthirsty.

"Yes, it is," agreed Charlotte. "But I can't help it. I don't know how the first spider in the early days of the world happened to think up this fancy idea of spinning a web but she did, and it was clever of her, too. And since then, all of us spiders have had to work the same trick. It's not a bad pitch, on the whole."

"It's cruel," replied Wilbur, who did not intend to be argued out of his position.

"Well, *you* can't talk," said Charlotte. "*You* have your meals brought to you in a pail. Nobody feeds me. I have to get my own living. I live by my wits. I have to be sharp and clever, lest I go hungry. I have to think things out, catch what I can, take what comes. And it just so happens, my friend, that what comes is flies and insects and bugs. And *further*more," said Charlotte, shaking one of her legs, "do you realize that if I didn't

catch bugs and eat them, bugs would increase
and multiply and get so numerous that they'd
destroy the earth, wipe out everything!"

"Really?" said Wilbur. "I wouldn't want *that*

to happen. Perhaps your web is a good thing after all."

The goose had been listening to this conversation and chuckling to herself. "There are a lot of things Wilbur doesn't know about life," she thought. "He's really a very innocent little pig. He doesn't even know what's going to happen to him around Christmastime; he has no idea that Mr. Zuckerman and Lurvy are plotting to kill him." And the goose raised herself a bit and poked her eggs a little further under her so that they would receive the full heat from her warm body and soft feathers.

Charlotte stood quietly over the fly, preparing to eat it. Wilbur lay down and closed his eyes. He was tired from his wakeful night and from the excitement of meeting someone for the first time. A breeze brought him the smell of clover—the sweet-smelling world beyond his fence. "Well," he thought, "I've got a new friend, all right. But what a gamble friendship is! Charlotte is fierce, brutal, scheming, bloodthirsty—everything I don't like. How can I learn to like her, even though she is pretty and, of course, clever?"

Wilbur was merely suffering the doubts and fears that often go with finding a new friend. In good time he was to discover that he was mistaken about Charlotte. Underneath her rather bold and cruel exterior, she had a kind heart, and she was to prove loyal and true to the very end.

## Reflections

1. Who was Charlotte? Describe her as Wilbur first saw her.
2. Why couldn't Charlotte see Wilbur as clearly as Wilbur saw her?
3. How did Wilbur feel when Charlotte killed the fly?
4. How did Charlotte defend herself for eating flies and other bugs? What were some of her arguments?
5. What did the goose mean when she said that Wilbur was an innocent pig? What do you think was to happen at Christmas time?
6. What did Wilbur mean when he said, "But what a gamble friendship is"? How did Wilbur feel about his new friend? Have you ever felt that way about a new friend?

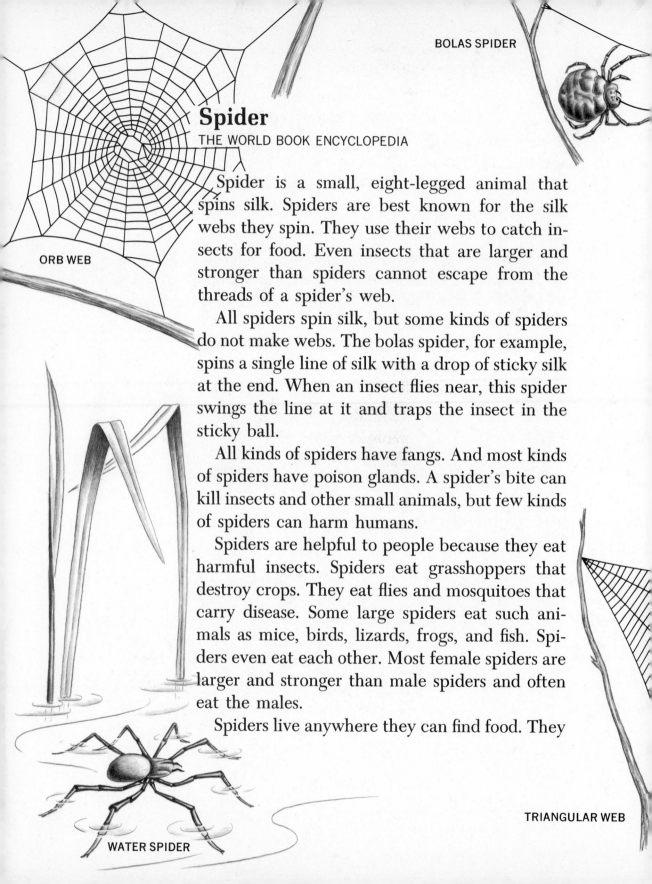

ORB WEB

BOLAS SPIDER

# Spider

THE WORLD BOOK ENCYCLOPEDIA

Spider is a small, eight-legged animal that spins silk. Spiders are best known for the silk webs they spin. They use their webs to catch insects for food. Even insects that are larger and stronger than spiders cannot escape from the threads of a spider's web.

All spiders spin silk, but some kinds of spiders do not make webs. The bolas spider, for example, spins a single line of silk with a drop of sticky silk at the end. When an insect flies near, this spider swings the line at it and traps the insect in the sticky ball.

All kinds of spiders have fangs. And most kinds of spiders have poison glands. A spider's bite can kill insects and other small animals, but few kinds of spiders can harm humans.

Spiders are helpful to people because they eat harmful insects. Spiders eat grasshoppers that destroy crops. They eat flies and mosquitoes that carry disease. Some large spiders eat such animals as mice, birds, lizards, frogs, and fish. Spiders even eat each other. Most female spiders are larger and stronger than male spiders and often eat the males.

Spiders live anywhere they can find food. They

WATER SPIDER

TRIANGULAR WEB

can be seen in fields, woods, swamps, caves, and deserts. One kind of spider spends most of its life under water. Another kind lives near the top of Mount Everest, the world's highest mountain. Some spiders live in houses, barns, or other buildings. Others live on the outside of buildings—on walls, on window screens, or in the corners of doors and windows.

There are more than 29,000 known kinds of spiders, but scientists believe there may be as many as 50,000 kinds. Some kinds are smaller than the head of a pin. Others are as large as a man's hand. One spider, a South American tarantula, measured 10 inches long with its legs extended.

TANGLED WEB

## Reflections

1. What is the purpose of a spider web? Where are some places that you've seen spider webs?
2. What is unusual about the bolas spider?
3. According to this article, what are ways in which one type of spider may be different from another?
4. How are spiders helpful to people?
5. Now that you have read a scientific article about spiders, think about Charlotte. What things did E. B. White describe that fit with the description in this article?

TARANTULA

225

# FROM CELLS TO SEQUOIAS

### ERNEST E. JUST (1883–1941)

Ernest Just, a professor of physiology at Howard University Medical School, was one of the first scientists to investigate the mystery of how a one-celled egg develops into a living thing made up of many cells. He investigated the structure of cells many years before there were modern microscopes.

### JOHN MUIR (1838–1914)

John Muir was interested in preserving the sequoias and giant redwood trees. Through his efforts, a bill was passed by Congress setting up Sequoia National Park. Muir Woods National Monument, a redwood forest in California, was named in his honor.

226

# Close-Up on Insects

**Beekeepers** raise bees for honey and beeswax. They set up hives for the bees to use as homes. The hives are placed outdoors near plants that particular bees like. Each plant gives the honey a special taste.

Beekeepers learn how to handle bees carefully so they won't be stung. But just to be safe, they wear veils and special clothing.

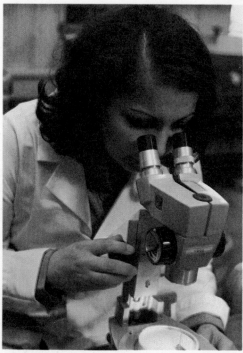

Scientists, called **entomologists,** study insects to find out what they eat, where they grow, where they lay their eggs. They try to find out which insects are harmful to plants and animals and which are helpful. Most entomologists work in laboratories. There they have tools and equipment to help them study insects very closely. Their work helps beekeepers raise bees that will make more and better-tasting honey.

# Ong, of Canada

VERA HENRY

*When the wild geese settled on the marsh on their way north, Holly knew that it would be for the last time. A new highway had been built, and the marsh was being drained to make a summer resort. Suddenly a shot rang out, and the whole flock flew away except the mate of the dead bird. She built a nest in the long grass and laid her eggs.*

*Holly's friend, Johnny Salt, was an Ojibwa Indian who lived on the nearby reservation. One day he accidentally destroyed the goose's nest and broke all the eggs but one. Holly took the egg home. Her grandfather, a retired captain who carved wooden figures for a living, suggested letting Jessica, a hen that had been trying to hatch a doorknob, sit on the egg.*

*When the gosling hatched, the first thing he saw was Tavish, Holly's collie, and immediately he adopted the dog as his mother. Holly decided to name the bird Ong after the sound that geese make.*

*Mrs. Plumley, the fat, red-headed housekeeper who cleaned and cooked for Holly and the captain, thought that draining the marsh would be good for the community and Holly, too. She felt that Holly's friends should be girls Holly's age, not a dog and a wild goose.*

### The Enemies

Ong and Mrs. Plumley were not friends. In the first place, she blamed him because Holly had caught a cold the time she fell in the pond.

The truth was Mrs. Plumley didn't really approve of wild geese. They flew around at night, making a racket like a jammed automobile horn and waking people out of a sound sleep.

It was going altogether too far when one of those nasty, snake-necked creatures tracked up the ground around her kitchen and then had the nerve—the absolute nerve—to knock at the door.

Ong on his part didn't think too much of Mrs. Plumley. She had odd red feathers that stood straight up around her head. When he knocked at the door with his beak, it was Holly or the captain he wanted.

If Mrs. Plumley happened to answer, she waved her apron and cried, "Shoo! Shoo!" in a voice like a loud mosquito.

As Ong grew larger, so did the feud. Whenever she saw him around the door, Mrs. Plumley took her broom and chased him away.

"Shoo! You nasty creature!" she cried, waving the straw broom. "Shoo!"

"Honk-honk," protested Ong and waddled away with as much dignity as possible.

Then one warm June day, Ong had had quite enough.

On this occasion all he had done was take bites from the green tomatoes growing in the garden. Mrs. Plumley took her broom and chased him almost out to his own pen under the russet apple tree.

Suddenly Ong halted. His black neck twisted in an indignant manner. His wings, which now were quite large and strong, began to beat. He rushed at his enemy, beak open, hissing angrily.

Mrs. Plumley was so surprised, she didn't know what to do. She waved the broom in vain. Then she turned and ran, with Ong pursuing her, hissing like a leaky tire. Just before she escaped into the kitchen and slammed the screen door, he nipped her plump leg.

It wasn't a very big nip, but Mrs. Plumley was as upset as if she had been bitten by a lion.

Holly and the captain tried to soothe her. For all her faults, Mrs. Plumley was a kind woman who made excellent chocolate cakes.

"I am sure he was only trying to play," Holly said. "Sometimes he chases Tavish like that."

The captain, who didn't seem quite so sure of Ong's good intentions, went back to his studio, where he carved a little wooden figure of a fat lady being pursued by a wild goose.

Instead of taking the figure down to Mrs. McNab's store or putting it on the studio shelf, the captain rather regretfully hid it in a drawer.

Next to flapjacks, there was nothing that the captain enjoyed as much as Mrs. Plumley's chocolate cake.

If Mrs. Plumley was a poor loser, Ong wasn't a very generous winner either.

From that time on, he terrorized poor Mrs. Plumley. Holly and the captain had to stand guard when she arrived in her little car in the morning or left at night.

Every so often during the day, Ong's long black neck would appear below the kitchen window, waving like the hose on a vacuum cleaner.

Mrs. Plumley found it quite unnerving. She said he looked as if he were laughing at her.

One day, looking out the window, Mrs. Plumley discovered Ong pecking at the valves on her car tires.

"It isn't anything personal, Mrs. Plumley," Holly explained. "Ong is just curious. You know how the handle of a bucket or that piece of rope hanging from the fence fascinates him."

"I'll fascinate him," Mrs. Plumley said grimly. "He's spoiled, that's what he is. What that creature needs is a good lesson."

The next time Ong tried to chase her, Mrs. Plumley was prepared. She had a can of black pepper in her apron, and she threw it at him.

As it happened, the breeze was blowing in the wrong direction, so as much pepper got on Mrs. Plumley as got on Ong.

Mrs. Plumley sneezed and sneezed and sneezed. Ong made strange strangled noises—"Hon-on-on-on-k! O-o-ng!"

After that day Mrs. Plumley and Ong simply ignored each other.

They never did get to be friends.

### First Flight

Ong was no longer content to waddle awkwardly after Tavish. He had discovered that he could fly.

It came as quite a surprise to him.

One afternoon Tavish, who missed the peace and quiet of his bachelor days, tried to sneak away for a ramble in the woods.

"W-on-k. W-on-k—Wait for me!" squalled Ong, running and trying to catch up, but Tavish was too far away.

"Wonk! Wonk!" cried Ong, beating his wings in indignation. He was up on a little hill, and then suddenly he was in the air.

He was so surprised, he came in for a crash landing. How had he done it? He wasn't quite certain. He knew that the robins and sparrows who sometimes shared his bathtub-swimming pool could soar through the air. But Tavish couldn't fly, and neither could Holly nor the

captain nor Mr. Salt. On the other hand, Mrs. Plumley came close to it sometimes when he chased her.

Ong tried again, moving his wings rapidly back and forth.

This was splendid. It was even better than swimming. Up-up-up! The best Jessica ever managed was the perch in the hen coop, but he was far higher than that. He wished he had known before that he didn't need to waddle on the ground.

He was so delighted, he forgot all about following Tavish. With a little practice he was able to go from his pen to the pond in the meadow without once touching the earth.

Holly laughed as she watched his acrobatics. Then she frowned. Now that he had discovered he could fly, Ong might wander too far.

"Do you think we should clip Ong's wings, Grandfather?" Holly asked later. "Suppose he flies away?"

"Do you want to turn him into a barnyard creature like Jessica?" the captain demanded.

"No," Holly admitted, "only the wild geese will soon fly south. Suppose he decides he wants to leave us?"

Her grandfather brushed the bangs back from her forehead. "Ong is almost full-grown. When you are older, you may want to leave here, too."

Holly shook her head. "This is my home. I am going to live here forever and ever."

She leaned sleepily against her grandfather. They were sitting as they often did out on the porch where they could watch the stars. The new highway was about half a mile away, and through the trees she caught glimpses of headlights that seemed to be a reflection of the dart of fireflies in the woods. She listened to the crickets chirrup, the croak of frogs in the pond, and the sad, lonely cry of the whippoorwill.

"Whip-poor-will! Whip-poor-will."

Her grandfather glanced at the luminous dial of his watch. "Time for Echo to go over," he said. "I sure wish I was still young enough to be an astronaut."

Holly watched the satellite pass overhead.

"Grandfather," she said, "now that they are sending spaceships to the moon, do you suppose they'll ever take along two of all the animals, like Noah did on the ark?"

Her grandfather slapped at his arm. "As far as I'm concerned, they're welcome to the mosquitoes, although Mrs. Plumley is right. There are less of them now the marsh has been drained."

Holly jumped up. "Oh, I forgot to put Ong in his pen! I'd better do it now."

As soon as it began to grow dark, Jessica and the other hens climbed up on a perch, tucked a head under a wing, and fell asleep. The phoebes, the swallows, the mourning doves, the thrush went to bed with the sun. But not Ong. Jessica had done her best to teach him proper habits, but Ong's webbed feet weren't meant for perching. And even after it began to grow dark, he liked to wander in the cool clover blossoms around his pen.

Ong wasn't in his pen. He didn't seem to be any place in the yard.

Holly took a flashlight and, with Tavish beside her, ran out to the pond, thinking Ong might have gone there for a late swim.

She called his name, "Ong, Ong, O-n-g! She threw back her head and gave an Indian war cry, but Ong didn't answer as he usually did. She began to be frightened.

Far off in the woods, she heard the yap of the fox. An owl hooted from a nearby tree. It wasn't safe for a silly young gander to wander alone at night.

"Find Ong, Tavish," she ordered. "Go find Ong."

Mrs. Plumley was fond of remarking that Tavish understood every single word that was said. Now he went over to Ong's pen and sniffed. He ran around in a circle with his long nose to the ground. Then he looked up in the air and barked.

Ong must have been trying out his wings.

"Find him, boy," Holly repeated. "Go look for him."

Tavish barked and disappeared into the night.

The grandfather's crutch tapped on the path. "Go to bed, Little One," he said gently. "Ong has probably found himself a nice quiet corner and gone to sleep. Tavish will find him."

Holly did as she was told and went to bed. Once she thought she heard Tavish bark. She closed her eyes and said a prayer, but it was a long time before she fell asleep.

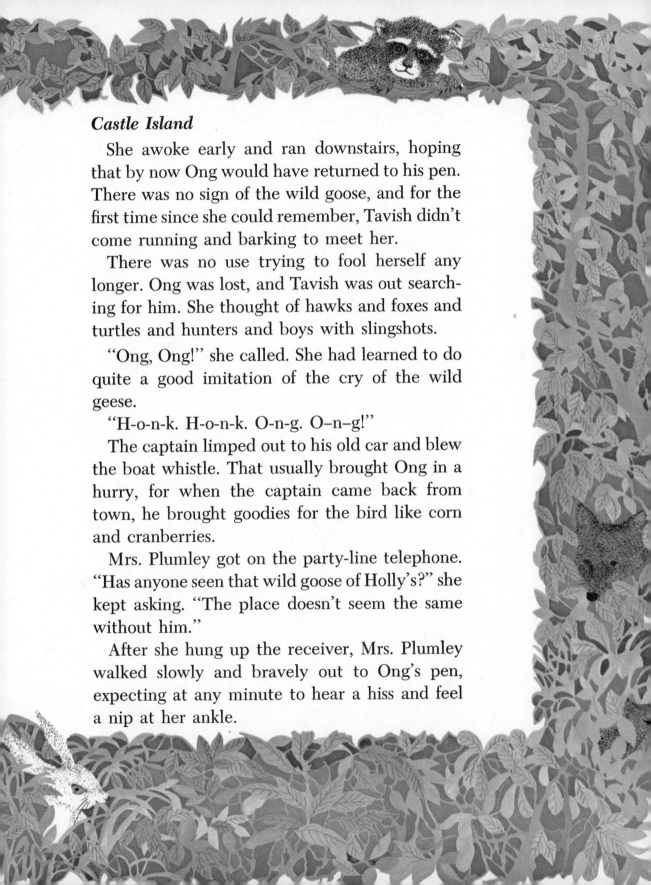

### Castle Island

She awoke early and ran downstairs, hoping that by now Ong would have returned to his pen. There was no sign of the wild goose, and for the first time since she could remember, Tavish didn't come running and barking to meet her.

There was no use trying to fool herself any longer. Ong was lost, and Tavish was out searching for him. She thought of hawks and foxes and turtles and hunters and boys with slingshots.

"Ong, Ong!" she called. She had learned to do quite a good imitation of the cry of the wild geese.

"H-o-n-k. H-o-n-k. O-n-g. O–n–g!"

The captain limped out to his old car and blew the boat whistle. That usually brought Ong in a hurry, for when the captain came back from town, he brought goodies for the bird like corn and cranberries.

Mrs. Plumley got on the party-line telephone. "Has anyone seen that wild goose of Holly's?" she kept asking. "The place doesn't seem the same without him."

After she hung up the receiver, Mrs. Plumley walked slowly and bravely out to Ong's pen, expecting at any minute to hear a hiss and feel a nip at her ankle.

When that didn't work, she went sadly back to the house.

Only Jessica, peacefully laying an egg in the hen house, seemed unconcerned. She had, it seemed, more important things to do.

All that long day Holly and the captain searched for Ong and Tavish. They drove along back roads, blowing the boat whistle. Holly ran down the Indian trail and the beach, calling and calling.

Mrs. Plumley scolded, but gently, because Holly and the captain barely touched the good dinner she had fixed for them. Then she walked slowly out to her little car and drove off to her own home in town.

When it began to grow dark, Jessica flew up on her perch, tucked her head under her ruffled feathers, and went to sleep.

Mr. Salt, looking very grave, stopped by at the farmhouse. He was on his way to a council meeting. He said there was no sign of either Tavish or Ong around the bay or in the Indian reservation. His people promised to keep watch.

For a long time after she went to bed, Holly lay awake, listening to the night sounds. She could hear the wind in the pines and the tree toads and the far-off sound of the lake. She heard the captain moving around downstairs, making another pot of coffee. Sometimes he worked all night. She could hear the deep thump-rumble of frogs in the swamp. No matter how hard she tried, she could not hear Tavish or Ong.

In the morning they were still missing.

Johnny Salt came over in his red sports car. "I'm taking the day off to look for Ong and Tavish," he said. "The boss is giving me his boat. I'm going over to Castle Island. It's the only place we haven't looked."

"I don't see what good that would do, Johnny," the captain said. "An old dog like Tavish could never swim that far, even if he thought Ong might be there."

"Please!" begged Holly, trying not to cry. "Let me go with Johnny."

"All right, Little One," the captain said gently, "but wear slacks and something to cover your arms. That place is full of poison ivy."

On any other day Holly would have enjoyed the boat trip. Mrs. Plumley had insisted on packing a picnic lunch with peanut butter and carrot sandwiches for Holly and thick beef and a dill pickle for Johnny Salt.

Back on the beach the bulldozers and workmen dwindled in size until they looked like toys. Sea gulls screamed overhead, dipping and skimming along the waves. Holly trailed her fingers in water, green as the early leaves of spring.

Huge, jagged rocks jutted out from the water around Castle Island. The waves here were much higher and rougher than they had been in the bay.

While Mr. Salt circled the island, Holly looked through the powerful field glasses at the rocky beach, but there was no sign of Tavish or Ong. She called and called, but her voice was snatched away by the wind.

The sun, reflected on the water, was extremely hot. She was grateful for the big straw hat Mrs. Plumley had made her wear.

"I'm afraid we might as well start back," Johnny said at last. "I'm apt to wreck the boat if I try to take it in any closer."

He reached for the motor cord.

"Listen!" cried Holly. "Listen."

Did she just imagine that she heard a faint bark? It was hard to be certain with the shrill crying of the gulls and the crash of waves.

She cupped her hands to her mouth. "Tavish!"
she called. "Ong—Tavish!"

"Your ears must be better than mine," Johnny
Salt said gently.

"I know he is somewhere back there in the
woods!" Holly cried. "I know I heard him!"

Johnny Salt started to shake his head, and then
he stopped.

"I hear something, too," he admitted. "It's not
a fox. Maybe, as my ancestors would say, it is
some kind of evil spirit. Make sure your life belt
is fastened, Holly. The boss will kill me if I even
scratch his boat, but I'm going to try to land."

He took the oars, and as skillfully as if the big
boat had been a birchbark canoe, he guided it
towards the beach. When they reached shallow
water, he anchored and carried Holly piggyback
onto the beach.

A bedraggled, furry body hurled itself through
the bushes, almost knocking Holly down. Yelping
with joy, Tavish leaped on Johnny, then ran back
to Holly. He licked at Holly's face as she knelt
and wound her arms about him.

"I thought I had lost both you and Ong," Holly
sobbed.

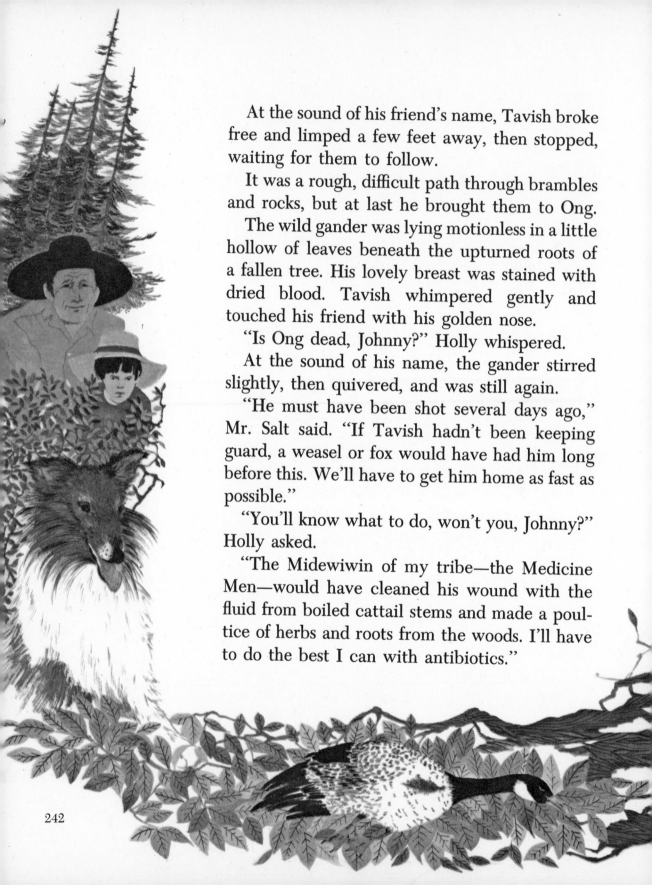

At the sound of his friend's name, Tavish broke free and limped a few feet away, then stopped, waiting for them to follow.

It was a rough, difficult path through brambles and rocks, but at last he brought them to Ong.

The wild gander was lying motionless in a little hollow of leaves beneath the upturned roots of a fallen tree. His lovely breast was stained with dried blood. Tavish whimpered gently and touched his friend with his golden nose.

"Is Ong dead, Johnny?" Holly whispered.

At the sound of his name, the gander stirred slightly, then quivered, and was still again.

"He must have been shot several days ago," Mr. Salt said. "If Tavish hadn't been keeping guard, a weasel or fox would have had him long before this. We'll have to get him home as fast as possible."

"You'll know what to do, won't you, Johnny?" Holly asked.

"The Midewiwin of my tribe—the Medicine Men—would have cleaned his wound with the fluid from boiled cattail stems and made a poultice of herbs and roots from the woods. I'll have to do the best I can with antibiotics."

242

## Flapjacks and Medicine Men

On the boat trip back, Holly cradled Ong in her arms while Tavish crouched at her feet, his burr-matted head against her, his eyes never leaving her face.

"Good Tavish," Holly said. "You couldn't bring Ong home, so you stayed to protect him. But how did you find him on Castle Island?"

While the captain and Johnny Salt dressed Ong's wound, Mrs. Plumley tried to feed Tavish, but though he was half starved, time after time he left his food to return to Ong.

He lifted his golden nose in the air and barked and whined, trying to tell his friends what had happened.

"I wish I could understand you, boy," the captain said. "Even if by some miracle you realized Ong was hurt and on the island, I don't see how you managed to swim so far. No wonder you look all worn out."

Mr. Salt pried Ong's yellow beak open, and the captain poured down a little medicine.

The bird seemed to shudder. He made a feeble sound—"Ark-ark."

Holly ruffled his neck feathers. "You're safe home now, Ong," she told him. "You must never leave again."

Ong was quite ill. Each day Holly carried him to a cool patch of clover under the russet apple tree. All day he squatted motionless, barely touching the berries or corn Holly brought him. He even ignored the captain's flapjacks.

Sometimes when Holly caressed him, ruffling his neck feathers gently to let in air rather than stroke them as one would a dog, he lifted his head and gave a faint, sad sound of thanks.

Tavish spent most of the time lying on the ground beside his friend, whining encouragement and keeping guard as he must have done on the island.

When the antibiotics didn't seem to work, Johnny Salt brought a worn, leather, beaded bag from the reservation. He took a grayish powder out of it and sprinkled it on Ong's wound.

He grinned at the captain. "The Midewiwin of my tribe were wise men. In time the scientists of the world may catch up with them."

Whether it was the antibiotics or the Medicine Man's little leather pouch, that day Ong staggered to his feet and took a few weak steps. When Johnny carried him down to the pond in the meadow, he drifted around, occasionally spraying the water over his dull feathers.

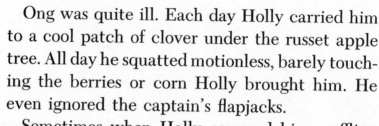

He began to eat again. Mrs. Plumley made him cornmeal mush. Holly and Johnny Salt brought him little treats of cranberries and gumdrops. Every morning he ate one of the captain's flapjacks and demanded more.

"If we'd given him the flapjacks in the first place instead of all that medicine, he'd be better by now," the captain grumbled. "That's what he needed to get him back on his feet."

One afternoon when Mrs. Plumley was walking towards her car, ready to go home, she heard a hissing sound behind her, and then she felt a little nip on her ankle.

She was so pleased, she almost cried.

Ong was well again.

### Reflections

1. Suppose that you had to depend entirely on this story for information about Canadian geese. What have you learned here about their appearance (size color, shape), their manner of walking and flying, and their personality and behavior?

2. How do you feel when you see a sick animal?

3. How did Mr. Salt feel about the Midewiwin of his tribe? Give details from the story to support your answer.

4. The author of this story often uses *similes*. To give you a vivid idea about something, the author says it was like something else. For example, she says that Mrs. Plumley didn't like geese because at night they made a racket "like a jammed automobile horn." Find three other similes in the first section of the story.

# Haiku

Now wild geese return . . .
     What draws them crying crying
All the long dark night?

       —Roka

     Out of the sky, geese
    come honking in the spring's cold
    early-morning light.

         —Soin

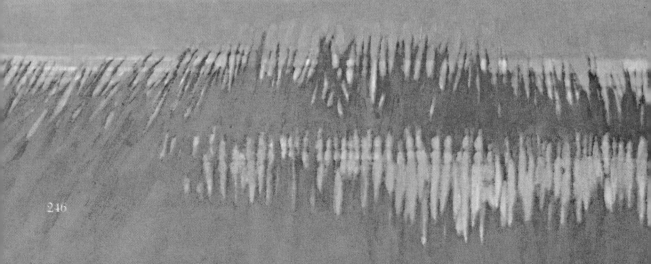

Wild geese have eaten
　　　All of my barley . . . Alas,
They are flying on!

　　　　　—Yasui


Night over the pond
of the temple garden . . . geese
adrift and asleep. . .

　　　　　—Shiki

247

# Bird Artist

**JOHN JAMES AUDUBON (1785–1851)**

Even as a boy, John James Audubon liked painting the birds he saw. Later he painted over four hundred life-sized pictures of birds in the North American wilderness. The National Audubon Society, devoted to preserving our wildlife, was named in Audubon's honor.

WILD TURKEY

MALLARD DUCK

AUDUBON, PAINTED BY HIS SONS JOHN AND VICTOR

GREAT HORNED OWL

# Chicks and Ducks

(top) This **poultry farmer** raises hens on a chicken farm. She earns her living by selling eggs which will be bought in grocery stores, perhaps hundreds of miles from the farm.

Poultry farmers supply food and shelter for their flocks of hens. They learn about different kinds of hens and raise those that are easiest to care for and lay the most eggs. They also have to make sure their animals stay healthy.

(bottom) A **bacteriologist** helps people who raise animals for food by studying how to keep the animals healthy. This bacteriologist, Jessie I. Price, found out that many ducks on Long Island, New York, were dying. She studied the bacteria that were causing the deadly disease and worked to develop a vaccine against it. Dr. Price's work is important to the whole duck-farming industry.

# The Animal Parade
DONALD CULROSS PEATTIE

When naturalists use the word animal, they mean any living thing that is not a plant. They mean

- the four-footed, warm-blooded mammals;
- the two-legged, feathered birds;
- the four-footed, cold-blooded turtles and lizards, salamanders and frogs;
- the six-legged insects;
- the eight-legged spiders;
- the millipedes and centipedes which are supposed to have a hundred legs (well, a hundred more or *less*!);
- the no-legged fishes and snakes;
- the no-backboned creatures. These include not only insects and spiders but a lot of ocean life as well. Octopus, jellyfish, starfish, crab, lobster, the sea anemones (which look confusingly like deep-sea flowers), the corals, the sponges, and many more creatures are animals that live in the ocean.

These animals are all alive, just as alive as you and I are. But how long they live varies.

How old, then, is "old"? A lively grandmother or a brisk grandfather of seventy will say, "You're just as old as you feel." This has some cheerful truth in it. But a cat near twenty doesn't feel much like hunting mice any more. The field mouse itself finds life too much for it before it can finish its second winter. But there are very simple creatures that live a long time. The sea anemone is one. A well-known English biologist kept one for sixty-six years. That's a long life, but not a very merry one! A sea anemone spends most of its time attached to a rock. When it does creep on its one "foot" or pedal disk, it goes so slowly, you cannot see it move.

A mayfly, though it lives as a fly but a day or so, has a life of light and air and dancing. A clam can live for twenty years, but who wants to be a clam? A salamander may live half a century, but it doesn't see much of the world. An eagle can live that long, too. But soaring over mountain and forest, it reaches heights of adventure and experience impossible to the cold-blooded salamanders. So, length is no measure for life. It is what you get out of life and what you put into it that matters.

Yet to all live creatures, life is so precious that they will struggle or fight to the end to keep it. And the winners at the great game of endurance are admired. That is why people like to exaggerate the ages of old animals. It is hard to know for sure about wild creatures. The records kept of animals we keep as pets are more exact. Even so, it is easy to boast about a pet's age. It may have been in the family so long that no one is very sure any more just how old it is.

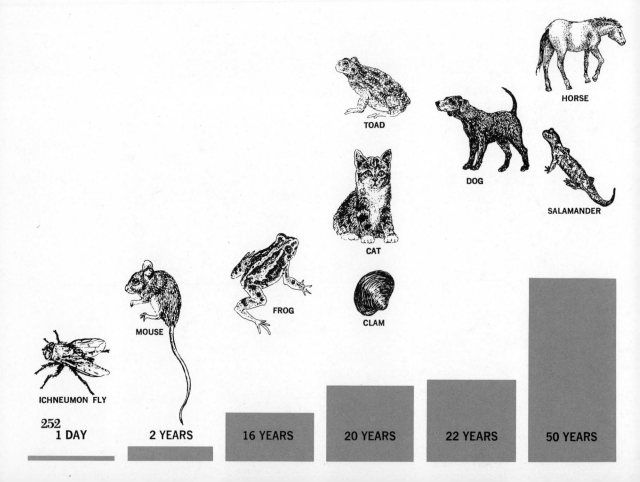

ICHNEUMON FLY

MOUSE

FROG

CAT

CLAM

TOAD

DOG

HORSE

SALAMANDER

1 DAY    2 YEARS    16 YEARS    20 YEARS    22 YEARS    50 YEARS

Parrots are often said to live to a hundred, but there is no real proof of that. They probably have lives half as long. The elephant, too, is often thought to grow as old as he is big, but no one has learned of an elephant older than sixty-nine.

But that *is* old, very old, for an animal. The record age for a horse is fifty years. For an owl it's sixty-eight. The record age for a dog is twenty-two, for a toad twenty, for a lobster fifty, for a pelican fifty-one. And for a bullfrog it is sixteen.

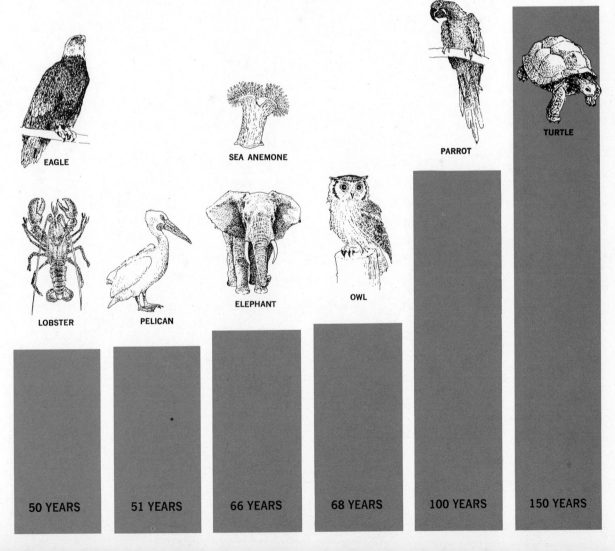

EAGLE

SEA ANEMONE

PARROT

TURTLE

LOBSTER

PELICAN

ELEPHANT

OWL

50 YEARS    51 YEARS    66 YEARS    68 YEARS    100 YEARS    150 YEARS

The giant land tortoise beats all the records. Most people believe that these slow old hardshells can live well over a hundred years. That's a long time to go crawling about the earth, your blood running chill and sluggish, with no braver way to meet danger than to draw into your shell!

It is better, people will feel, to stand upright on two feet and face the world even for a shorter time. And people do live longer than any other mammals. Even the wrinkled elephant is second. Every year discoveries in medicine and science prolong human life. Well may we give thanks for our own share of the grand adventure.

## Reflections

1. About 700,000 species of animals live on Earth. Name six or seven large groups of animals very different from each other.
2. If you had the choice of being any animal other than a human being, which animal would you choose? Why?
3. The writer of this piece says that length is no measure for life. Why do you think he feels this way?
4. Suppose that a great many different animals (a fish, an eagle, a lizard, a flea, a tiger, etc.) held a meeting to decide which one had the most pleasant life. What might they say they liked about their lives?
5. According to this article, people live longer than any other mammal. What are some reasons for the prolonged life of people?

# I Shall Not Live in Vain

EMILY DICKINSON

If I can stop one heart from breaking,
I shall not live in vain;
If I can ease one life the aching,
Or cool one pain,
Or help one fainting robin
Unto his nest again,
I shall not live in vain.

# GROUPING WORDS IN SENTENCES

In every English sentence we read, one word comes first, and others follow from left to right across the page. Try the sentence below by reading down each column of words. You will find that the words make a sentence.

| Each | laughter | who |
|------|----------|-----|
| day | to | love |
| brings | all | fun |

Now read these sentences aloud.

1.  A funny brown puppy     is playing     down the street.
2.  That blue coat     by the door     is mine.
3.  My green and blue notebook     will soon be found.
4.  The big red apple     on the oak desk
    is ready     for eating.

Words in the sentences above have been so spaced in each line that the words which fit together are grouped together. This is not the usual way to print words. But it is an easy way to read them. We learn to group the words that go together with our eyes and in our thinking. Such grouping of words is something that we bring to the written line. Seldom, except sometimes in poetry, does a line of print bring special arrangements of words to us.

Certain words themselves act as stop-and-go traffic signs in sentences. They signal ways for us to group other words within a sentence. A little practice will show you how the signal words work. If you can solve the puzzles that follow, you will learn some good ways to group words as you read.

## Puzzle One

All the sentences below have some blanks. Try working some of these words into the blanks: *a, an, the, this, that, these, those, his, no, all, her, our, my, their, one, two,* or *three.* Sometimes only one of the words will fit; sometimes two words may fit together in one blank space.

1. —— boys have —— secret meeting place.
2. Allen keeps —— games and models in —— place.
3. —— apple tree grows by —— cabin.
4. John went there, but he forgot —— ball and —— bat.
5. —— boys are —— ones I mean.
6. —— own house is near —— secret place.

Notice that each blank comes close to a noun.

Now use each of the italicized words listed in the first paragraph above in a sentence. These signal words are grouped with nouns and other words that follow them when we read. For example:

1. The boys     have     a secret meeting place.
2. Those boys     are     the ones I mean.
3. No apple tree     grows     by their cabin.

One way, then, to group words is to keep words like *a, an,* and *the* with the words that follow them.

## Puzzle Two

Words of another kind are missing in the paragraph that follows. Copy the paragraph and supply the word or group of words that you think fits best in the blanks.

The frisky squirrel lives —— our backyard. One day I chased him. He ran —— the tree. He jumped —— limb —— limb. Then he ran —— the tree. He scooted —— the yard, —— two bushes, and jumped —— the fence. He ran —— the rocks. I could not catch him. So I went —— the house, —— the stairs, and sat down —— my window to rest.

Words like *up, from, to, by, over, under, with, at, after, upon, across, off, on, between, from, into, down, before,* and *beneath* are called prepositions. Try fitting some of these into the blanks above. Prepositions are most often used to show direction or place. In reading, we group prepositions with the words that follow them in the sentence.

## Puzzle Three

Words like *who, that, when, if, since, so, after, although, where, whose, which, whom, because,* and *as* also act as signals. We group them with the words that follow them. It works like this:

1. John,     who is my cousin,     visits us often.
2. The model car     that came in the mail     is mine.
3. Mary,     when you finish,     come over to my house.
4. I will go     if you come with me     to his house.

Rewrite the four sentences above, grouping other words with *who, that, when,* and *if.*

Learn to group words like *who, that, when, if, since, what, so, as, after,* and *although* with the words that follow them. They help you keep sentence parts together.


**Puzzle Four**

Sometimes, in our reply to certain questions, we say or write sentences with just two words.

|  |  |  |
|---|---|---|
| John is. | He could. | They might. |
| They are. | She may. | He does. |
| I have. | She can. | I do. |

More often, however, verbs like *is, are, have, could, may, can, might, does,* and *do* and others like *would, must,* and *should* are signals that other verbs are coming.

| | |
|---|---|
| John *is eating.* | She *does enjoy* our company. |
| She *may have eaten.* | He *might have been seen.* |
| Judy *could have gone.* | Karen *has been swimming.* |

What other words listed above can you use in the six sample sentences instead of *is, may, has, does, might,* and *could?*

Watch for words like *is, are, have,* and the others in the list. You can often expect them to signal that other verbs are coming. Learn to group these words together as you read.

Good readers must make word groups in their thinking. Using correct word groupings, you will have a better understanding of what you are reading. You will also read with the rhythm of natural speech.

# The Friendly Cricket

Costa Rican Folk Song

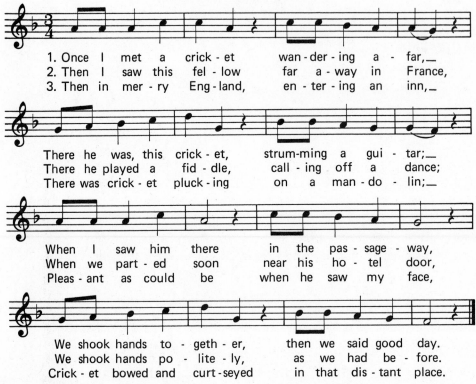

1. Once I met a crick-et wan-der-ing a far,__
2. Then I saw this fel-low far a-way in France,
3. Then in mer-ry Eng-land, en-ter-ing an inn,__

There he was, this crick-et, strum-ming a gui-tar;__
There he played a fid-dle, call-ing off a dance;
There was crick-et pluck-ing on a man-do-lin;__

When I saw him there in the pas-sage-way,
When we part-ed soon near his ho-tel door,
Pleas-ant as could be when he saw my face,

We shook hands to-geth-er, then we said good day.
We shook hands po-lite-ly, as we had be-fore.
Crick-et bowed and curt-seyed in that dis-tant place.

4. On a day last summer, when to Spain I'd come,
   There was Mister Cricket banging on a drum;
   When he spied me there, sipping at my tea,
   He approached my table, bowed, and greeted me.

5. Cricket is a trav'ler, as you surely know,
   So I always find him ev'rywhere I go;
   As he comes toward me, strolling down the street,
   We shake hands together, any time we meet.

# A Different Drummer

# The Magic Bagpipe
GERRY and GEORGE ARMSTRONG

Every year on the Isle of Skye, a great celebration was given at Dunvegan Castle in honor of the MacLeod chief's birthday. Part of the celebration was a bagpipe competition, and its winner was declared the Piper to the Chief.

Donald MacCrimmon had been taking lessons from Mister MacSkirl, who was going to give him his old set of bagpipes. But when Mister MacSkirl realized that the boy had become the better player, he told Donald to forget about the pipes.

On his way home, Donald saw an old woman struggling to get out of the river. He scrambled down the bank and hauled her to safety.

The old woman took Donald to her home. When she heard his story about the bagpipes, she gave him the handsomest set of pipes he had ever seen. But she warned him that the bagpipes could be played only by him!

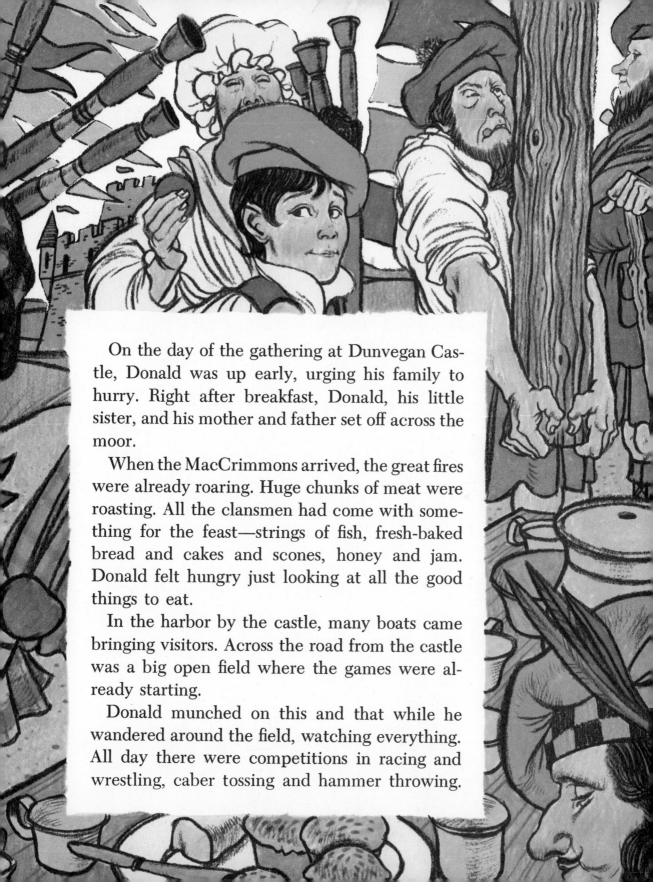

On the day of the gathering at Dunvegan Castle, Donald was up early, urging his family to hurry. Right after breakfast, Donald, his little sister, and his mother and father set off across the moor.

When the MacCrimmons arrived, the great fires were already roaring. Huge chunks of meat were roasting. All the clansmen had come with something for the feast—strings of fish, fresh-baked bread and cakes and scones, honey and jam. Donald felt hungry just looking at all the good things to eat.

In the harbor by the castle, many boats came bringing visitors. Across the road from the castle was a big open field where the games were already starting.

Donald munched on this and that while he wandered around the field, watching everything. All day there were competitions in racing and wrestling, caber tossing and hammer throwing.

Then, late that afternoon, Mister MacKenzie—who had been chosen because he had the loudest voice—shouted, "Pipers! Get ready!" and the contest Donald had waited for began.

Piper MacClure was first. Donald would be last, after O'Neil and Mister MacSkirl.

Donald waited happily, enjoying the music. He did not notice MacSkirl a few steps away. The old man stared at the boy from underneath his bushy eyebrows. He had a good set of pipes himself, but Donald's pipes were the best he had ever seen.

Finally, while O'Neil was playing, Mister MacSkirl spoke to Donald. "I'm sorry that I didn't fix up my old pipes for you," he said.

"Oh, that's all right, sir," said Donald happily. "I have a bagpipe set of my own now."

"So I see. But it's not a very good one. I'll tell you what I'll do, my boy. I'll trade with you."

And what did MacSkirl do then but jerk Donald's pipes from him and shove his own bagpipes at the boy! Then off he started. Of course, MacSkirl had not the least idea of how Donald had come by his set of bagpipes—he only wanted it for himself.

Donald started to race after the man. "No, no!" he called. "Please, Mister MacSkirl, I don't want to trade."

Just then MacSkirl's name was called, and he marched out on the field, leaving Donald weeping with anger.

Suddenly the boy heard such a strange noise that he stopped crying. What could it be? MacSkirl was playing, but it didn't sound like bagpipe music. It sounded like a cat fight!

There were squeals, shrieks, and gurgles. The bagpipe was wheezing and gasping like a sick cow. MacSkirl's fingers were slurring over every hoarse note.

At first the crowd listened in surprised silence. Then someone tittered and someone else giggled. And in a moment the whole crowd was rocking with laughter.

MacSkirl was bewildered. The pipes fell from his shaking hands. He pulled his bonnet down over his ears and fled.

Donald watched in amazement. Then he heard his own name called, "Donald MacCrimmon!" He ran out on the field, picked up his pipes, tucked them lovingly under his arm, and, puffing out his cheeks, began to play.

The laughter and hooting died as the people turned to listen to Donald. At first his music was as slow and sad and lonely as a single gull wheeling in a bleak sky.

The crowd grew very quiet as Donald paced slowly up and down, and the music sang of hardship and loneliness and disappointment. It made the listeners think of the cold wind sweeping over a moor and the gray waves rolling against the rocks.

Then Donald quickened his step, and the people lifted their heads as his music changed. It rolled out proud and glad, proud of the very hardness of life because it offered a challenge to overcome. People began to tap their feet and nod and smile. This music made them proud of their beautiful Isle of Skye, proud of being Scotsmen, proud of belonging to the MacLeod clan. The music swelled until everyone could feel it going through him, and the ground trembled with the warm, stirring tune.

Then Donald stopped.

For a minute there was silence, and Donald thought, "No one liked it. But I know I played well."

He lifted his chin proudly and started to march off the field.

Suddenly, as if there had been a signal, the crowd came to life with a roar. People rushed out on the field. Donald felt himself seized by friendly hands. He was lifted up on someone's shoulder and carried around the field. People cheered and screamed and stamped their feet. Bonnets flew into the air.

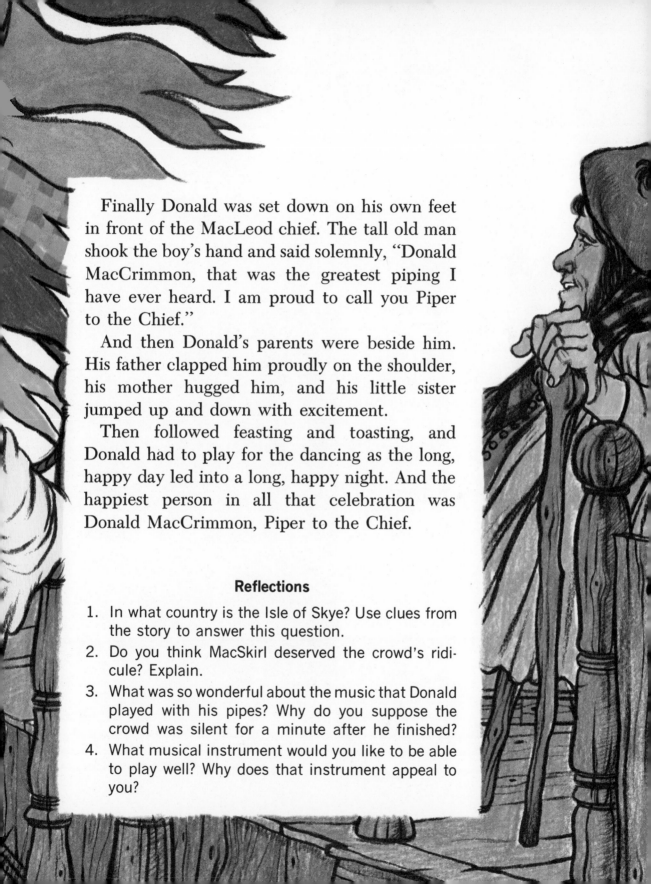

Finally Donald was set down on his own feet in front of the MacLeod chief. The tall old man shook the boy's hand and said solemnly, "Donald MacCrimmon, that was the greatest piping I have ever heard. I am proud to call you Piper to the Chief."

And then Donald's parents were beside him. His father clapped him proudly on the shoulder, his mother hugged him, and his little sister jumped up and down with excitement.

Then followed feasting and toasting, and Donald had to play for the dancing as the long, happy day led into a long, happy night. And the happiest person in all that celebration was Donald MacCrimmon, Piper to the Chief.

### Reflections

1. In what country is the Isle of Skye? Use clues from the story to answer this question.
2. Do you think MacSkirl deserved the crowd's ridicule? Explain.
3. What was so wonderful about the music that Donald played with his pipes? Why do you suppose the crowd was silent for a minute after he finished?
4. What musical instrument would you like to be able to play well? Why does that instrument appeal to you?

# *Music Makers*

## LOUIS ARMSTRONG

Louis (Satchmo) Armstrong made jazz music an accepted part of American culture. Like jazz, Armstrong was born in New Orleans, Louisiana. And as trumpeter and singer, his name is permanently tied to the history of American jazz.

Louis Armstrong became a legend in his own lifetime. He took jazz out of New Orleans and introduced it as an art form around the world. Wherever jazz is played, Satchmo is remembered as a great musician.

## DANNY KAYE

A singer, an actor, and a comedian, Danny Kaye began entertaining children for UNICEF in 1954. Since then he has made sick and unhappy children smile and laugh in countries throughout Africa, Asia, and Europe.

Born and raised in Brooklyn, New York, Mr. Kaye does not have to know the languages spoken in these countries. He communicates with the language of music and his own natural warmth. He makes people laugh by "double-talking"—running nonsense syllables together to sound like sentences.

Anyone who has seen the movie *Hans Christian Andersen* has seen Danny Kaye. Who else could better portray this famous author of fairy tales?

## LEONARD BERNSTEIN

Leonard Bernstein was the first music director of the New York Philharmonic Symphony Orchestra to be born in the United States. Best known as a conductor, he also won fame in other roles. He is a composer, a pianist, and a lecturer on music. In addition to writing symphonic music, he wrote the score for the musical, *West Side Story.* And he has been seen on television all over the country, lecturing on music and conducting the Young People's Concerts.

At times, Bernstein is even able to combine his musical talents. For example, he has played the solo part in piano concertos while conducting the orchestra from the piano bench.

Leonard Bernstein, born in Lawrence, Massachusetts, showed his talents at an early age. At fifty, he retired to give more time to composing and lecturing.

**MARIA TALLCHIEF**

Maria Tallchief's Indian name, Princess Wa-Xthe-Thonba (Princess of Two Standards), fits her life perfectly. She was born in the Osage Indian reservation town of Fairfax, Oklahoma. And she became the New York City Ballet Company's *prima ballerina*.

When Maria was about seven, her family moved to Los Angeles. There she studied both piano and ballet dancing. But ballet won out. At seventeen, Maria Tallchief made her debut with the Ballet Russe de Monte Carlo. She joined the New York City Ballet Company at its start in 1948, and became its leading dancer in 1954. Today, as a teacher of ballet, she passes on to others her knowledge and love of the dance.

# Bola and the Oba's Drummers

LETTA SCHATZ

*Bola had been allowed to leave his small village for the first time and to come with his mother to the market in the great town. At their stall in a far corner of the crowded West African marketplace, the deep sound of many drums reached Bola's ears. Then over the sea of bobbing heads, Bola saw the huge Royal Umbrella and the Royal Drummers, weaving and wheeling as they beat upon their drums. And in their midst, dancing as the drums commanded, was the Oba, the mighty king himself. But what truly held Bola's eyes were the two smallest drummers. They were boys about his own age. In that instant Bola knew he wanted to be a drummer, too, and to play at the Oba's palace. Without stopping to think about what he was doing, Bola followed the boy drummers through the palace gate to the veranda in the vast courtyard of the palace.*

## The Royal Drummers

One of the boys smiled. He had a merry, narrow face that folded into deep, smiling lines.

"Welcome," he said. "Greetings on our first meeting. I am Tunji. And this is my older brother, Bamiji. Are you new to the town?"

"I live in Ado-Ido village," Bola answered softly, still awed to be talking to one of the drummers. "My name is Bola. I came to market with my mother. Then I heard your drumming. Ah! How I would like to drum as you do! Is it hard to learn?"

"Hard?" the older boy, Bamiji, exclaimed. There was no mistaking that he and Tunji were brothers. Their faces were alike, but their expressions were different. Bamiji had a superior look. "One must be born a drummer," he said scornfully. "It has been the trade of our family for generations beyond remembering. Our father is Head Royal Drummer, and he has been teaching us since our hands could hold the stick. All

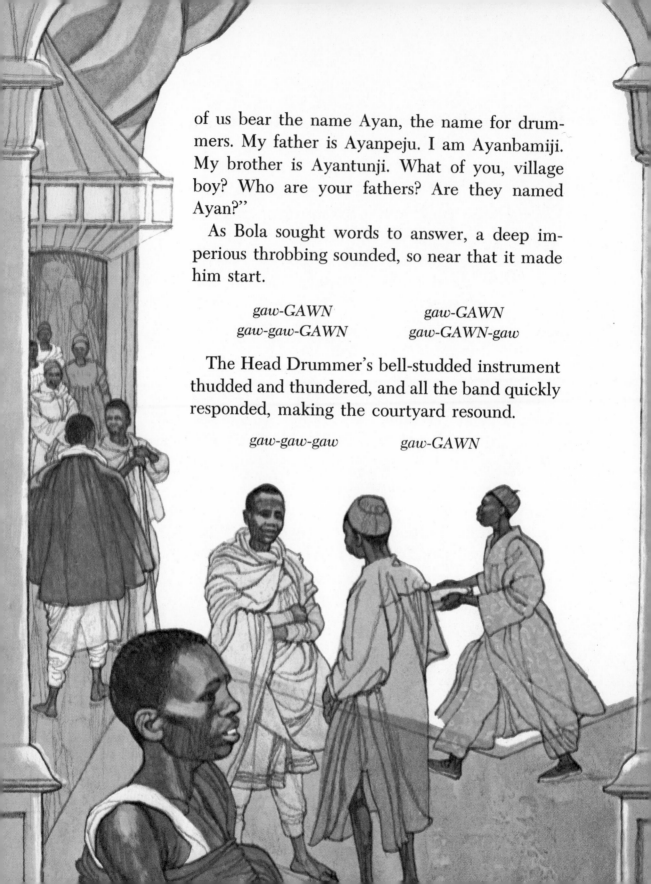

of us bear the name Ayan, the name for drummers. My father is Ayanpeju. I am Ayanbamiji.
My brother is Ayantunji. What of you, village
boy? Who are your fathers? Are they named
Ayan?"

As Bola sought words to answer, a deep im-
perious throbbing sounded, so near that it made
him start.

*gaw-GAWN*      *gaw-GAWN*
*gaw-gaw-GAWN*      *gaw-GAWN-gaw*

The Head Drummer's bell-studded instrument
thudded and thundered, and all the band quickly
responded, making the courtyard resound.

*gaw-gaw-gaw*      *gaw-GAWN*

"What is happening? Why are they drumming?" Bola asked.

"It is Chief Onikoyi," said Tunji, the younger boy. "See. He is arriving late."

Bola looked. A wizened old man with a wise, lined face was passing through the great arched gate. He was dressed in flowing white robes and narrow-ankled trousers embroidered in gold. Though his legs were feeble, his bearing was proud.

"The drummers are announcing him," Tunji explained. "Listen, they are saying,

'Chief Onikoyi,
Chief of Ikoyi,
Wise man of Ikoyi,
The sea never dries,
Neither does his wisdom.'"

"Aiee! Did the drums truly say all that?" Bola gasped. He had heard an exciting rhythm, nothing more.

"Of course," Tunji answered. "The Oba must know who is entering or leaving. When people of importance come, we announce their names and sing their praises. When they leave, we do the same. That is our duty."

"Nnhn." Bola shook his head in admiration. "It must be wonderful to have such duties."

"Would you like to try my drum?" Tunji asked.

Bola dipped his head in a speechless yes. Breath caught in disbelief, he gingerly reached for the precious instrument that Tunji handed him. Never had he even seen a drum so near; yet now his own two hands were holding one.

The drum was longer than he had thought—almost the length of his arm. It had a circle of leather stretched over the top and another one over the bottom. Down its length ran straight leather thongs, connecting one drumhead to the other.

Bola passed his hand lightly over the thin, tightly stretched strings. They were so close to each other that they almost touched, like a springy fence encircling the drum. He pressed down on them and felt a hard bulge beneath his palm. Through the thong fence he could just make out the body of the drum: it was carved from a solid log and shaped like two thick bowls,

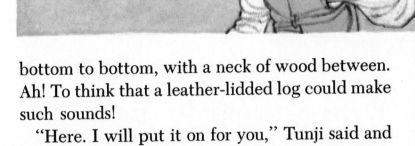

bottom to bottom, with a neck of wood between. Ah! To think that a leather-lidded log could make such sounds!

"Here. I will put it on for you," Tunji said and slipped the drum strap over Bola's left shoulder.

The wide cloth strap pulled tight, and Bola's shoulders felt for the very first time the wonderful tug of a drum hanging down. It hung suspended under his arm, its roundness just fitting into the hollow.

"Ayantunji! Ayanbamiji!" It was Father Ayan, the Head Drummer, calling.

"Yes, Father."

Tunji and Bamiji turned to go. "Come," Tunji said, beckoning to Bola as to an old friend. "We had better get back now."

Tunji ran after his brother. Puzzled, Bola followed the two boys, who were rapidly weaving their way through the people on the broad, dusky veranda.

"What is it? Why the hurry?" Bola asked.

"It is the chiefs," Tunji said over his shoulder. "They have come out of the king's chambers and are beginning to depart. Chief Adeyinka is going. And Chief Adeniyi. And now Chief Adepoju has come into the courtyard. . . ."

Bola was amazed. From the depth of the great dim veranda, they could not see the courtyard, yet Tunji and Bamiji knew exactly what was happening there.

"Haw-wu! Did the drums tell you all that?" Bola asked.

"Of course. Anyone with ears could hear it," Bamiji said. "Ah-ah! Now the Balogun is going! Come along, Tunji. Move your feet. Father will be very vexed if we are not there to drum the Balogun's praises!"

They passed between the pillars. The light of the courtyard struck their eyes after the darkness of the veranda. Bola looked up. The sun was beginning to dip low. He had not realized how long it had been since he left his mother's stall in the market. Mother's parting words clanged a warning in his head. How angry she would be if he were late.

Bola touched Tunji's arm. "I must go now," he said. "Thank you! Thank you many times!"

"Come again," Tunji said. "Any time you please. If you want, I will teach you to drum. I have never taught anyone before, but, if you wish, I will try."

"Truly?" Bola asked. "You do not joke?"

"Truly. It is a promise," said Tunji.

From the palace gate Bola waved back, then raced toward the market as if his feet were on wheels, stopping now and again to ask the way.

## The First Lesson

The next week, as Bola reached the great wall, there was Tunji, sitting by the palace gate. Tunji jumped up and ran to greet Bola, a wide smile of welcome on his face.

"Greetings of the morning! Morning, did I say? Look. It is almost afternoon."

Bola smiled back, the friendly welcome settling the flutters inside him. "Greetings of the morning," he said.

Bola looked about. The palace seemed quiet. The drummers were seated at their place beside the gate. A few people waited patiently on the great broad veranda, hoping to see the Oba. But today the courtyard was almost empty.

"Where are all the people?" Bola asked. "Last week there were so many! And where is your brother? I do not see him."

"There is no council meeting today. Last market day the council met, and next market day it shall meet again. Today is just a day like all others. The chiefs came to greet the Oba, but they have gone now. As for Bamiji . . ." Tunji shrugged. "He is at school."

"How does it happen that you are not at school then?"

Again Tunji shrugged. "My father likes to keep one of us here with him. Next year, perhaps, he will send me. What of you? Do you not go to school?"

"No. Our village has no school. And besides, my father does not have money enough. But he says if the next cocoa crop is good, he will send me to school. There is one three miles from our home." Bola looked at Tunji's drum. "But if I could drum like you, I would not care if I never went to school. Last time you said . . . do you remember? You said, perhaps . . ." All week Bola had been boasting how Tunji would teach him to drum. Now suddenly he was afraid to say it. "You said, if I wished to drum . . ."

"Ah! Myself, I would rather go to school." Tunji said. "They have many books there with wonderful tales. And they play football on the school field. I would like to be a football player."

Bola looked at Tunji in amazement. Bola could not believe that anyone who could be a drummer should wish to be anything else!

"But if you want to learn," Tunji said, "let us get you a drum. Come."

The drummers sat in their shady spot on the veranda, talking to each other. They barely looked up as Tunji passed between them and opened a door in the palace wall. Bola had not even noticed this door before. Slowly he followed his new friend.

He was in a long room—dark except for the light from the open door—a long, narrow room, part of the hollow palace walls. The room was crowded with chairs and mats and even some pots, but this Bola barely noticed at all. It was at the wall he stared. The walls were studded with pegs from which hung drums of all sizes and shapes, big and small, old and new.

"My eyes! They will grow weak from looking!" Bola sighed. "This is like a treasure house. What do you do with so many drums?"

"Come on a festival day," Tunji said, "then you will see. Today only six drummers are here. But often there are twelve or even more. Some festivals use special instruments. And sometimes," Tunji grinned, "sometimes one of the men plays so hard, he splits the drum. We always keep some extra ones."

Bola's eyes roamed the drum-festooned walls. "Nnhn." There was one exactly like the one the Head Drummer played, a great leather-lidded tube surrounded by gleaming bells, its wide strap richly embroidered. Bola stared at it. He reached out, not quite daring to touch it.

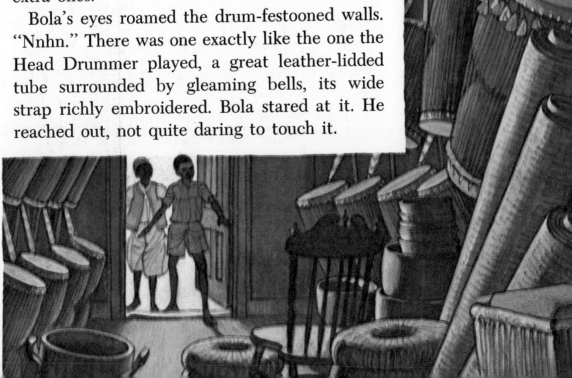

"Can you play this one, Tunji?"

"Iya Ilu?! The Mother Drum? Kai! My father would not let me use Iya Ilu. Nor Bamiji either. Mother Drum is the one that leads all the others and is played only by the most skilled of men. I am learning to play that one—Ishaju." There was pride in Tunji's voice as he pointed to a medium-sized cylinder hanging on the wall.

"Do all the drums have names?" Bola asked.

Tunji clicked his tongue. "Ttt! Does not each of us have a name of our own? Each drum has a different voice. Each has a part of its own to play. Naturally they have names." Tunji reached up. From a peg on the wall, he took down a small instrument, twin to his own, and from a peg beside it, a crook-shaped stick.

"Here," he said, handing them to Bola. "Kanango is the drum for learners. You can use this one for today."

"Ah-ah! Will your father not be angry?"

"Angry? Why? You will not take it away."

The two boys slipped quietly through the door, past the drummers, and down along the dusky veranda. They settled in a sheltered spot, close to the walls where the shadows were deepest.

Bola hugged the string-encircled drum to him. Kanango. Even its name was musical.

"Please, Tunji," he asked shyly, "will you show me how to make the drum speak?"

"Ah! You want to fly before you have feathers! To learn to make a drum speak takes much time. First . . ." Tunji beat out a simple rhythm.

"Listen. You must play exactly what I do." Tunji sounded very important, like a proper master.

"When you can copy rhythms, *then* you will be ready to copy speech."

*GAWN-gaw-gaw*—Tunji beat the simple rhythm.

*GAWN-gaw-gaw*—Bola copied it on his drum.

Then Tunji beat a more complicated rhythm: *gaw-GAWN-gaw gaw-gaw*. And Bola repeated it perfectly.

Tunji looked up and grinned. "Not bad. But let us see you play this one," he challenged: *gaw-GAWN-gaw GAWN-gaw-gaw gaw-gaw*.

Bola listened carefully. He began to play.

"No. That does not sound right," Tunji said. "The stick should be loose. Don't grab it with your fist. Let it hang in the loop between your thumb and first finger. Then it will strike lightly. Watch."

Bola watched and listened as Tunji again played the rhythm. Then Bola began again to

283

copy Tunji. He tried to hold the stick as Tunji did. How strange it felt, bobbing about in his hand, held only by the tips of forefinger and thumb.

"Better. Much better. Keep it loose," Tunji said.

Pleased with Tunji's praise, Bola loosened his fingers still more. The little crook suddenly took on a life of its own. It jumped from Bola's hand and clattered to the ground.

Tunji laughed. "Not quite so loose!" he said.

Bola reached for the stick, then glanced up at the sky.

The sun was beginning to move downward. His time at the palace was passing away.

"Please, Tunji. Now can you show me how to make the drum talk?"

"Ttt! How can you make it speak if your stick runs away?" Tunji asked, smiling a teasing smile.

"If you will show me, Tunji, I am sure I can do it properly. Let us try again. You will see," Bola pleaded.

This time Bola copied Tunji's rhythm perfectly. Tunji changed the pattern slightly, but Bola was not tricked. He repeated the new rhythm, beat for beat.

Again and again Tunji changed the rhythm. Each time Bola followed like an echo. Tunji tried longer, more difficult patterns. Repeatedly he challenged, "Ha! Listen, Bola! I bet you cannot play this!"

But Bola listened, putting all his being into his ears. The stick moved to his will as if it were part of him. Each time he echoed the rhythm Tunji played perfectly.

Several times the drums by the gate cried out, announcing the arrival and departure of important visitors. The quiet courtyard suddenly echoed with sound that rebounded from the palace walls and seemed even to shake the ground. One of the chiefs came, stayed awhile, then left again. Then another chief made a brief call. Two merchants came together. Then the Supervisor of Police came. Each time Bola looked up and listened closely to the drummers, the vivid throbbing echoing through him, setting him a-quiver. Would he ever be able to play like this?

The sun moved lower. Tunji beat out the longest rhythm yet. Bola repeated it.

"Well done!" Tunji exclaimed. "Ah, but you learn quickly. Now, if you wish to try to make Kanango speak . . ."

Bola flushed warm with pleasure. "Oh, please! Even just a word or two. How do you do it? How can a drum speak? I listen and listen. But I do not hear the words you hear when the drums sound."

"Ah! It seems hard to believe," Tunji said. "I suppose it is because your ears have not yet learned to listen properly. I hear it so plainly. It seems so simple.

"You know that in the Yoruba language, all words have tunes. If I wish to say your name, my voice must rise high, so all will know that *ola* means 'honor.' Otherwise, if we say the *o* and speak it low and the *la* in a middle tone, people will think your name means 'tomorrow.' Or if we say the *o* with a middle tone and then say the *la* very low, they will think your name means 'wealth.'

"Every word has its tune. The drum just copies the tune of the words. To make it speak high, we pull the strings tight. That tightens the drumhead and makes its voice high. Now listen. It will say 'Bola.' Watch."

Tunji seemed to be hugging his Kanango under his arm. His lower arm pressed down on its strings until they were squeezed tight against the body of the drum. Tunji tapped the drumhead with his stick, two quick, light taps. High and clear Kanango spoke out, two high, short sounds. Bola could hear it. Ah! It was truly speaking the tune of his name. Again Tunji tapped. But now the sound was different, not quite so high as before. Bola looked at the drum. How had Tunji changed the sound?

"See. If I loosen the strings that connect the drumheads," Tunji said, "if I loosen them just enough, then the drum speaks in a middle tone, halfway between high and low. And if I do not touch the strings at all—listen to it then."

Bola listened. "I hear it!" he exclaimed. "Now the voice is low! Wonderful! Truly wonderful! Let me try."

Bola pressed down on the leather thongs and felt them give, felt them bend toward the drum, their shape marking stripes on the flesh of his arm. He pressed until the pliant cords could give no more, then he tapped the drumhead lightly with his stick. Once. Twice. Again he plainly heard the tune of his name, two high syllables, "Bo-la." Again he played it. "Bo-la."

"Good!" Tunji exclaimed. "They must have won!"

Puzzled, Bola looked up at his friend. What was Tunji talking about?

"Won?" he asked.

Tunji nodded. "I can always tell just by looking," he said. "Bamiji's team won their football match today. See . . ." Tunji pointed toward the palace gate. Bamiji had just come trotting through the entrance, a grin on his face.

Bola was dismayed. Could school already be finished for the day? He tipped his head back. Kai! The sun had slid so much lower since last he looked. Bola jumped to his feet, slipping the drum from his shoulder as he rose.

"Ah-ah! I dare not be late!" he said.

"Too bad," said Tunji, taking Kanango. "When Bamiji tells of a match, you think you are seeing it. Will you come next market day?"

"I will try," Bola said.

"Till next time then," Tunji said, tapping his drum with the stick. An hour ago Bola would have thought it just an idle tapping, but now his ears could hear what they had not heard before.

"Till next time," sang the drum, echoing the tune of Tunji's words. "Till next time."

## Reflections

1. Do you think Tunji was a good teacher? Explain why or why not. Would you like to have Tunji for a teacher?

2. What were the full names of Tunji and Bamiji? How were their names formed? If the same system were used in this country, what would be the name of each member of your family?

3. Do you think Bola will ever become a great drummer? Give reasons for your answer.

4. Here are three ways of expressing the idea that the ruler is approaching.
   a. A note with these words: "The king is coming."
   b. Someone saying, "The king is coming."
   c. A note with this drawing:

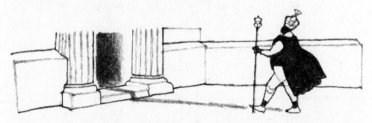

How else might someone who spoke the Yoruba language express this idea? Do you think that method would work with English? Explain why or why not.

# Animals in Art

IRV BARNETT

### *THE DREAM* (detail)

HENRI ROUSSEAU (1844–1910)

People share their world with animals, even their dreams. Rousseau imagined a jungle where a piper's notes draw wild animals to the source of the music.

THE MUSEUM OF MODERN ART, NEW YORK CITY. GIFT OF NELSON A. ROCKEFELLER

## GROUP OF BULLS, HORSES, AND STAGS
PREHISTORIC CAVE PAINTING

This detail of a cave painting in Lascaux, France, was done some twenty thousand years ago. In 1940 two boys discovered the Lascaux Caves while they were searching for their lost dog. Perhaps prehistoric man wanted some way to control the herds of animals which he hunted, and the rock paintings were part of a magic ceremony created to influence the animal spirits.

PHOTO: HINZ, BASEL

## AFRICAN DRUM FROM THE BAGA TRIBE
TWENTIETH-CENTURY CEREMONIAL DRUM

Sculpture is the most popular art form in Africa. Members of the Baga tribe in northwestern Africa carved one log to make this chieftain's ceremonial drum. It is as tall as a man and makes a deep booming sound when played. For each different ceremony the drum is redecorated with new patterns. But the little horse supporting the drum on his colorful saddle is kept the same.

ROYAL ONTARIO MUSEUM, TORONTO, CANADA

## BUFFALO DANCE OF THE MANDAN INDIANS
KARL BODMER (1809–1893)

Karl Bodmer, a Swiss artist, visited the Mandan Indians of North Dakota in the mid-nineteenth century and painted this dance. The buffalo provided food, clothing, and shelter for the Indians. When the vast buffalo herds disappeared from the plains, the Mandans performed this dance to bring them back. The two bravest men in the tribe had the honor of wearing the entire head of the buffalo.

293

## AKBAR IN BATTLE
SIXTEENTH–CENTURY COURT PAINTING

Emperor Akbar, the greatest Mogul ruler of India, employed painters to illustrate scenes from his life. This painting shows Akbar advancing into battle. The men in the fortress are fleeing to their boats to escape from Akbar's thundering elephants.

## PLOWMAN OF AREZZO
SIXTH–CENTURY B.C. ETRUSCAN BRONZE

The Etruscans were a rich and powerful people that lived in central Italy about twenty-five hundred years ago. This little bronze group shows an Etruscan farmer walking behind his two yoked oxen. Originally the farmer was holding on to the beam of the plow, which was fitted into his hands.

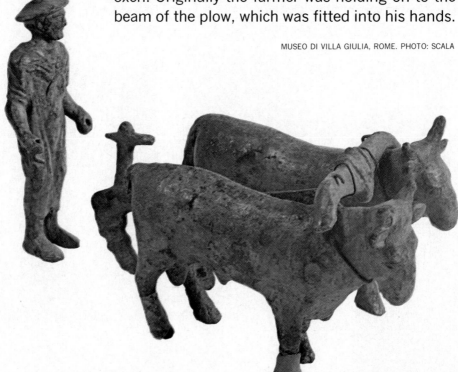

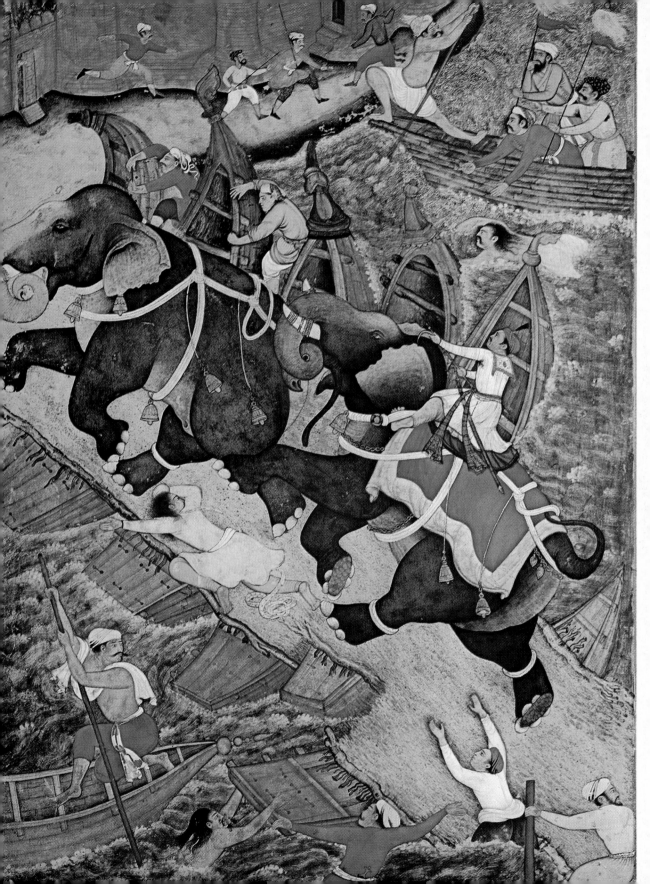

## *BOY TAKING FLEAS OUT OF A DOG*
GERARD TER BORCH (1617–1681)

This boy and his dog lived in Holland in the seventeenth century. The boy is carefully grooming his pet so he will be clean and healthy, and the little spaniel is happy to stay just where he is.

## THE HORSE FAIR
ROSA BONHEUR (1822–1899)

Rosa Bonheur's animal paintings are known for their remarkable accuracy. *The Horse Fair* is considered her masterpiece. It was originally called *The Horse Market in Paris* when it was begun in 1852. For a year and a half Rosa Bonheur went to the horse market twice a week to make sketches. She dressed as a man in order not to attract attention among the horse dealers and buyers. Looking at the painting, you almost hear the frantic sounds and sense the horses straining against the men.

THE METROPOLITAN MUSEUM OF ART, NEW YORK CITY. GIFT OF CORNELIUS VANDERBILT

## THE UNICORN AT THE FOUNTAIN
FIFTEENTH–CENTURY TAPESTRY

This tapestry is one of a set made for the royal family of France. It is woven with wool, silk, and metallic threads. The unicorn, an imaginary animal, has always been thought to have magical powers. In this scene the hunters have sighted a unicorn by the fountain and are gathering around to watch him.

## BABOON AND YOUNG
PABLO PICASSO (1881–1973)

Picasso is an artist with an extraordinary imagination. When he saw a child's toy car, he realized that it could easily become a part of his baboon sculpture. Can you see where?

THE MUSEUM OF MODERN ART, NEW YORK CITY. MRS. SIMON GUGGENHEIM FUND

299

### *THE WINGED LION*

JANET ANDERSON (1960–     )

Mrs. Lili Knize, art instructor for the New Canaan public schools, asked one of her classes to draw imaginary animals. Janet Anderson, a fourth grader, created this colorful animal for the assignment.

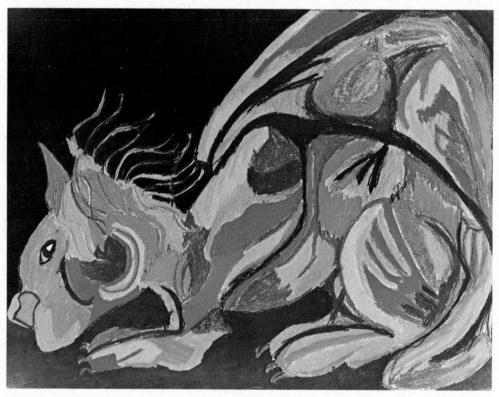

COURTESY MRS. LILI KNIZE, ART INSTRUCTOR, NEW CANAAN, CONNECTICUT, PUBLIC SCHOOLS

# Time for Fun

PRISCILLA FITZHUGH

### *OLD STAGECOACH* (detail)

EASTMAN JOHNSON (1824–1906)

People have always had time for fun. What they enjoy does not differ from century to century nor from continent to continent. If this were an abandoned bus instead of an old stagecoach, twentieth-century children would probably be climbing all over it just as these nineteenth-century boys are doing.

MILWAUKEE ART CENTER, LAYTON COLLECTION

## *ACROBATS*

KATSUSHIKA HOKUSAI (1760–1849)

These Japanese drawings are actually woodcuts. They appeared in the *Manga*, a series of sketchbooks containing Hokusai's drawings. The acrobats are obviously enjoying themselves as they perform their warm-up exercises.

## ONE HUNDRED CHILDREN AT PLAY

SOUTHERN SUNG DYNASTY (1127–1279)

This picture of Chinese children at play was done with ink and dyes on silk. If you look closely, you can see that children in the twelfth century played the same games that children the world over still play today: follow the leader, marching to music, and dressing up in costumes.

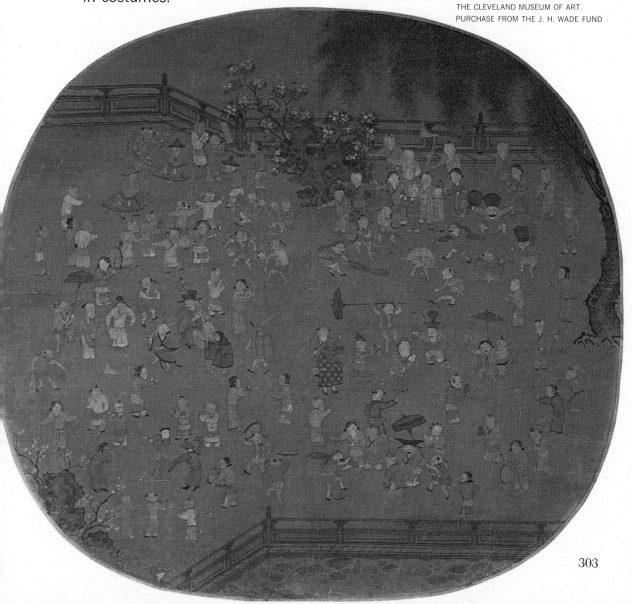

303

### THE SOAP BUBBLE BLOWERS
JEAN–BAPTISTE CHARDIN (1699–1779)

The two French boys in this picture are having fun in an age-old way. If you've ever blown soap bubbles, you know that half the fun is seeing how big the bubble gets before it bursts or floats away. The younger boy is more interested in watching the older boy than he is in trying the game himself.

### CHILD'S GAME
PAUL KLEE (1879–1940)

Sometimes an artist can have great pleasure himself by painting another person having fun. This painting seems to express the joy of being a little girl in the country on a sunny day.

## FOOTBALL PLAYERS

HENRI ROUSSEAU (1844–1910)

These old-fashioned figures seem to be moving like marionettes on their tree-bounded stage. This football game is a product of Rousseau's imagination rather than a picture of an actual sporting event.

## FOOTRACE

ROBERT DELAUNAY (1885–1941)

All you can see in this painting of a race are the five runners. The track, the spectators, the finish line are all left to your imagination.

### *YOUNG AMERICA*

ANDREW WYETH (1917– )

Born in Chadds Ford, Pennsylvania, Andrew Wyeth has painted the people and the land around there all his life. He was trained as a painter by his father, who was also a famous artist.

This boy on a bicycle was a close friend of the Wyeth family. His idea of fun was riding across the open farm country, the wind pressing against him and rustling the decorations on his bicycle.

### HAMMERSMITH BRIDGE ON BOAT RACE DAY
WALTER GREAVES (1841–1930)

Incredible crowds have gathered on this bridge to watch the boat race on the Thames. The most daring of the spectators have climbed up on the cables for a better view. The boat race is not the only spectacle here. The crowd is also being entertained by the minstrels and dancers.

## CHILDREN'S GAMES
PIETER BRUEGHEL THE ELDER (1520?–1569)

In this painting the whole town is a playground. A flood of people has filled every inch of this Flemish village. The children are using everything in sight for their game playing. As far as you can see, to the faint bluish church spire at the end of the long busy street, games are going on.

### DREAM RIDE

WILLIAM JAMES GLACKENS (1870–1938)

The charming details in this painting could not have taken place except in someone's fantasy. This girl might be riding her rocking horse in the nursery. But anyone knows that when you are playing games and having fun, rocking horses and broomsticks can become dappled ponies and horseless riders get there just as fast.

# The Mouse That Soared

HELEN LOUISE MILLER

## Characters

ORVIE MOUSE *Hugh*

MAMMA MOUSE *Angie*

*James* FRISKY

*Derrick* WHISKERS } *mice who play the Three Blind Mice*

*Mark* RISKY

*Salley* SCAMPER, *a mouse who plays the Farmer's Wife*

*Ben* LONG TAIL

*Dougie* SHORT TAIL

*Blackmon* NIBBLER

*Terry* SCRIBBLER

*Capers* FLUTTER } *other mice*

*Lisa* FURRY

*Stacia* SQUEAKY

*Leigh* SQUEALY

*Kenny* BILL

*Todd* JAKE } *boy rocketeers*

*Paul* THOMAS CAT

ANNOUNCER (*offstage voice*)

REPRINTED FROM *EASY PLAYS FOR BOYS AND GIRLS* BY HELEN LOUISE MILLER, COPYRIGHT © 1963 BY PLAYS, INC., PUBLISHERS, BOSTON, MASSACHUSETTS.

Setting: *Merry Mouse Meadow*
(*At curtain rise the game Three Blind Mice
is in progress.* FRISKY, WHISKERS, *and*
RISKY, *who are blindfolded, join hands and
go around in a circle, singing "Three Blind
Mice."* SCAMPER, *as the Farmer's Wife,
brandishes a cardboard carving knife and
tries to break through the circle. When they
finish the song, the Farmer's Wife chases
the Three Blind Mice as they break the
circle and run in all directions, until one is
caught. During the game,* ORVIE *sits under
a tree, ignoring the others, pretending to
read a torn scrap of newspaper. Other mice
stand around stage and watch the game.*)

315

FRISKY. That was fun! Let's play again.

WHISKERS (*as he takes off his blindfold*). Come on, Orvie, you play this time.

ORVIE. No, thanks. I want no part of that stupid game!

SCAMPER (*offering* ORVIE *the carving knife*). But it's fun. Take my part.

ORVIE. No, thanks.

NIBBLER. Oh, come on, Orvie. We need your voice. You're such a good squeaker.

ORVIE. I wouldn't sing that disgusting song!

SCAMPER. Disgusting! What's disgusting about it?

ORVIE. Everything! It makes us mice look silly and stupid.

LONG TAIL. I never thought of that.

ORVIE. Well, think about it. Actually, mice are very clever creatures. We have to be to stay alive.

SHORT TAIL. Maybe we could play Hickory Dickory Dock!

ORVIE. That's almost as bad.

FURRY. Hickory dickory dock,
The mouse ran up the clock.
The clock struck one,
The mouse ran down.
Hickory dickory dock!

RISKY. What's wrong with that?

ORVIE. Don't you see? The mouse was a coward. Afraid of a little old clock! He ran away.

WHISKERS. I never thought of that!

ORVIE. You're all too busy running away to think of anything. You're even afraid of old Thomas the Cat!

RISKY. Sh-h-h! Don't even mention him. He might hear you.

ORVIE. And what if he does? He's half blind and almost toothless. Yet you're all scared to death of him.

LONG TAIL. Mice are just naturally timid!

ORVIE. That's not true. Think of our great mouse heroes. Why doesn't anybody write songs about them?

SCRIBBLER. I don't know any mouse heroes.

ORVIE. Shame on you! What about our great ancestor who wasn't afraid of a lion?

SQUEAKY. Oh, I know about him. He even saved the lion's life.

ORVIE. And what about the brave mice who sailed with Columbus and came along with the Pilgrims on the *Mayflower?* Does anybody ever hear about them?

FURRY. No, never!

ORVIE. Take my own ancestor—Orville Mouse, the First.

SCRIBBLER. Tell us about him, Orvie. Maybe I could write a song about him.

ORVIE. He lived in the little bicycle shop where the famous Wright brothers built the first airplane. He was named for Orville Wright.

FURRY. How exciting!

ORVIE. You just wait and see! One of these days I'm going to make all you mice sit up and take notice.

SQUEAKY. I'll bet you would be a real mouse hero, if only you had the chance.

SQUEALY. But nothing exciting ever happens here in Merry Mouse Meadow.

(*There is a loud noise offstage. All the mice except* ORVIE *flee in terror.*)

ORVIE. Cowards! Cowards!

ALL (*ad lib*). What was that? (*Etc.*)

ORVIE. Don't you know?

FRISKY. It sounded like the end of the world.

ORVIE. It was a rocket taking off in the next field.

WHISKERS. A rocket! What rocket?

ORVIE. Don't you ever read the papers? Here, Scribbler. (*Hands him scrap of newspaper.*) Read this.

SCRIBBLER (*reading*). "The Junior Rocket Club meets every Saturday morning in Pleasant Acres near Merry Mouse Meadow where they have built a launching pad. The president of the club told reporters they are planning to send up a mouse in their next experiment."

SQUEAKY. Run for your lives! Run for your lives!

ORVIE (*as they start to run off*). Stop! Stop! Where are you going?

SHORT TAIL. I don't know, but I'm getting out of here fast.

LONG TAIL. You heard what it said. They're looking for a mouse to go up in a rocket!

ORVIE. There's nothing to be afraid of. You're all perfectly safe.

SCAMPER. How do you know?

ORVIE. Because they're going to take *me*.

RISKY. You!

ORVIE. Yes, me! I am going to volunteer.

FURRY. What!

ORVIE. This is my big chance. Just think, I'll be the very first mousetronaut!

NIBBLER. You wouldn't dare!

SCRIBBLER. You'll be blown to bits!

RISKY. What will your mother say?

ORVIE. She will be proud of me, and so will the rest of you when you see my name in headlines.

SCRIBBLER. "Orvie in orbit!" Yes, it has a wonderful sound.

WHISKERS. But you will be killed!

ORVIE. Nonsense! I'll live to tell even my great-grandchildren about my adventure in space.

SCAMPER. You will bring honor and glory to Mouseland.

RISKY. Do you really think you can do it, Orvie?

ORVIE. I know I can, but I will need all of your help.

ALL (*ad lib*). Tell us what to do. We'll help you. . . . (*Etc.*)

ORVIE. Good! Now first of all, I will need special equipment.

FLUTTER. I've heard there isn't any air in space. What will you breathe?

SQUEAKY. Couldn't we give him some cans of air to take along?

SQUEALY. It's not that simple. Orvie will need his own space suit.

NIBBLER. He will need a helmet.

SCRIBBLER. And gloves.

FURRY. And boots.

SQUEALY. What are we waiting for? Let's go round up the things he needs.

LONG TAIL. Come along, Orvie. You'll have to try them on for size.

(*All* MICE *except* SCRIBBLER *and* NIBBLER *exit.*)

NIBBLER. Do you really think he can make it?

SCRIBBLER. Other animals have done it. Remember that monkey who went up in 1961? What was his name?

NIBBLER. His name was Enos. His picture was in all the papers at the time.

SCRIBBLER. If a monkey can do it, so can a mouse.

NIBBLER. Anything apes can do, mice can do better!

SCRIBBLER. Sh-h-h! I hear somebody coming.

NIBBLER. Quick! Let's hide.

(NIBBLER *and* SCRIBBLER *hide as* BILL *and* JAKE *enter.*)

JAKE. Everything is set for the big test flight. All we need is our mouse.

BILL. We'll catch one. There are traps all around the base.

JAKE. But they're still empty. Those mice are getting smarter every day.

BILL. Maybe we could catch a field mouse right here.

JAKE. What do you think you are, Bill, a cat?

BILL. There's just one thing that bothers me, Jake.

JAKE. What's that?

BILL. I want to bring our mouse back alive. I don't want him to burn up on the way down.

JAKE. That's always the big re-entry problem, but I think we have it licked. The mouse will be safe in his little nose cone, and he will come down by parachute.

BILL. Sh-h-h! (*Pointing.*) Look! Look! Look over there.

JAKE. What? Where?

BILL. I thought I saw a mouse. Maybe we can sneak up on him.

JAKE. Oh, come on, Bill. We don't have time. We're due at the launching pad right now. Hurry up.

(*As* JAKE *and* BILL *exit,* NIBBLER *and* SCRIBBLER *creep out.*)

NIBBLER. What was all that talk about burning up on the way down?

SCRIBBLER. It has something to do with what scientists call friction. A fast-moving object falling through the atmosphere can burn itself up. That's what happens to a shooting star.

NIBBLER. Then it could happen to Orvie! We can't let him go!

SCRIBBLER. Simmer down. Every spaceman must face these dangers. But the scientists are finding new answers all the time.

NIBBLER. I hope those boys know what they're doing. Poor Orvie!

SCRIBBLER. Here he comes! And look! His mother is with him.

(ORVIE *enters wearing a space suit. He is accompanied by* MAMMA MOUSE *and other* MICE.)

MAMMA MOUSE. Oh, Orvie, are you sure you're all right?

ORVIE. I'm fine, Mamma. Now, don't worry.

SHORT TAIL. We'll go with you to the launching pad.

LONG TAIL. We'll see you off.

SCRIBBLER. No, we'd better stay here.

NIBBLER. We just found out there are mousetraps all over the base.

SCAMPER. How will we know what happens to Orvie?

WHISKERS. We can listen on the radio.

FRISKY. I brought my transwhisker!

MAMMA MOUSE (*throwing her arms around* ORVIE). Oh, Orvie! Orvie! I can't let you go!

ORVIE. Now, now, Mamma. Don't cry. When I come back, you'll be the proudest Mamma Mouse in all the world. Here, Squeaky, you look after her.

SQUEAKY. I'll take good care of her, Orvie.

ORVIE. And now I must be off. Thanks for all your help.

ALL. Good luck, Orvie. (ORVIE *exits, as* MICE *all wave and sing to the tune of "Good Night, Ladies."*)

Good luck, Orvie! Good luck, Orvie! Good luck, Orvie,
Come back here safe and sound.

MAMMA MOUSE. Oh, dear! I think I'm going to cry.

SQUEAKY. Now, now, Mamma Mouse, you must be brave.

RISKY. You come and sit by me, and we'll listen to the radio.

(MICE *form semicircle around* FRISKY *and radio.*)

FRISKY. It's too soon for any news.

FLUTTER. While we are waiting, I think we should plan a celebration for Orvie when he comes down.

FURRY. We'll give him a banquet.

SHORT TAIL. And call out the band!

LONG TAIL. We'll have music and speeches.

SCRIBBLER. I've already started a poem. Listen. It's called "Ode to Orville." (*Takes paper from pocket and reads.*)

> Out by the Rocket Firing pad
> The Meadow Mousie stands.
> The mouse a mighty mouse is he
> With large and venturesome plans,
> And the courage of his tiny heart
> Is strong as iron bands!

(*All applaud.*)

SCAMPER. Let's hear the rest of it.

SCRIBBLER. That's as far as I can go till I see what happens.

WHISKERS. Turn on the radio now, Frisky. It must be close to launching time.

(FRISKY *turns on the radio. There are static sounds from offstage. He pretends to listen closely.*)

FRISKY. I can't quite get the station, but I think they said they're starting the countdown.

ALL (*singing to tune of "John Brown Had a Little Indian"*).

> One little, two little, three little seconds,
> Four little, five little, six little seconds,
> Seven little, eight little, nine little seconds,

Ten little seconds to go!
Ten little, nine little, eight little seconds,
Seven little, six little, five little seconds,
Four little, three little, two little seconds,
One little second to go!

(*Loud crash and whistling sound from offstage.*)

ALL (*ad lib*). He's off! He's off! (*They look up.*) Whee-ee! There goes Orvie! (*Etc.*)

MAMMA MOUSE (*jumping up in a frenzy*). Orville! Orville Mouse! You come back here this very minute! Do you hear me?

SQUEAKY. There, there. Take it easy, Mamma Mouse.

MAMMA MOUSE. He'll be killed! I know he will! Oh dear! Oh dear!

FRISKY. Sh-h-h! I think I'm getting something on the radio.

(*All crouch down and listen.*)

ANNOUNCER (*offstage, on loudspeaker*). A perfect takeoff! Everything is going just exactly as planned, and all precautions have been taken to bring our mouse passenger back to earth safely.

SQUEALY. Hear that, Mamma Mouse? There's nothing to worry about.

LONG TAIL. Orvie is going to be a hero for sure.

SHORT TAIL. We must give him a medal.

FLUTTER. Where will we get one?

RISKY. I know! I know! Let's give him Thomas Cat's bell!

WHISKERS. How would we get Thomas Cat's bell?

RISKY. If Orvie can be a hero, so can we! We'll take it right off Tom's neck. All in favor?

ALL. Aye!

FLURRY. Sh-h-h! I think I hear the cat coming. Quick, let's hide.

(ALL *hide behind bushes as* THOMAS CAT *enters.*)

THOMAS CAT. I smell something funny! Not a mouse in sight!

(MICE *dash out and attack* THOMAS CAT. *In the scuffle, two of them sit on* THOMAS CAT *as* SQUEALY *takes the bell from around his neck!*)

SQUEALY. We have it! We have it!

THOMAS CAT. Let me up! Let me up!

MICE. Promise to do us no harm.

THOMAS CAT. I promise. (*They let him up.*) Now what was that all about? Why did you take my bell?

NIBBLER. It's for Orvie.

SCRIBBLER. Orvie is a hero now. We want to give him a medal.

THOMAS CAT. Orvie has always been a hero. He was the only mouse who was never afraid of me. If you had told me the bell was for Orvie, I would have given it to you without all this fuss.

SCAMPER. Thanks, Thomas. You may join us at the radio for news of Orvie's return to earth.

THOMAS CAT. We don't need the radio for that. Orvie has already landed safe and sound.

MAMMA MOUSE. How do you know?

THOMAS CAT. I've just come from the field. Orvie is fit as a fiddle.

ALL. Hurrah! Hurrah! Hurrah!

THOMAS CAT. As soon as he has had his medical checkup, he'll be home.

FRISKY. Come on, everyone. We must get our band instruments and have a parade to welcome Orvie home.

MICE (ad lib). Yes, let's. Come on, hurry! (Etc.)

(FRISKY, WHISKERS, FURRY, FLUTTER, SQUEAKY, and SQUEALY exit.)

THOMAS CAT (to MICE as they exit). Bring me my fiddle. I want to take part in the celebration.

MAMMA MOUSE. Are you sure Orvie has not been hurt?

THOMAS CAT. He's as right as rain, ma'am.

SCRIBBLER. Dear me, I must finish my poem. (Takes pad of paper from pocket and begins to scribble rapidly.)

MAMMA MOUSE (looking offstage). Here they come with their instruments.

(MICE *return with sheets of paper and rhythm instruments, including fiddle for* THOMAS CAT.)

FRISKY. We're all tuned up and ready to go with "Three Blind Mice."

RISKY. But Orvie hates that song.

FLUTTER. We made up some new words, and here's a copy for each of you. (*Gives sheet to each one.*)

MAMMA MOUSE (*looking off left*). He's coming! He's coming! (*Running to meet* ORVIE *as he enters.*) Oh, Orvie, Orvie! Welcome home!

ALL (*singing to accompaniment of their rhythm instruments*).

One brave mouse! One brave mouse!
See how he soars! See how he soars!
He soars right up in the morning light,
Away he goes like a flying kite!
Did ever you see such a wonderful sight
As one brave mouse!

ALL (*ad lib*). Welcome home, Orvie! Are you all right? Congratulations! (*Etc.*)

ORVIE. Thank you. Thank you.

SCAMPER. As a small token of our admiration, we wish to present you with this medal. (*Hangs the bell around* ORVIE's *neck.*) May you wear it with pride and honor.

ORVIE. But this is Thomas Cat's bell. How did you get it?

THOMAS CAT. They mobbed me and took it by force.

ORVIE. But they've always been scared to death of you!

SCRIBBLER. Not any more, Orvie. Some of your courage must have rubbed off on us. All we needed was a hero to look up to. Listen! (*Reads poem.*)

> Our thanks to you, dear Orvie Mouse,
> For the lesson you have taught.
> In your brave deed each timid mouse
> Found courage that he sought.
> From this day forth, we sing your praise,
> O mighty mousetronaut!

(*Applause as curtain falls.*)

## THE END

### Reflections

1. In what ways does a play differ from a story? Give as many ways as you can.
2. Would you prefer to read a play, see it performed, or be an actor in it? Give the reasons for your answer.
3. Why does Orvie think that mice are clever? Do you agree with him? Why or why not?
4. What did the other mice learn from Orvie? How do you know? Give evidence from the play.
5. What is a *mousetronaut?* What do you think a *transwhisker* is? Since you cannot find these words in a dictionary, how were you able to figure out their meanings?

# Dream-Song

Sunlight, moonlight,
Twilight, starlight—
Gloaming at the close of day,
And an owl calling,
Cool dews falling
In a wood of oak and may.

Lantern-light, taper-light,
Torch-light, no-light:
Darkness at the shut of day,
And lions roaring,
Their wrath pouring
In wild waste places far away.

Elf-light, bat-light,
Touchwood-light and toad-light,
And the sea a shimmering gloom of gray,
And a small face smiling
In a dream's beguiling
In a world of wonders far away.

*Walter de la Mare*

# A World of Wonders

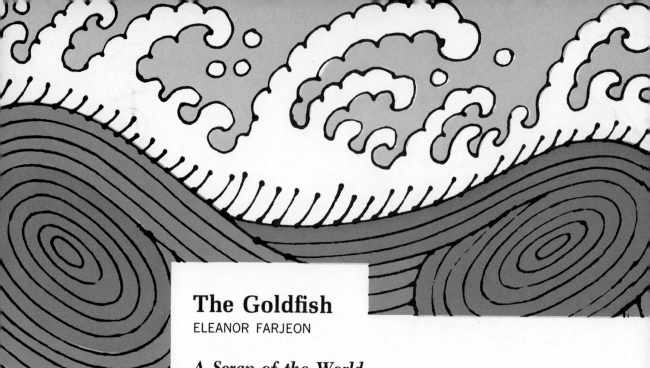

# The Goldfish

ELEANOR FARJEON

### A Scrap of the World

There was once a Goldfish who lived in the sea in the days when all fish lived there. He was perfectly happy and had only one care, and that was to avoid the net that floated about in the water, now here, now there. But all the fish had been warned by King Neptune, their father, to avoid the net. In those days they did as they were told.

So the Goldfish enjoyed a glorious life, swimming for days and days in the blue and green water. Sometimes he swam low down close to the sand and shells and pearls and coral and big rocks. Here the anemones grew like clusters of gay flowers, and the seaweed waved in frills and fans of red, green, and yellow. Sometimes he swam high up near the surface of the sea, where the whitecaps chased each other and the great waves rose like mountains of glass and tumbled over themselves with a crash.

When the Goldfish was as near the top as this, he sometimes saw swimming in the bright blue water far, far above him a great Gold Fish. This fish was as golden as himself but as round as a jellyfish. At other times, when that distant water above was dark blue instead of bright, he saw a Silver Fish. He had never met such a fish under the sea. She, too, was often round in shape, though at times, when she seemed to swim sideways through the water, he could see her pointed silver fins.

The Goldfish felt jealous of the other Gold Fish, but with the Silver Fish he fell in love at sight. He longed to be able to swim up to her. Whenever he tried to do this, something queer happened that made him lose his breath. With a gasp he sank down into the ocean, so deep that he could see the Silver Fish no longer. Then, hoping she might come down to swim in his own water, the Goldfish swam for miles and miles in search of her, but he never had the luck to find her.

One night as he was swimming about in very calm water, he saw overhead the motionless shadow of an enormous fish. One great long fin ran under its belly in the water, but all the rest of it was raised above the surface. The Goldfish knew every fish in the sea, but he had never before seen such a fish as this! It was bigger than the Whale and as black as the ink of the Octopus. He swam around it, touching it with his little nose. At last he asked, "What sort of fish are *you*?"

The big black shadow laughed. "I am not a fish at all. I am a ship," he said.

"What are you doing here if you are not a fish?"

"Just now I am doing nothing, for I am becalmed. But when the wind blows, I shall go sailing around the world."

"What is the world?"

"All that you see and more."

"Am I in the world, then?" asked the Goldfish.

"Certainly you are."

The Goldfish gave a little jump of joy. "Good news! Good news!" he cried.

A passing Porpoise paused to ask, "What are you shouting for?"

"Because I am in the world!"

"Who says so?"

"The Ship Fish!" said the Goldfish.

"Pooh!" said the Porpoise. "Let him prove it!" and passed on.

The Goldfish stopped jumping because his joy had been lessened. "How can the world be more than I can see?" he asked the Ship. "If I am really in the world, I ought to be able to see it *all*—or how can I be sure?"

"You must take my word for it," said the Ship. "A tiny fellow like you can never hope to see more than a scrap of the world. The world has a rim you can never see over. The world has foreign lands full of wonders that you can never look upon. The world *is* as round as an orange, but you will never see how round the world is."

Then the Ship went on to tell of the parts of the world that lay beyond the rim of things. He told of men and women and children and of flowers and trees. He also told of birds with eyes in their tails, of white and black elephants, and of temples hung with tinkling bells. The Goldfish wept with longing because he could never see over the rim of things. He could not see how round the world was, and he could not behold all at once all the wonders that were in the world.

How the Ship laughed at him! "My little friend," said he, "if you were the Moon yonder, or if you were the Sun himself, you could only see one half of these things at a time."

"Who is the Moon yonder?" asked the Goldfish.

"Who else, but that silver bit of light up in the sky?"

"Is that the sky?" said the Goldfish. "I thought it was another sea. And is that the Moon? I thought she was a Silver Fish. But who then is the Sun?"

"The Sun is the round gold ball that rolls through the sky by day," said the Ship. "They say he loves the Moon and gives her his light."

"I will give her the world!" cried the Goldfish. And he leaped with all his tiny might into the air, but he could not reach the Moon. He fell gasping into the sea. There he let himself sink like a little gold stone to the bottom of the ocean, where he lay for a week weeping his heart out. The things the Ship had told him about were more than he could understand, but they filled him with great longings—longings to possess the Silver Moon and to be a mightier fish than the Sun and to see the whole world from top to bottom and from side to side, with all the wonders within and beyond it.

### The World of the Goldfish

Now it happened that King Neptune, who ruled the land under the waves, was strolling through a grove of white and scarlet coral. He heard a chuckle that was something between a panting and a puffing. Peering through the branches of the coral trees, he beheld a plump Porpoise bursting its sides with laughter. Not far off lay the Goldfish, swimming in tears.

King Neptune, like a good father, preferred to share in all the joys and sorrows of his children. He stopped to ask the Porpoise, "What tickles you so?"

"Ho! ho! ho!" puffed the Porpoise. "I am tickled by the grief of the Goldfish there."

"Has the Goldfish a grief?" asked King Neptune.

"He has indeed! For seven days and nights he has wept because—ho! ho! ho!—because he cannot marry the Moon, be mightier than the Sun, and possess the world!"

"And you," said King Neptune, "have you never wept for these things?"

"Not I!" puffed the Porpoise. "What! Weep for the Sun and the Moon that are nothing but two blobs in the distance? Weep for the world that no one can behold? No, Father! When my dinner is nowhere, I'll weep for *that;* and when I see death coming, I'll weep for *that;* but for the rest, I say pooh!"

337

"Well, it takes all sorts of fish to make a sea," said King Neptune. He stooped and picked up the Goldfish.

"Come, child," he said, "tears may be the beginning, but they should not be the end of things. Tears will get you nowhere. Do you really wish to marry the Moon, be mightier than the Sun, and possess the world?"

"I do, Father, I do!" cried the Goldfish.

"Then since there is no help for it, you must get caught in the net. Do you see it floating yonder in the water? Are you afraid of it?"

"Not if it will bring me all I long for," said the Goldfish bravely.

"Risk all, and you will get your desires," promised King Neptune. He let the Goldfish dart through his fingers. He saw him swim boldly to the net which was waiting to catch what it could. As the meshes closed upon the Goldfish, King Neptune stretched out his hand and slipped a second fish inside the net. Then, stroking his green beard, he continued his stroll among his big and little children.

And what happened to the Goldfish?

He was drawn up into the Fisherman's boat that lay in wait above the nets. In the same net a Silverfish was taken. She was a lovely creature with a round body and silky fins like films of moonlit cloud.

"There's a pretty pair!" thought the Fisherman. He carried them home to please his little daughter. And to make her pleasure more complete, he first bought a globe of glass and sprinkled sand and shells and tiny pebbles at the bottom. He set among them a sprig of coral and a strand of seaweed. Then he filled the globe with water, dropped in the Goldfish and the Silverfish, and put the little glass world on a table in his cottage window.

The Goldfish, dazed with joy, swam towards the Silverfish. He cried, "You are the Moon come out of the sky! Oh, see how round the world is!"

And he looked through one side of the globe and saw flowers and trees in the garden. He looked through another side of the globe and saw on the mantelpiece black and white elephants of ebony and ivory. Through another side of the globe he saw on the wall a fan of peacock's feathers, with eyes of gold and blue and green. Through the other side, on a bracket, he saw a little Chinese temple with many bells. He looked at the top of the globe and saw a man, a woman, and a child smiling down at him over the rim.

And he gave a little jump of joy and cried to his Silver Bride:

"Oh, Silverfish, I am greater than the Sun, for I give you, not just half, but the whole of the world! I give you the top and the bottom and all the way around, with all the wonders that are in it and beyond it!"

And King Neptune under the sea, who had ears for all that passed, laughed in his beard and thought:

"It was a shame to let such a tiny fellow loose in the vast ocean. He needed a world more suited to his size."

And ever since then, the world of the Goldfish has been a globe of glass.

### Reflections

1. At the beginning of this story, what mistaken idea did the Goldfish have about the sun and the moon?
2. What happened to the Goldfish each time he tried to reach the Silver Fish?
3. How did the Porpoise feel about the news that there was a whole world he would never be able to see?
4. Why did King Neptune want the Goldfish to get caught in the net? Why did he slip another fish into it?
5. Do you think the Goldfish was brave to swim into the net? Explain.
6. How much of the world did the Goldfish finally get to see? How much did he think he saw? Why?

# Once . . .
NATALIA M. BELTING

### *From the Hawaiian Islands*
Once, when the sky was very near the earth,
a woman hoeing in her garden took off her
    necklace
and hung it in the sky.
The stars are her silver necklace.

### *From India*
The dark gray clouds,
the great gray clouds,
the black rolling clouds are elephants
going down to the sea for water.
They draw up the water in their trunks.
They march back again across the sky.
They spray the earth with the water,
and men say it is raining.

**From Siberia**

When it storms,
a camel walks across the skies.
He has two riders.
One beats a drum. It is the thunder.
One waves a scarf. It is the lightning.

**From Malaya**

The rainbow is the fishing line of the king of
    dragons.
The king of dragons sits in the high places above
    the earth,
in places where no man has ever been.
He fishes in the waters below the earth;
And the rainbow is his fishing line.

# The Snake Who Wanted to Fly

DAN STORM

A Snake once met two Buzzards sitting on a rock and said to them, "How fortunate you two are. You can travel through the air, while I go always with my stomach to the ground. How wonderful it must be to sail through the blue sky, flying, flying, looking down over the whole world. How unlucky am I, always crawling, crawling on the ground. It takes me all day to go even a short distance. But with you, *zzzssst*, you only have to think of being in some place to be nearly there."

The two Buzzards listened to the Snake and felt sorry for him, for they are kind birds who never kill anything and are a great help to animals and mankind in cleaning up the country. They tried to make this Snake more contented with his lot.

The younger Buzzard said, "Yes, flying seems pleasant enough. But there is nothing pretty to see. When we are up in the air, we are no closer to the blue sky than you are here on the ground."

"That is true," the older bird said. "Things are not always as pretty as they look. Sometimes it is tiresome living in the air. We are not welcome on the ground, you know. With you it is different. Everyone is afraid of you."

"Aha, yes," sighed the Snake, "but I am at heart like you two fellows. By nature I am really a bird. That is what I am. Oh, if I could only fly just once, it would be so wonderful."

The two Buzzards drew closer together on the stone where they were sitting on their heels like two cowboys and began to think very hard. "It is certainly impossible for you to fly," said one Buzzard. "That is certain. But there ought to be some way we could take you for a ride in the air."

"Yes, yes!" cried the Snake. "One of you take me on your back. I am not very heavy."

"You are too heavy for me," said one.

"Me, too," said the other. "We Buzzards are not very strong—mostly feathers. Feel . . ."

Now, indeed, it began to look as if the Snake would have to give up his idea of a trip into the air. Suddenly the older bird said, "Wait! There is one way we can take you for a little *paseo* into the sky. We will both carry you, Señor Snake, that is what we will do!"

So the two birds went nearby on the desert and brought back a dried-up yucca stalk. This stick was about six feet long, but very light and strong. Each bird took an end of the stick in his mouth, and they told the Snake to follow them up a small hill.

When all three were at the top of the little hill, the older Buzzard said, "Take a tight hold here in the middle of the stick, Brother Snake, with your mouth. We will each take hold of an end of the stick and will fly with it in our beaks, together. Hold on tight."

The Snake did as he was told, and the Buzzards shook out their wings. "Ready, Brother Snake! Here we go, taking off. *Cuidado!*" And with that the two birds went running down the hill, flapping their wings and shouting to each other, "Both together, *compadre*."

The Snake dragged most of himself on the ground behind while he held on for dear life to the middle of the stick with his mouth. As they neared the bottom of the hill, the two Buzzards were at top running speed. With a strong beating of their wings, they rose together into the air, and the birds, Snake, stick, and all, were flying, flying higher and higher into the air.

The three had not gone far when a great crowd of all kinds of birds appeared behind them. They had come from afar to see what this strange group of fliers might be. The Snake was hanging onto the stick with his long teeth, swinging lightly back and forth high above the earth. This was what he long had wanted.

The Eagle, who was in the band of birds, flew over close to the Snake and began asking him all kinds of questions and saying things to make him angry. "Flap your wings, Brother Snake," he said. "Do I see feathers sprouting at your tail?"

The Eagle was about to say something more to the Snake, when the little Dove came and stood on the yucca stick right close to the Snake's head and said to him, "Don't answer the Eagle. He is trying to make you talk and open your mouth. If you did that, you would lose your hold on the stick and fall to the ground."

The little Dove did not want to see even its worst enemy have any trouble, but the Snake, with his new experience in flying, seemed to think that now he knew all about it. Seeing the Dove so close to him, he forgot for a moment that he was not a bird and opened his jaws to make a grab for the Dove.

No sooner had he done this than he dropped from the stick and fell through the air, turning over and over, down, down, down. He was flying, but he could go only in one direction, and that led him right into a prickly pear bush down on the plains. The breath was knocked out of him, and countless cactus thorns were knocked into him by his fall. Soon he gathered himself together and crawled back to his den in the rocks. And in the days that followed, every time he pulled a thorn out of himself, he cared a little bit less about his flying trip.

### Reflections

1. Which characters in this story seem good-natured and kindhearted? Which one is stupid? Give reasons to support your opinion in each case.
2. A number of Spanish words are used in this story. They appear in *italic* type. Find them and reread the sentences that come before and after them (the *context*). What meaning do you think each foreign word has on the basis of its context?
3. What caused the Snake's downfall?
4. Pretend that one year after the Snake's sad experience, he was overheard asking two fish to take him swimming. Tell what you think might happen.
5. Have you ever wished to be someone else or to do something beyond your range? Tell about it.

# Anansi's Hat-Shaking Dance

HAROLD COURLANDER

If you look closely, you will see that Kwaku
Anansi, the spider, has a bald head. It is said that
in the old days he had hair but that he lost it
through vanity.

It happened that Anansi's mother-in-law died.
When word came to Anansi's house, Aso, his wife,
prepared to go at once to her own village for the
funeral. But Anansi said to Aso, "You go ahead;
I will follow."

When Aso had gone, Anansi said to himself,
"When I go to my dead mother-in-law's house,
I will have to show grief over her death. I will
have to refuse to eat. Therefore, I shall eat now."
And so he sat down in his own house and ate a

huge meal. Then he put on his mourning clothes and went to Aso's village.

First there was the funeral. Afterwards there was a large feast. But Anansi refused to eat out of respect for his wife's dead mother. He said, "What kind of man would I be to eat when I am mourning for my mother-in-law? I will eat after the eighth day has passed."

Now this was not expected of him, because a man isn't required to starve himself simply because someone has died. But Anansi was the kind of person that when he ate, he ate twice as much as others and when he danced, he danced more vigorously than others and when he mourned, he had to mourn more loudly than anybody else. Whatever he did, he didn't want to be outdone by anyone else. And although he was very hungry,

he couldn't bear to have people think he wasn't the greatest mourner at his own mother-in-law's funeral.

So he said, "Feed, my friends, but as for me, I shall do without." So everyone ate—the porcupine, the rabbit, the snake, the guinea fowl, and the others—all except Anansi.

On the second day after the funeral, they said to him again, "Eat; there is no need to starve."

But Anansi replied, "Oh no, not until the eighth day, when the mourning is over. What kind of man do you think I am?"

So the others ate. Anansi's stomach was empty, and he was unhappy.

On the third day they said again, "Eat, Kwaku Anansi; there is no need to go hungry."

But Anansi was stubborn. He said, "How can I eat when my wife's mother has been buried only three days?" And so the others ate, while Anansi smelled the food hungrily and suffered.

On the fourth day Anansi was alone where a pot of beans was cooking over the fire. He smelled the beans and looked in the pot. At last he couldn't stand it any longer. He took a large spoon and dipped up a large portion of the beans, thinking to take it to a quiet place and eat it without anyone's knowing. But just then the dog, the guinea fowl, the rabbit, and the others returned to the place where the food was cooking.

To hide the beans, Anansi quickly poured them in his hat and put it on his head. The other people came to the pot and ate, saying again, "Anansi, you must eat."

He said, "No, what kind of man would I be?"

But the hot beans were burning his head. He jiggled his hat around with his hands. When he saw the others looking at him, he said, "Just at this very moment in my village, the hat-shaking festival is taking place. I shake my hat in honor of the occasion."

The beans felt hotter than ever, and he jiggled his hat some more. He began to jump with pain, and he said, "Like this in my village, they are doing the hat-shaking dance."

He danced about, jiggling his hat because of the heat. He yearned to take off his hat, but he could not because his friends would see the beans. So he shouted, "They are shaking and jiggling the hats in my village, like this! It is a great festival! I must go!"

They said to him, "Kwaku Anansi, eat something before you go."

But now Anansi was jumping and writhing with the heat of the beans on his head. He shouted, "Oh, no, they are shaking hats; they are wriggling hats and jumping like this! I must go to my village! They need me!"

He rushed out of the house, jumping and pushing his hat back and forth. His friends followed after him saying, "Eat before you go on your journey!"

But Anansi shouted: "What kind of man do you think I am, with my mother-in-law just buried?"

Even though they all followed right after him, he couldn't wait any longer, because the pain was too much, and he tore the hat from his head.

When the dog saw, and the guinea fowl saw, and the rabbit saw, and all the others saw what was in the hat, and saw the hot beans sticking to Anansi's head, they stopped chasing him. They began to laugh and jeer.

Anansi was overcome with shame. He leaped into the tall grass, saying, "Hide me." And the grass hid him.

That is why Anansi is often found in the tall grass, where he was driven by shame. And you will see that his head is bald, for the hot beans he put in his hat burned off his hair.

All this happened because he tried to impress people at his mother-in-law's funeral.

### Reflections

1. What kind of personality did Anansi have? Give both his good and his bad points.
2. Do you think Anansi deserved what happened to him? Give reasons for your answer.
3. Describe how Anansi felt when his friends laughed at him.
4. What do you suppose Anansi's wife said to him on the first night they were both at home? Make up the conversation that you think they might have had.

# Animal Lovers

Most people like animals, but only a lucky few have jobs working with them. Here are some people who train them and sell them and take care of them when they are sick.

**Veterinarians,** or animal doctors, take care of animals when they are sick. They also work to keep the animals well. Veterinarians are trained to recognize the diseases animals might get, and to cure them. Animal doctors must be understanding and gentle. They must treat both the animals and their owners with kindness.

**Pet-shop owners** sell more than puppies and kittens. Some sell exotic birds or fish. Some sell hamsters or even friendly snakes. Shop owners must feed and care for their animals until someone comes to buy them.

*(top left)* Some pets are sent to obedience school for training. **Dog trainers** work with the owners and their animals so that both understand the rules. Some dogs are trained at special schools to be seeing-eye dogs that help blind people.

*(bottom left)* **Zoo keepers** take care of animals and birds living in the zoo. They know what kind of house or cage each one needs and how hot or cold it should be. They also know what food each animal eats.

*(bottom right)* A circus is another place where people work with animals. This **lion tamer** has a dangerous but exciting job.

# Too Much Nose

HARVE ZEMACH

## Three Gifts

Once there was a poor old father, who was both
very poor and very old. He had three sons, and
one day he called them to his side and said, "Sons,
it is time for you to leave here and make your
own way in the world. But before you go, I have
some things to give you, some things of very
great value."

The three lads were surprised to hear this.
"What things, Father?" they asked, "and where
are they?" The old man told them to pull the
wooden chest out from under his bed and take
what they found in it. They dragged out the chest
and got it open, and what they found was an old
broken hat, crushed on top and missing its brim;
a ragged coin purse, full of holes; and a rusty
horn.

"Now see what I've given you!" exclaimed the
father to his eldest son.

The eldest son held up the hat and smiled sadly.
"I see, Father," he said, "it was once a good hat,
but now it is not even fit to sit on the scarecrow's
head."

"So it seems," said the father, "but if you put
it on, you can go wherever you care to go and
do whatever you please to do, and no one will
see you as long as you have it on." Then he turned

to his second son and said, "Now see what I have given *you!*"

The second son shook some dust out of the ragged coin purse. "If I had a coin to carry in it," he said, "it would soon fall out, there are so many holes. But no matter, since I haven't got a coin."

"So it seems," said the father, "but every time you put your fingers in, you'll find a silver coin there, and after that as many as you wish." Then he said to his third son, "And see what I have given *you!*"

"Father, it's a very nice horn," the third son said, "and when I am starving hungry, I shall blow tunes on it to make myself forget about eating."

"Silly boy! That's not what it is for," said the father. "Whenever you want anything, you need only to sound the horn, and Someone will bring you whatever you want."

Then the old father gave his blessings to his sons, and they went their separate ways. The second son tucked the coin purse under his belt and headed for a nearby town. There, as he was passing below the windows of a palace, a maid looked out and called to him. "Can you play at cards?" she asked him.

"As well as most," he replied.

"Good, then come up, for the queen wants somebody to play with her."

The young man went in and up the stairs and was shown where to sit at a table across from the queen. She gave him a sharp look and began dealing the cards. They played for an hour, and the queen kept winning. Each time she won, she cried, "The queen wins! Three silver coins for the queen!" And when the game was over, she said, "You unlucky man, you have lost thirty pieces of silver. But never mind, I can see you are too poor to pay."

"Oh, I can pay all right," said the second son. He opened his coin purse and reached into it thirty times and each time brought out a shiny silver coin.

The queen was amazed. "How is it possible," she asked, "that such a poor-looking fellow can find so much silver in that ragged old purse?"

"It is no ordinary purse," he answered proudly and told her the secret of his father's gift.

"I don't believe it. Here, let me see for myself," said the queen, and she snatched the coin purse from the young man's hands. Then, before he could say a word, she called the guards and ordered them to turn the fellow out.

When the guards had done with him, the second son went to find his elder brother. He told his brother about the queen and begged to borrow his hat, promising to return it shortly.

As soon as he got the hat, he put it on and became invisible. Then he went back to the palace. It was the dinner hour, and because of the hat no one was able to see the second son enter and sit down at the table right next to the queen. He waited until the queen was served her soup. Then, before she could eat the first spoonful, he lifted the bowl to his own lips and replaced it empty on the table.

The queen thought that very strange, and even stranger when the rest of her dinner disappeared the same way, each dish in turn. Finally she cried out, "Who are you, invisible one, and what do you want?"

"It is I who played cards," said the young man, "and I'll give you no peace until you return my coin purse."

"I would gladly return it," said the queen, "but how do I know it is you who speaks and not someone else? First you must let me see you; then I'll return your purse."

So the young man took off his hat and showed himself to the queen. "Now you see it is I," he said, "so give me my coin purse."

The queen went and got the ragged purse, but before giving it to him, she said, "Tell me, young man, how did you make yourself invisible?"

"Oh," he said, "it is this broken old hat that has the power. As soon as you put it on, no one can see you."

"I don't believe it," said the queen.

"But it's true," said he. "You just put it on and . . ."

"Impossible!" said the queen. "Here, let me see for myself." And she snatched the hat out of his hands and thrust it on her own head.

"There, just as I told you," said the young man. "Now you are invisible."

"So I am," cried the queen, and she rushed out of the room.

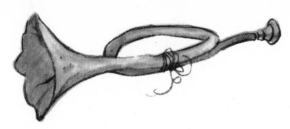

### That Rusty Horn

Before the young man realized what had happened, she called for the guards and had him thrown out of the palace. The young man picked himself up and stumbled away to find his other brother. When he found him, he begged to borrow the rusty horn, just for a little while. His brother grumbled about it but finally agreed, and the second son hurried back to the palace.

He took a deep breath and blew the horn as hard as he could. At once Someone appeared, looming up before him, and asked in a mysterious voice, *"What is your wish?"*

"I want an army with cannons to overthrow the palace," cried the youth.

Instantly there was a sound of soldiers marching and a rumble of cannons. The soldiers surrounded the palace, closing in from all directions, and aimed the cannons. The queen and her company were terrified.

"What's this all about?" cried the queen as soon as she saw the second son standing under her window.

"Give me back my purse, and give me back my hat," said he, "or I shall overthrow the palace!"

"Wait," said the queen. "I have them right here. Just come inside, and I'll give them to you straightaway."

So the young man marched up to collect his things. The queen fluttered about the room, opening and closing cabinets and looking under chairs. "You gave me such a fright," she said, "that I can't remember where I put them. Are they behind that bench? No? Well, under the table in the corner?"

The young man went to look, and while he was looking, the queen said, "How did a poor fellow like you manage to call together such an army?"

"Because I've got this horn," said he, "and if you don't hurry up and find my things, I'll have the cannons batter down the palace in right earnest!"

"That rusty horn?" said the queen. "You won't make me believe it can even make a sound."

"Oh, yes, it can," said he. "You just hold it this way and blow very hard."

"Really?" said she. "Let me try!" And she grabbed it away from him and sounded it. And instantly Someone appeared and said to her, *"What is your wish?"*

"I want two stout men," cried the queen, "and I want them to drive that shabby-looking fellow out of the palace!"

It was done. And now the second son had nothing left and was ashamed to go back to his brothers. So he wandered away outside the town, and he wandered on and on. The sun set, and he could not see his way along the road. He finally stumbled into a vineyard, where he slept all night under a fig tree.

He woke up early the next morning and found the fig tree covered with ripe figs, though it was not yet the season for figs. "Some good luck at last," he thought, for he was hungry from his wanderings. He plucked some figs and began to eat. They were so delicious that he hardly noticed a certain tickling feeling in his nose. But suddenly he dropped the whole bunch and jumped to his feet.

His nose had grown to a terrible size!

Poor fellow! Now he could not even show himself to people and would have to spend the rest of his days wandering. He left the vineyard and hurried down the road. Before long he saw some cherry trees. One of them was all covered with ripe cherries. He was still hungry, so he plucked some and began to eat. And with every cherry that he ate, his nose got an inch smaller. By the time he was done, it was back to its regular size.

"Aha!" he said out loud. "Now I know what to do!"

First he filled a bottle with juice squeezed out of the ripe cherries. Then he ran back to the

vineyard and collected a basketful of figs. Then he returned to the palace, going around to the back door. "Figs for sale!" he cried. "Delicious ripe figs!"

The queen's servants bought the whole basketful. They sent word to the queen of their luck in finding figs for sale at this time of year, and the queen said to serve them right up. Everyone in the palace feasted on the figs, and the queen, of course, ate more than anyone else.

Well, it happened to them, just the way it happened to the second son when he had eaten the figs. Their noses grew and grew.

There was a terrible fuss in the palace. They sent for doctors, and all the doctors for miles around came hurrying to the palace and tried all their medicines, one after another. But nothing did any good.

Meanwhile the second son waited until all the doctors had given up and gone. Then, with a beard pasted on his chin and a hat pulled down over his eyes, he came to the palace again and called out, "Noses! I can heal noses! Whoever has got too much nose, let him come to me!"

The queen and her servants rushed to the window. "A doctor!" exclaimed the queen. "Maybe he can help us." They called him inside and begged him to heal their noses.

"All right," said he. "I have a special medicine, just for healing noses like yours. But it is very strong stuff. I'm afraid it may be too strong for a queen."

"Nonsense," said the queen, "if it really heals noses, then I must have some. I shall pay you anything you ask."

"Oh, yes," said he, "you'll have to pay a lot, because it is the only medicine of its kind in the world. But I do think that it's terribly strong stuff to give to a queen."

"Well, then, start by healing the noses of my servants," said the queen. She thought she ought to see if the medicine worked before she paid anything for it.

So the second son held up the bottle of cherry juice and gave each of the queen's servants just enough to make each nose return to its ordinary size. "There! You see!" he said. "Isn't it wonderful medicine! One drop . . . two drops . . . and *presto!* the nose is healed."

The queen looked on. She saw how well the medicine worked, but it made her jealous to hear the doctor boast about it. "You think yourself very clever," she said, "but you are not the only one who can work wonders. I've got even greater wonders than yours."

"Is that possible?" said the pretended doctor. "What could be more wonderful than my medicine for noses?"

"Why, I have a hat," said she, "that makes you invisible when you put it on. I also have a purse

that gives you a silver coin every time you reach into it and a horn that calls forth Someone, who brings you anything you need."

"You are joking," said he. "Such things don't exist."

"Yes, they do. I have them right here!" said the queen, showing him the coin purse and the hat and the horn.

Quick as a wink, the second son flipped the hat onto his head, snatched up the purse and the horn, and vanished from the palace. Then he went and found his brothers and gave them back the hat and the horn. And he lived comfortably for the rest of his life by means of his magical coin purse.

As for the queen, you can be sure she was furious. But nobody could tell what made her more angry—losing the treasures she had taken from the second son or being left forever with too much nose!

**Reflections**

1. At first, why were the three sons disappointed in the things their father gave them? What did he tell them that made them feel better?

2. What kind of person was the queen? Tell why you think so.

3. If you could choose, which one of the three gifts would you pick for yourself? Why?

4. If you were the queen, what would you have done when everyone's nose became longer?

5. Do you think this experience will change the queen? If so, how?

6. Do you think "Too Much Nose" is a good title for this story? Explain.

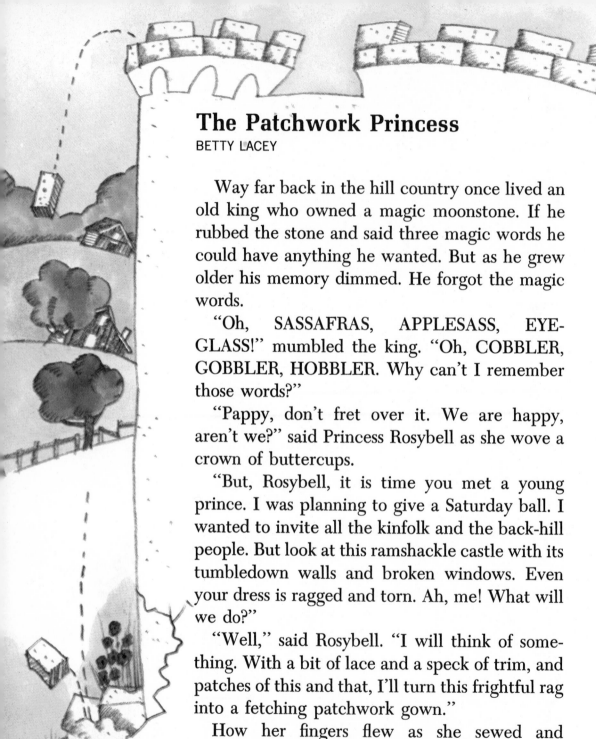

# The Patchwork Princess

BETTY LACEY

Way far back in the hill country once lived an old king who owned a magic moonstone. If he rubbed the stone and said three magic words he could have anything he wanted. But as he grew older his memory dimmed. He forgot the magic words.

"Oh, SASSAFRAS, APPLESASS, EYE-GLASS!" mumbled the king. "Oh, COBBLER, GOBBLER, HOBBLER. Why can't I remember those words?"

"Pappy, don't fret over it. We are happy, aren't we?" said Princess Rosybell as she wove a crown of buttercups.

"But, Rosybell, it is time you met a young prince. I was planning to give a Saturday ball. I wanted to invite all the kinfolk and the back-hill people. But look at this ramshackle castle with its tumbledown walls and broken windows. Even your dress is ragged and torn. Ah, me! What will we do?"

"Well," said Rosybell. "I will think of something. With a bit of lace and a speck of trim, and patches of this and that, I'll turn this frightful rag into a fetching patchwork gown."

How her fingers flew as she sewed and patched! When she had finished, she put on the dress. And putting on the buttercup crown, she

hurried out to show the king.

"I'm bedazzled!" the king exclaimed. "Now, if only the castle were shiny new. Oh, WISHES, DISHES, FISHES! Why can't I remember those words?"

"Don't fret, Pappy. We'll just do it ourselves. Let's call in all the kinfolk and back-hill people to help."

How they worked! How they patched! How they cooked! How they cleaned!

"I'm bedazzled!" exclaimed the king, when he saw what they had done. "Now we will have the ball!"

Just then the sky filled with dark rolling storm clouds. Thunder and lightning filled the air. A raindrop fell, then another and another. Water covered the garden. It broke the windows and

... Sassafras, applesass
eyeglass....? cobbler
gobbler, hobbler...?

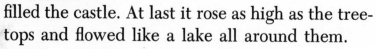

filled the castle. At last it rose as high as the tree-
tops and flowed like a lake all around them.

"Oh, SOGGY, FOGGY, BOGGY!" muttered
the king, looking out on the sea of water. "What
will we ever do?"

"Quick," commanded the princess. "We need
a craft. Let's build a raft."

Following her orders, they all worked together
to build a huge raft. It was big enough for all the
people. There was even enough room for a cackling chicken or two.

The rain stopped. Darkness came. The raft
floated slowly away from the castle. The children
cried, the mountain men muttered. And the old
king complained, "Oh, MOAN, GROAN,
DRONE. Why can't I remember those words?"

Seeing the people's sadness, Rosybell stood up
in the middle of the giant raft. "No need to be
sad," she said. "Let's take a chance and have that
dance!"

They lighted torches all around the edge of the
giant raft. The fiddlers tuned up their fiddles. Before long everyone was dancing and singing.

By dawn, tired from dancing, the weary people had fallen asleep. Up and down went the raft.
Up and down.

"We're at sea. Oh look, we're at sea!" someone
shouted. "We'll surely drown!"

"Oh, HOMESICK, HEARTSICK, SEASICK,"

moaned the old king, his face turning rather green. "What will we ever do?"

"No fear!" exclaimed Rosybell. "We can make a sail and catch this gale."

With coats and shawls, petticoats and mufflers—with even the king's royal deerskin robe—they stitched together a sail. It caught the wind and carried the raft across the sea to a distant shore.

"Oh, LAND, SAND, GRAND!" sighed the king as they waded to firm ground. "I wonder whose kingdom this is?"

They didn't have to wonder very long. The soggy stragglers from the raft were quickly surrounded by sword-wielding, shield-bearing guards. In their midst stood a handsome prince in shining, silver armor.

"What bedraggled clan is this that has washed up on my shore? Take these poor ragamuffins to the castle kitchen," the handsome prince commanded. "Perhaps they will make good servants."

"Wait!" pleaded the old king. "I am the king of the backcountry, and these are my kinfolk and back-hill people. And this is my daughter, the Princess Rosybell."

Rosybell stood before the prince, her patchwork gown in shreds, the buttercup crown wilted down around her dripping hair.

"Unbelievable!" said the prince.

"When my kingdom fell to ruin, Rosybell showed us how to fix it up," said the king.

"Extraordinary!" said the prince.

"When the flood came, Rosybell saved our lives by suggesting we make a raft," recalled the kinfolk.

"Remarkable!" said the prince.

"When sadness overcame us, she made us merry by starting the dance on the raft. When we thought we were lost at sea, she thought of making a sail," said the back-hill people.

"Incredible!" said the prince.

"It's not only incredible," said the king, "It's PRODIGIOUS, PORTENTOUS, AND PHENOMENAL! I wish you could see her as the beautiful princess she really is."

In an instant, Rosybell stood wearing a gown of finest gossamer. It was sprinkled with diamonds. And on top of her hair was a crown of real gold.

The king had remembered the magic words!

"Enchanting!" said the prince. He took the princess by the hand and led her up to his castle. And he was followed by the happy king and his magic moonstone. He was followed by the merry-making kinfolk and the laughing back-hill people. He was followed by the sprightly fiddlers, the skipping children and their dogs. He was even followed by a cackling chicken or two.

In that castle there was a hall where they held that Saturday ball. And they danced happily ever after.

### Reflections

1. Why did the king think he couldn't give a ball?
2. Suppose the king had not remembered the magic words. What do you think could have happened? What would Rosybell have done?
3. What would you suggest the king do to prevent forgetting the magic words again?
4. Suppose you had the power to create a magic stone. What words would you think up to make the magic work?

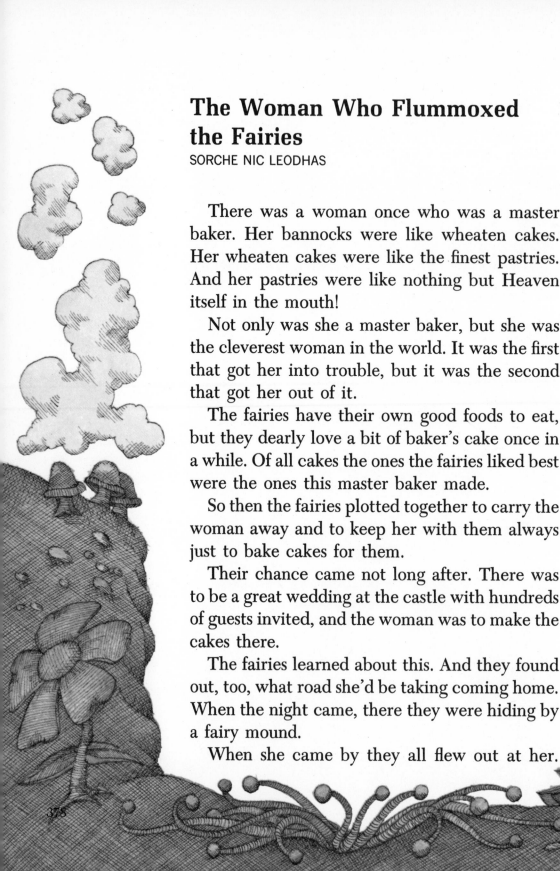

# The Woman Who Flummoxed the Fairies

SORCHE NIC LEODHAS

There was a woman once who was a master baker. Her bannocks were like wheaten cakes. Her wheaten cakes were like the finest pastries. And her pastries were like nothing but Heaven itself in the mouth!

Not only was she a master baker, but she was the cleverest woman in the world. It was the first that got her into trouble, but it was the second that got her out of it.

The fairies have their own good foods to eat, but they dearly love a bit of baker's cake once in a while. Of all cakes the ones the fairies liked best were the ones this master baker made.

So then the fairies plotted together to carry the woman away and to keep her with them always just to bake cakes for them.

Their chance came not long after. There was to be a great wedding at the castle with hundreds of guests invited, and the woman was to make the cakes there.

The fairies learned about this. And they found out, too, what road she'd be taking coming home. When the night came, there they were hiding by a fairy mound.

When she came by they all flew out at her.

The fairies drifted fern seed into her eyes. All of a sudden she was that sleepy that she could go not one step farther without a bit of a rest!

"Mercy me!" she said with a yawn. "It's worn myself out I have this day!" And she sank down on what she took to be a grassy bank to doze just for a minute. But it wasn't a bank at all. It was the fairy mound, and once she lay upon it she was in the fairies' power.

She knew nothing about that nor anything else till she woke again, and found herself in fairyland.

"Well now," she said, "and did you ever! It's all my life I've wanted to get a peep into fairyland. And here I am!"

They told her what they wanted, and she said to herself, indeed she had no notion of staying there the rest of her life! But she didn't tell the fairies that.

"To be sure!" she said cheerfully. "Why you poor wee things! To think of me baking cakes for everyone else, and not a one for you! So let's be at it," said she, "with no time wasted."

"Let me see now," said she, looking about her. "Well, 'tis plain you have nothing for me to be baking a cake with. You'll just have to be going to my own kitchen to fetch back what I'll need."

Yes, the fairies could do that. So she sent some for eggs, and some for sugar, and some for flour, and some for butter. Others flew off to get other things she told them she had to have. At last all was ready for the mixing. The woman asked for a bowl. But the biggest one they could find for her was the size of a teacup, and a wee dainty one at that.

Well then, there was nothing for it, but they must go and fetch her big yellow crockery bowl from off the shelf. And after that it was her wooden spoons and her egg whisp and one thing and another, till the fairies were all tired out.

At last everything she wanted was at hand. The woman began to measure and mix and whip and beat. But all of a sudden she stopped.

"'Tis no use!" she sighed. "I can't ever seem to mix a cake without my cat beside me, purring."

"Fetch the cat!" said the fairy king sharply.

So they fetched the cat. The cat lay at the woman's feet and purred. The woman stirred away at the bowl, and for a while all was well. But not for long.

The woman let go of the spoon and sighed again. "Well now, would you think it?" said she. "I'm that used to my dog setting the time of my beating by the way he snores at every second beat that I can't seem to get the beat right without him."

"Fetch the dog!" cried the king.

So they fetched the dog and he curled up at her feet beside the cat. The dog snored, the cat purred, the woman beat the cake batter, and all was well again. Or so the fairies thought.

But no! The woman stopped again. "I'm that worried about my babe," said she.

"Fetch that babe!" roared the fairy king without waiting for her to finish what she was saying. And they fetched the babe.

So the woman began to beat the batter again. But when they brought the babe, he began to scream the minute he saw her, for he was hungry, as she knew he would be.

"I'm sorry to trouble you," said the woman, raising her voice above the screaming of the babe. "But I can't stop beating now lest the cake go wrong. Happen my husband could get the babe quiet if . . ."

The fairies didn't wait for the king to tell them what to do. Off they flew and fetched the husband back with them. He, poor man, was all in a whirl, what with things disappearing from under his eyes right and left, and then being snatched through the air himself the way he was. But here was his wife, and he knew where she was things couldn't go far wrong. But the baby went on screaming.

So the woman beat the batter. The baby screamed. The cat purred. The dog snored. And the man rubbed his eyes and watched his wife to see what she was up to. The fairies settled down, though 'twas plain to see that the babe's screaming disturbed them. Still, they looked hopeful.

Then the woman reached over and took up the egg whisp and gave the wooden spoon to the babe, who at once began to bang away with it, screaming just the same. Under cover of the screaming of the babe and the banging of the spoon and the swishing of the egg whisp the woman whispered to her husband, "Pinch the dog!"

"Tow! Row! Row!" barked the dog, and added his voice to the babe's screams, and the banging of the wooden spoon, and the swishing of the egg whisp.

"Tread on the tail of the cat!" whispered the woman to her husband.

So the woman swished, and the baby screamed. The wooden spoon banged and the dog yelped. The cat howled, and the whole of it made a terrible din. The fairies, king and all, flew round and round in distraction with their hands over their ears, for if there is one thing the fairies can't bear it's a lot of noise. And what's more the woman knew what they liked and what they didn't all the time!

So then the woman got up and poured the batter into two pans that stood ready. She laid by the egg whisp and took the wooden spoon away from the babe, and picking him up she popped a lump of sugar into his mouth. That surprised him so much that he stopped screaming. She nodded to her husband and he stopped pinching the dog and took his foot from the cat's tail. In a minute's time all was quiet. The fairies stopped flying round and round and sank down exhausted.

And then the woman said, "The cake's ready for the baking. Where's the oven?"

The fairies looked at each other in dismay. At last the fairy queen said weakly, "There isn't any oven."

"What!" exclaimed the woman. "No oven? Well then, how do you expect me to be baking the cake?"

None of the fairies could find the answer to that.

"Well then," said the woman, "you'll just have to be taking me and the cake home to bake it in my own oven, and bring me back later when the cake's all done."

The fairies looked at the babe and the wooden spoon and the egg whisp and the dog and the cat and the man. And then they all shuddered like one.

"You may all go!" said the fairy king. "But don't ask us to be taking you. We're all too tired."

"Och, you must have your cake then," said the woman, feeling sorry for them now she'd got what she wanted. "I'll tell you what I'll do. After it's baked, I'll be leaving it for you beside the road where you found me. And what's more I'll put one there for you every single week from now on."

"I'll not be outdone!" cried the fairy king.

"For what you find in that same place shall be your own!"

Then the woman picked up the pans of batter. The man tucked the bowls and spoons and things under one arm and the baby under the other. The fairy king raised an arm and the hill split open. Out they all walked, the woman with the pans of batter, the man with the bowls and the babe, and the dog and the cat at their heels. Down the road they walked and back to their own house. And never looked behind them.

When they got back to their home the woman put the pans of batter into the oven. Then she dished out the porridge that stood keeping hot on the back of the fire and gave the babe his supper.

There wasn't a sound in that house except the clock ticking, the kettle singing, the cat purring and the dog snoring. And all those were soft, quiet sounds.

So that's the way the woman flummoxed the fairies. A good thing she made out of it, too, for when the cake was baked and cooled the woman took it up and put it behind the fairy mound, as she had promised. And when she set it down she saw there a little brown bag. She took the bag up and opened it and looked within. It was full of bright shining yellow gold pieces.

And so it went, week after week. A cake for the fairies, a bag of gold for the woman and her husband. They never saw one of the fairies again, but the bargain never was broken and they grew rich by it. So of course they lived, as why should they not, happily ever after.

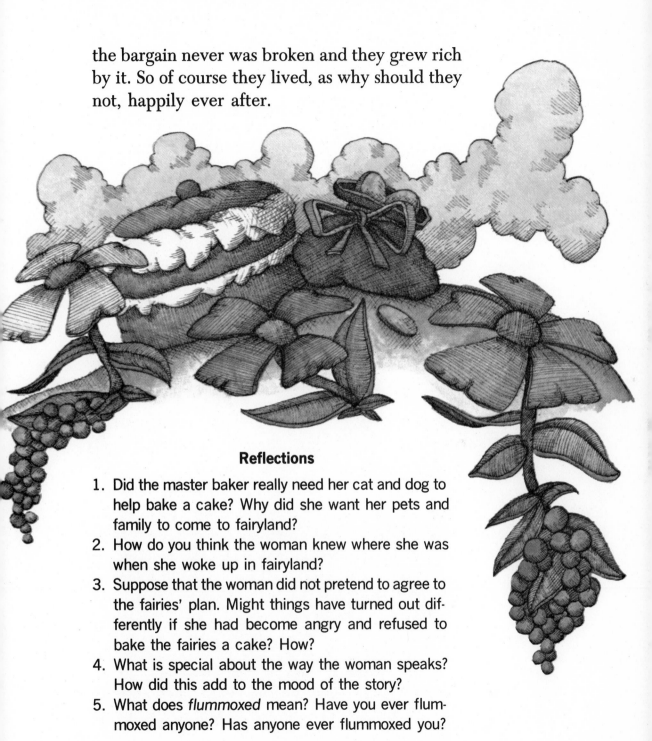

### Reflections

1. Did the master baker really need her cat and dog to help bake a cake? Why did she want her pets and family to come to fairyland?

2. How do you think the woman knew where she was when she woke up in fairyland?

3. Suppose that the woman did not pretend to agree to the fairies' plan. Might things have turned out differently if she had become angry and refused to bake the fairies a cake? How?

4. What is special about the way the woman speaks? How did this add to the mood of the story?

5. What does *flummoxed* mean? Have you ever flummoxed anyone? Has anyone ever flummoxed you?

# The Witch of Willowby Wood

ROWENA BENNETT

There once was a witch of Willowby Wood,
and a weird wild witch was she, with hair that
    was snarled
and hands that were gnarled, and a kickety,
    rickety
knee. She could jump, they say,
to the moon and back, but this I never did see.
Now Willowby Wood was near Sassafras Swamp,
where there's never a road or rut. And there
    by the
singing witch-hazel bush the old woman builded
her hut. She builded with neither a hammer or
    shovel. She
kneaded, she rolled out, she baked
her brown hovel. For all the witches' houses,
    I've oft heard
it said, are made of stick candy and fresh
gingerbread. But the shingles that shingled
    this old
witch's roof were lollipop shingles and
    hurricane-proof, too
hard to be pelted and melted by rain.
(Why this is important, I soon will explain.)

One day there came running to Sassafras
    Swamp a dark little
shadowy mouse. He was noted for being a
    scoundrel
and scamp. And he gnawed at the old woman's
    house where the
doorpost was weak and the doorpost was worn.
And when the witch scolded, he laughed her to
    scorn.
And when the witch chased him, he felt quite
    delighted. She
never could catch him for she was nearsighted.
    And so,
though she quibbled, he gnawed and he nibbled.
The witch said, "I won't have my house
take a tumble. I'll search in my magical book
    for a spell
I can weave and a charm I can mumble to get
    you
away from this nook. It will be a good warning
    to other
bad mice, who won't earn their bread
but go stealing a slice."
"Your charms cannot hurt," said the mouse,
    looking pert.

Well, she looked in her book and she
waved her right arm, and she said the most
   magical
things. Till the mouse, feeling strange,
looked about in alarm, and found he was
   growing some
wings. He flapped and he fluttered the longer
   she muttered.
"And now, my fine fellow,
you'd best be aloof," said the witch as he
   floundered
around. "You can't stay on earth and you
can't gnaw my roof. It's lollipop-hard and
   it's
hurricane-proof. So you'd better take off
from the ground. If you are wise, stay in the
   skies."
Then in went the woman of Willowby Wood,
in to her hearthstone and cat.
There, she put her old volume up high on the
   shelf, and
fanned her hot face with her hat. Then she
   said,
"That is that! I have just made a bat!"

# A Tale of Stolen Time

EVGENY SCHWARTZ

translated by LILA PARGMENT and ESTELLE TITIEV

## Plenty of Time

Once there lived a boy called Peter Zubov. He was a lazy boy and was way behind all the other children in his class. He didn't do his arithmetic homework or his spelling homework. Even in singing he was behind all the others. But Peter didn't worry. He would always say, "There's plenty of time. I'll catch up next week." But when the next week came, he would say again, "There's plenty of time. Next week I'll catch up."

One morning Peter came to school, late as usual. As he ran to the cloakroom, he called, "Aunt Natasha, take my coat."

From behind the coat hangers came a voice, "Who is it?"

"It's I—Peter," answered the boy.

"Why is your voice so hoarse today?"

"I don't know. I just suddenly became hoarse."

Aunt Natasha's head peered out from among the hangers. She took one look and gasped in surprise.

"What's the matter?" Peter asked.

"What's the matter indeed!" Aunt Natasha answered. "You told me you were Peter, but you must be his grandfather!"

"What do you mean—grandfather? *I'm* Peter Zubov. I'm in the fourth grade."

"Just look at yourself in the mirror."

Peter looked, and what he saw made him shake. He had turned into a thin, pale old man with a long gray beard and a moustache! His face was *covered* with wrinkles. He stood and stared at himself. His gray beard began to quiver. He turned and ran out of the room.

He ran straight home, thinking, "Surely Mother will recognize me." At last Peter reached his house, and he rang the bell quickly three times. The door opened, and there was his mother, who stood looking at him without saying a word. Peter, too, remained silent. His gray beard shook. He was ready to burst into tears.

"Whom do you want to see, sir?" asked Peter's mother.

In a faint whisper Peter asked, "Don't you know me?"

"I'm sorry, but I don't," answered his mother.

Peter turned away and walked off, thinking, "Maybe I'm not really Peter any more. I guess I'm just a lonely old man. I'm all alone, with no mother and no friends. How can I get along? Old people are usually doctors, lawyers, or teachers—but I have learned to be none of them. I've only gone as far as the fourth grade, and I certainly haven't learned very much—not as much as I should have. What will become of me?"

Peter kept walking and thinking, thinking and walking. He didn't notice that he had left the town behind him and that he was now in a forest. He walked on and on until darkness fell.

Peter began to feel tired. "It would be nice to rest a while," he thought. Just then he spied a tiny white house among the trees. He went in and looked about. No one was there. In the middle of the room stood a table with a lamp hanging over it. Four stools had been placed around the table. On the wall was a clock with a pendulum that said, "Tick-tock, tick-tock," as it swung to and fro. In one corner of the room, there was a pile of hay.

Peter crawled deep into the hay. He made himself a cozy, warm nest and cried for a while. Then he wiped the tears with his long gray beard and fell asleep.

Some time later he awoke. The lamp was shining brightly, and around the table sat four children, two boys and two girls. A large abacus lay before them. The children were counting on it, softly sighing and mumbling:

"Two years plus five years plus seven plus three. This is for you and this is for me."

"What strange children," thought Peter. "Why are they mumbling and sighing like old people? Why are they here at night in this lonely little forest hut?"

Peter lay as still as he could—not moving a muscle, scarcely breathing. He was trying to hear everything that the children were saying. Suddenly he realized that these were not real children.

These were not two little boys and two little girls sitting together around a table. They were four sorcerers who knew a terrible secret. They could change children who wasted their time into old people. They were always hunting for children who wasted their time. They had found Peter and another little boy and two little girls and had

turned them all into old people. Then they took
the time they had stolen from the children, and
now the sorcerers were the children and the
children were old, old people.

The sorcerers had counted up all the time and
were ready to put away the abacus when one of
them, who seemed to be the leader of the group,
picked up the abacus and went up to the clock.
First he turned the hands; then he pulled the
weights and listened carefully to the tick-tock of
the pendulum.

Once again he calculated on the abacus, counting until the clock struck the hour of midnight.
He shook the abacus, and again he counted. Then,
calling the others to him, he said in a very low
voice, "My fellow sorcerers, you know that the
children whom we transformed into old people
still have a chance to become young again."

"How?" asked the sorcerers.

"I'll tell you in a moment, but first I'll make
sure no one is listening to us." The sorcerer went
out of the house on tiptoe, walked around and

397

around, and then came back and locked the door with a key. He took a large stick and stirred through the hay where Peter was hiding. But the lamp gave only a poor light in the corner, and the sorcerer didn't find Peter.

"Now, come close to me," called the leader to the others. In a low voice he continued, "The world is so made that any person can save himself from trouble if he tries hard enough. If the children whom we transformed into old people meet here tomorrow at exactly midnight and turn the hands of the clock seventy-seven times, then they will become children once again, and—*we* will die."

All were silent. Then one sorcerer, a girl, said, "But how will they find out what they have to do?"

Another mumbled, "They won't get here exactly at midnight. They'll be at least one minute late."

The third one added, "They can't even count to seventy-seven. They'll get mixed up."

"Just the same," warned the leader, "look sharp and listen carefully. If the children so much as touch the hands of the clock, we will become motionless—unable to move a finger. Now, let's not waste any time—to work, to work!"

The sorcerers hid the abacus and ran off like children, though they moaned and sighed just like very old people.

### No Time to Waste

Peter waited until the sound of their steps had died away. Then he ran out of the house as fast as he could. Hiding behind bushes and trees from time to time to see if he was being followed, he finally reached the town. Now to find three old people who were really schoolchildren!

The town was still asleep. No lights shone in the windows; no people walked in the streets. Only a policeman stood on the corner. Daylight was just beginning to break. In the distance a streetcar began to clang.

After some time Peter noticed an old woman who came hobbling down the street with a large basket over her arm. Peter ran to her and asked, "Tell me, Granny, are you a fourth grader?"

"What? What?" shrieked the old woman.

"Aren't you really a little girl?" Peter whispered.

The old woman stamped her foot and flung her basket at Peter. He dodged the blow and ran off.

By now the town was awake. Buses were running, people were dashing to work, and trucks were grinding their gears. Peter had seen this happen many times before, but it was only now that he understood that people hurried because they didn't want to waste time. He looked around him. He saw a number of old people coming down the street, but he could tell at a glance that they were really old people, not children who had been transformed by witches.

Here comes an old man carrying a briefcase. He's probably a teacher.

Here comes an old man with a brush and pail—a painter.

There goes a red fire engine with the fire chief in it. Surely *he* never wasted a minute.

Peter walked up and down without seeing a trace of young old men or old young children.

By now it was noon, and Peter decided to walk over to the square to rest a bit. Just then he noticed an old woman sitting on a bench crying bitterly. Peter wanted to go up to her, but he thought he had better wait a while.

After a bit the old woman dried her tears and sat swinging her legs as she took a piece of raisin bread out of her pocket. She kept picking out the raisins and eating them, but she threw the bread away. Then her eye fell on something lying in the snow—a ball that someone had forgotten. She picked it up, and, turning it round and round, she wiped it carefully with her handkerchief and began to play with it, throwing it up into the air and catching it.

Peter ran up to her saying, "I bet you're really a fourth grader."

The little old woman jumped up and down. "I am. I'm in the fourth grade. I'm Maria Popova. What's your name?"

Peter told her who he was and told her, too, all that had happened to him. Then off they went together to look for two more schoolchildren. After searching and searching for a long time, they came upon a big house with a large back-yard that had a woodshed at one side. Not far from the shed was a little old woman playing hopscotch. Peter and Maria looked at each other, and then together they ran as fast as they could towards the little figure, crying, "Granny, are you a schoolgirl?"

"Schoolgirl? Yes, I'm in the fourth grade, and my name is Nadya. What are your names?"

Peter and Maria told Nadya all that had happened, and then the three of them, holding hands, ran off to find the fourth child. They looked everywhere, in gardens, in the movies, in the Children's Theater, but not a trace of him could they find.

Meanwhile, time was running out. It was beginning to get dark. People were turning on the lights in their houses. Daytime was almost gone. Would they never find the fourth child and become young again? Were they doomed to remain old people?

Suddenly Maria called out, "Look, look up there!" pointing to the top of a passing trolley car. High up on the very top of the trolley sat an old man. His hat was pulled over one ear, his beard was waving in the wind, and he whistled as he rode along. The three children were very tired after all their searching. There, without a care in the world, sat the one they were looking for. There was nothing to do but run after the trolley. Luckily, the traffic light turned red just then, and the trolley stopped.

Up the children clambered and pulled the old man down. "You're a schoolboy, aren't you?" they demanded.

"Of course I am—third grade. What do you want?"

They told him the whole story, and since the trolley was going in the right direction, they all

got in. When the trolley came to the woods, the
four old people jumped out and ran off in search
of the little house. Once again, they were in
trouble. They lost their way. It became darker
and darker. They wandered about, stumbling and
falling.

"Oh dear," said Peter. "Yesterday I was in such
a hurry and so afraid to lose a minute that I didn't
look carefully enough to remember the road to
the house. Now I see that sometimes it's wisest
to take time in order to save trouble later."

The children were very tired and very unhappy. At that moment a gust of wind chased the
clouds from the sky and let the full moon shine
down on the woods. Peter climbed up into a tree
to look around, and there, not more than a few

yards away, stood the little white house, its windows shining through the fir trees.

Peter climbed down, whispered to the others to follow him, and quietly they went toward the sorcerers' house. Through the window they could see the clock—it was five minutes before twelve. The sorcerers were sleeping in the hay, guarding the time they had stolen.

Softly, ever so softly, the children opened the door and crawled on hands and knees toward the clock. When it was just one minute before twelve, they stood up. Exactly at midnight Peter stretched out his fingers to the hands of the clock and began turning them back from right to left, counting, "One, two, three . . ."

The sorcerers jumped up with a shriek—but they could move no further. They were rooted to that spot. And as they stood there, they began growing taller and taller, until they were as big as grown people. Wrinkles covered their faces, and their hair had turned gray.

"Lift me up, lift me up," cried Peter. "I'm getting smaller and smaller, and I can't reach the hands of the clock!"

The children lifted him up, and he went on counting, ". . . thirty-one, thirty-two, thirty-three." When he got to forty, the sorcerers had turned into bent, old people. Now they were getting shorter and shorter, bending closer and closer to the ground.

On the seventy-seventh turn of the clock's hands, the wicked sorcerers gave a horrible shriek and then disappeared completely.

The children looked at one another and jumped for joy. They were themselves. They were children once more.

**Reflections**

1. What serious fault did Peter have? What excuse did he always give?

2. What made Peter realize that he had turned into an old man?

3. This story is set in Russia, not America. One of the clues is the fact that the cloakroom at Peter's school has an attendant whom the children call "Aunt" Natasha, even though she is not related to them. Where else does Peter follow the Russian custom of calling a stranger by a relative's title?

4. The title of this story is "A Tale of Stolen Time." Who stole time in the story and from where?

5. How did Peter know that the "old people" were really children?

6. What do you think Peter learned about the value of time? What is the difference between "wasting time" and "taking time"?

# PICTURES FROM WORDS

In any story you read, words are used to describe the setting, or the place where the events of the story happen. Writers use words to describe people and things. We have to use our own imagination with words when we read sentences. For example, in these sentences, watch the word *carriage*. Think of the pictures you get as you read.

1. Mother left the baby *carriage* by the door.
2. George Washington rode in a *carriage* from Alexandria to his home, Mount Vernon.
3. You should see my dad's new car. What a *carriage!*
4. That's some *carriage* you have there. Did you make it?

Which picture below do you match with each of the sentences above? Would the third picture be suitable for the first, second, or fourth sentences? Why or why not?

## Word Pictures

Good writers use certain ways to help you understand what they mean. Here is one way.

1. The boy was chattering away *like an excited monkey.*
2. Tony sailed into the room *like a great eagle.*
3. She sat down *like a tired elephant.*

In each of these sentences, a person is described as similar to, or like, something else. How do you think an excited monkey chatters? How does a boy sail into a room like a great eagle? Do you think he walks swiftly? Is he silent? If you sit down like a tired elephant, do you sit on the edge of your chair, or do you drop heavily and rest your arms on the arms of your chair?

When we say one thing is like another, or similar to another, we call *like* or *as* and the words following it a simile (sim'ə lē). Writers often use similes. Your everyday speech is full of similes. You can easily make up some. Copy each of the following sentence starters; then complete each one. See how your similes are different from or similar to those your classmates write.

1. I am the air in a balloon, and I am going to come out like ——.
2. I am an egg being tossed into an electric fan, and I am going to smash like ——.
3. I am a great spotlight, and I shine as ——.
4. I am a shooting star, and I speed through the night like ——.
5. I am hungry enough to eat like ——.

Discuss the different word pictures your words made in the sentences above. Writing similes gives you a chance to use your imagination. Were some of your similes funny? Were some sad? Were some surprising?

## Changing the Meaning of Words

Sometimes people make their language more interesting by changing the meaning of a word or group of words. The words define one thing in a way that is like a simile but without *like* or *as*. This is how it works.

1. John's head is a computer.
2. He is a regular adding machine.
3. Tina is a walking encyclopedia.

As we read, we know that in fact John's head is not a computer, that no boy is an adding machine. We know a girl is not a walking encyclopedia. But we accept these words because they are a good, clear way of describing, or defining, one thing in terms of another. When we say to our best friend, "Gee, what a nut you are!" we know in fact that he is not a nut. If we said this to a stranger, we might get into trouble.

This use of words, calling someone or something by another name, is called metaphor. You make a metaphor by letting one word, or group of words, name something else.

Use a metaphor to complete each word group that follows the sentences below. The first one is done for you.

1.  Mr. Demos has a cold way of being unfriendly.
    His heart is <u>an iceberg</u>.

2.  Mrs. Demos has a warm way of being friendly.
    Her heart is ——.

3.  Mrs. Jenkins, the librarian, knows dozens of stories.
    She is ——.

4.  The dog knows a dozen tricks.
    Old Rover is a ——.

5.  The car squeaks, rattles, pops, and wheezes.
    The car is ——.

How are your metaphors in the sentences above alike?

Which one of the sentences below has a metaphor and which one a simile?

1.  Her skin is like marble.
    Her skin is marble.

2.  The car squeaks like a dozen mice.
    This car is a nest of squeaking mice.

3.  Old Rover is like a clown.
    Old Rover is all clown.

As long as you speak or read, you will use similes and metaphors. Know how words used in these two ways work to help you break the reading code.

411

# Roads Go Ever Ever On

Roads go ever ever on,
  Over rock and under tree,
By caves where never sun has shone,
  By streams that never find the sea;
Over snow by winter sown,
  And through the merry flowers of June,
Over grass and over stone,
  And under mountains in the moon.

*J. R. R. Tolkien*

# To Catch the High Winds

# The Day Jean-Pierre
# Went Round the World

PAUL GALLICO

### Plans and an Accident

For weeks and weeks Cecile Durand had been dreaming of her family's annual two-week holiday in Paris and telling her pet guinea pig, Jean-Pierre, all about it.

Most children, when they think of a holiday, look forward to going to the country and playing in the woods or to paddling at the seashore, finding shells, and digging in the sand. But Cecile lived in the country, not far from the sea. Her father owned a flower farm near Nice, which is on the Mediterranean. Her holiday was just the

other way round. It was to journey to a city to visit her aunt, Louise Tissaud, who lived in a tall, old house in Paris.

There had been great excitement when it came to the preparations, like finding and purchasing a suitable box for Jean-Pierre. Cecile held long conversations with the guinea pig, telling him all about what Paris was like.

There was only one small thing to mar Cecile's happiness. She had thought she would be able to carry Jean-Pierre's box on her lap, or Jean-Pierre himself in her pocket, as she often did. Monsieur Durand explained it was a rule of the airlines that no animals were permitted inside the cabin. Jean-Pierre would have to go with the luggage. But since the flight to Paris was very short, he would not mind.

With this Cecile had to be satisfied. But she decided to take her own precautions. She prepared special instructions in both French and English.

Dear Anyone,

Please, this is my own guinea pig, Jean-Pierre, whom I love better than anyone, except my parents. He is an Abyssinian guinea pig. He is special. He is also magic and can understand. If he is lost or misses the plane, or anything should happen, please do not leave him in this box, but take him out and give him love.

He is used to being cuddled at night and spoken to. He drinks milk but likes it made a little warm for him, please. He eats anything from the garden, like carrots, lettuce, cabbage, radishes, pieces of marrow, bits of apple, pear, and grapes—also crumbs of bread or cake or a little cheese. But best of all he likes pomegranate seeds, if you have any. If not, it does not matter. Please do not give him too much, as he will make a pig of himself if you let him.

He should be kept warm. If he sneezes, it is not because he has caught a cold but because he is excited. His big meal is at suppertime. That is all I have to say, except do not forget to give him lots of love and hugs and do not let him be lonely.

Thank you very much,
Jean-Pierre's mother,
Cecile Durand

To this she added her address, care of Madame Tissaud. Cecile put the two letters in separate envelopes, addressed one in French and the other in English, "To Whom It May Concern." These she quietly attached to the inside of Jean-Pierre's traveling box the morning they left.

They were driven to the airport by the head gardener who looked after things during Monsieur Durand's absence.

The loudspeaker went, "Plank, plonk, plink," and a voice announced, "Passengers for Paris on Flight 1200, proceed to Gate 5. Please have your boarding cards ready."

There were many planes parked on the apron of the airport, but Cecile knew the Caravelle at once, for she had flown before. She was allowed to run ahead and up the stairs into the aircraft so she could occupy a seat by a window. Soon they were all strapped in and the sweets offered by the air hostess popped into Cecile's mouth. They taxied to the end of the runway, and with a great roar the jet plane thundered away and climbed into the sky.

In less than an hour they would be in Paris, over six hundred miles away. Cecile gave herself up to dreaming about being reunited with Jean-Pierre, safe and sound in his little traveling box somewhere in one of the luggage compartments of the giant Caravelle that was carrying them to Paris.

Only, alas, he wasn't! An airline official had seen Jean-Pierre's box sitting on the loading bay. By mistake he had picked up the box, and it was soon on a plane bound for Bangkok, Thailand!

After landing and discovering that Jean-Pierre wasn't among the baggage, it began to seem to Cecile as though she were in a nightmare. Instead of happily proceeding in a taxi to Aunt Louise's house, here they were at the airport, and no Jean-Pierre. There was much talk and confusion. No one seemed to know what had happened. Finally the chief of the airline promised to call the Durands the first moment he heard of Jean-Pierre's whereabouts.

And with that the Durands had to be satisfied. They collected their bags and took a taxi to Aunt Louise's.

### A Surprise from Thailand

Cecile sat by the telephone all the next day, except when called to meals. She had slept very badly. Once, dreaming that she heard the telephone, she had leaped out of bed. There were also false alarms when friends of her aunt rang during the day.

On the third morning she had the surprise of her life. And it did not come over the telephone, after all. It arrived in a letter addressed to Cecile.

Her aunt handed it to her, saying, "My goodness, Cecile, you have friends in strange places!"

Cecile took it and ran to her father. "Look, Papa, look! I've got a letter! It's such a funny-looking one. It must be from Jean-Pierre."

There was a beautiful stamp on the envelope, showing it came from Thailand. The handwriting was small, delicate, and easy to read. In perfect French it began:

Dear Mademoiselle Durand,

I am writing to tell you of your little guinea pig, who was entrusted to my care until we were able to put him on a TWA plane for Paris, to be returned to you. You must be a very kind little girl to love your pet so much and leave such perfect instructions in case he should become lost.

He was given to me because I, too, own many pets. My name is Sirima Desjardins, and I am Siamese. My husband, Marcel, is French. He is Chief European Assistant to the Royal Forestry Department and is in charge of more than one hundred elephants.

I am sure you would be interested in my pets. I have a python (he is sweet—and also likes to drink warm milk) and a dwarf deer, a ruffed lemur who would make you laugh, he looks so funny, and a honey bear. Jean-Pierre visited my python and played with the lemur. I also have my favorite elephant on which I ride.

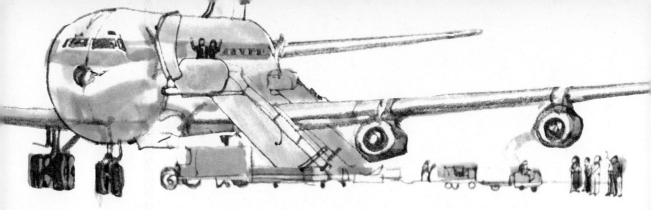

Her name is Nang-Hiaw, which means "Old Wrinkled-Skin," and indeed her gray hide looks like the map of a thousand rivers.

Yesterday morning, after I fed Jean-Pierre, I took him on Nang-Hiaw (for some twenty of my husband's elephants are working on the edge of the airport here), and I think he liked it. I held him tightly to my cheek all the time. He wasn't frightened even when Nang touched him with the sensitive tip of her trunk. He only wrinkled up his nose and sneezed.

When we returned to the airport, the king and queen of our country had just flown in from the north, and Jean-Pierre saw them both. As they came down the steps from the airplane, we all cheered, and Nang-Hiaw saluted them with her trunk. They waved to us and to Jean-Pierre, too.

Then I returned Jean-Pierre to the director of the airport, who put him aboard a TWA airliner bound for Paris. Perhaps you will have him back safe in your arms even before this letter arrives. But I thought you would like to know how he spent his time in our lovely country.

Wishing him a safe journey and a happy arrival,

> Yours in distant friendship,
> Sirima Desjardins

## A Circus Guinea Pig

But Jean-Pierre's adventures weren't over. Because of bad weather and other complications, instead of going to Paris, he landed in Australia! A few days after the letter from Thailand, the phone rang, and Cecile was very surprised when she picked it up and an operator said, "Hello, Mademoiselle Cecile Durand on the line? Go ahead, Sydney."

A man said in French: "Hello, Cecile, can you hear me?"

Cecile replied that she could, for it was just as plain as if it were from across the street.

"This is Monsieur Flippo speaking. Perhaps you have never heard of me, but I am a famous circus clown. I have your little guinea pig, Jean-Pierre, right here with me, safe and sound.

"When Jean-Pierre arrived in Sydney, nobody knew where he was from or where he was going or what to do with him. But when they read your clever little letter inside the cage, they knew that someone would have to look after him until they found out. And who do you think they went to? Old Monsieur Flippo, the circus clown, with his educated kangaroos and his trained pigs.

"Our circus is playing in an amusement park not far from the airport. So they sent the little fellow over to me. I fed him and gave him his warm milk, and then, where do you think he spent the night?"

"Where?" Cecile asked, prepared for almost anything but certainly not for what he said next.

"In Angelique! Angelique is one of my kangaroos. You see, my Angelique's baby died, and she was unhappy. Jean-Pierre was lonely and cold, so that's exactly where I tucked him. They got on fine. And do you know what happened the next day?"

Cecile was almost breathless with excitement by now but managed to say, "No, what?"

"He looked so funny, the guinea pig, with his head sticking out of Angelique's pouch, that I put him in the act."

"You mean Jean-Pierre was in the circus!" Cecile gasped.

"Right! He was a sensation! Three thousand children laughed, cheered, and clapped when I took him out of Angelique's pouch and showed him to them. (I shall have to get a guinea pig of my own.) Oh, he was marvelous! Such stage presence! Like an old trouper. Well, then, the next day they came from the airport to say that they had found out where he belonged and that he must go home. They said they would put a call through to you so I could tell you all about it. If you like, you can speak to him, Cecile."

"Oh, Jean-Pierre, Jean-Pierre, Jean-Pierre!" Cecile cried into the telephone. "Jean-Pierre, can you hear me?"

For a moment there was a silence from the other end of the line, and then—could it be possible? She heard a faint little chirrup, followed by the tiniest noise of small teeth clicking together. They were actually Jean-Pierre noises that Cecile knew so well. And then, best and most wonderful of all, in quick succession came three small but unmistakable Jean-Pierre sneezes.

"There you are!" It was Monsieur Flippo again. "He said hello to you. Tonight he will sleep in Angelique for the last time, and early tomorrow, that's Monday morning, he is starting his journey back home to you. How's that?"

"Oh, thank you, thank you, thank you, Monsieur Flippo!" said Cecile.

Then there was a click at the other end of the line, and it was over.

The next news Cecile received of Jean-Pierre was this cablegram.

YOUR GUINEA PIG JEAN-PIERRE STOPPED OFF HERE INTERNATIONAL AIRPORT HONOLULU EN ROUTE PARIS VIA SAN FRANCISCO NEW YORK STOP IN ADDITION TO THINGS YOU WROTE HE LIKED TO EAT HE ALSO GOES FOR PINEAPPLE PAPAYA COCONUT BREADFRUIT YAMS MALAY AND CUSTARD APPLES AVOCADOS POI MANGOES GUAVA POHA TAMARIND PASSION FRUIT LICHEE MACADAMIA NUTS AND SUGARCANE ALL PRODUCTS HAWAIIAN ISLANDS STOP HE ENJOYED SOME OF EACH ONLY HOPE NOT GIVE HIM STOMACHACHE STOP DEPARTED HERE OKAY GOOD WISHES SAFE ARRIVAL Y A CHIN TRAFFIC SUPERINTENDENT INTERNATIONAL AIRPORT HONOLULU

If Jean-Pierre could be said to have a fault, it was that he was a bit greedy. If allowed, he would eat until his sides swelled out and one was afraid he would burst.

Unhappily he did get a bad stomachache. When he finally arrived in New York, his nose was hot. His eyes were watery. He huddled in a corner of his cage, shivering miserably. No one knew what to do. Then the airport officials remembered a Professor Jones, who had hundreds of guinea pigs. If there was one man who knew all about what might be the matter, it was this professor.

Hurried phone calls were made. Then, in a special ambulance with police escort, Jean-Pierre was rushed to the laboratory of Professor Jones in downtown New York. Fortunately Cecile knew nothing of this.

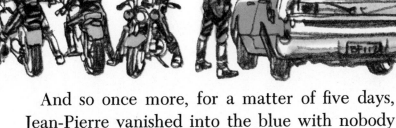

And so once more, for a matter of five days, Jean-Pierre vanished into the blue with nobody able to trace hide nor hair of him.

Strange to say, Cecile took even this calmly and occupied herself with enjoying the rest of her holiday. For she was certain that a guinea pig who was magic enough to telephone her from Australia would come safely home to her.

And then the day for the Durands' return to the south of France was at hand. The holiday was over. They were all packed and ready to leave for the plane back to Nice. Aunt Louise came to the cab to see them off and listened to the final instructions from Cecile as to exactly what to do and how to look after Jean-Pierre, should he arrive after they had departed.

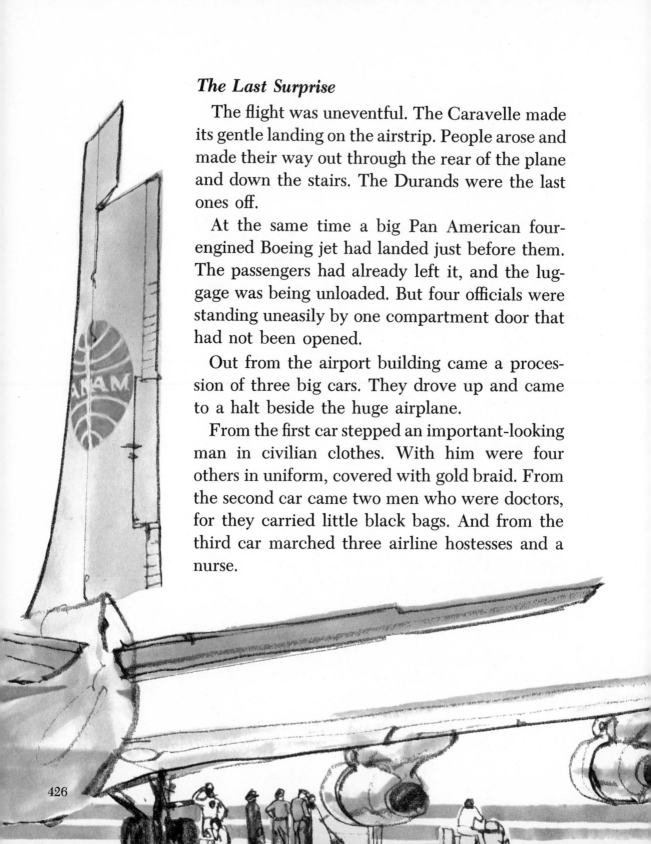

### The Last Surprise

The flight was uneventful. The Caravelle made its gentle landing on the airstrip. People arose and made their way out through the rear of the plane and down the stairs. The Durands were the last ones off.

At the same time a big Pan American four-engined Boeing jet had landed just before them. The passengers had already left it, and the luggage was being unloaded. But four officials were standing uneasily by one compartment door that had not been opened.

Out from the airport building came a procession of three big cars. They drove up and came to a halt beside the huge airplane.

From the first car stepped an important-looking man in civilian clothes. With him were four others in uniform, covered with gold braid. From the second car came two men who were doctors, for they carried little black bags. And from the third car marched three airline hostesses and a nurse.

"Goodness," said Monsieur Durand, "there must be someone very important and very ill aboard that plane."

Cecile said, "Oh, Papa, let's stay and watch a moment!"

As the important-looking man in civilian clothes approached the plane, the four attendants waiting there snapped to attention. The doctors stepped up closer. The hostesses and the nurse stood ready. The man motioned for the compartment door to be opened. Up it flew. From inside it a hand passed out—a small box—well, a kind of cage. It had so many stickers on it, the wood could hardly be seen, but at one end was a square of wire mesh, and poking his pink, healthy nose up against it was . . .

"Jean-Pierre! Jean-Pierre!" screamed Cecile at the top of her lungs. She ran to the plane and threw her arms about the little box, hugging it to her.

"Jean-Pierre, you've come back to me! I knew you would!" She opened the cage, reached inside, and took him out. The guinea pig was overcome with joy at being back with Cecile again. He squealed, clicked, chirruped, shrieked, and sneezed all at the same time, and then snuffled his way into her neck.

The important-looking man went over to Monsieur and Madame Durand and asked, "Are you Monsieur Durand, and is this Cecile?"

"Yes, of course," said Monsieur Durand. "Would you like to see my passport to prove it?"

"No, no," said the man, "take the animal. They were so nervous in New York, they put him on the wrong plane again, the one that flies directly from New York to Nice. But we were told about the mistake and were going to send him on to Paris. You're lucky to have Jean-Pierre back."

Cecile held Jean-Pierre up in her two hands and looked into his golden-yellow eyes and cried, "Oh, Jean-Pierre, no other girl has ever had such a splendid guinea pig!"

Jean-Pierre sneezed happily six times in a row to celebrate the happy end to his adventures.

### Reflections

1. On a map or a globe, trace Jean-Pierre's route around the world. Approximately how many miles did he travel?

2. Why was it fortunate that Cecile wrote her instructions in both French and English? What do you think might have happened to Jean-Pierre if Cecile had put just her name and address on his cage?

3. What animals did Sirima Desjardins have as pets? Which animal would you most want to have as a pet? Give reasons for your answer.

4. Since no punctuation is used in cablegrams or telegrams, how is the end of a sentence indicated?

5. Suppose Jean-Pierre were entrusted to your care for a day. Write a letter to Cecile, telling her how you cared for him.

# International Mail

H. ALEXANDER FRAENKEL

How easy it is to mail a letter. Drop an addressed and stamped envelope into a mailbox. As if by a miracle, it goes wherever you send it. But it has taken more than two thousand years for this to happen.

Back in 559 B.C., in Persia, only a lucky few used a postal system. King Cyrus stationed riders a day apart throughout his kingdom. Then messages were passed from rider to rider. Sometimes very private messages were written on a man's shaved head. When his hair grew back, he was sent on his way. When he arrived, his head was shaved once more. Then the message could be read.

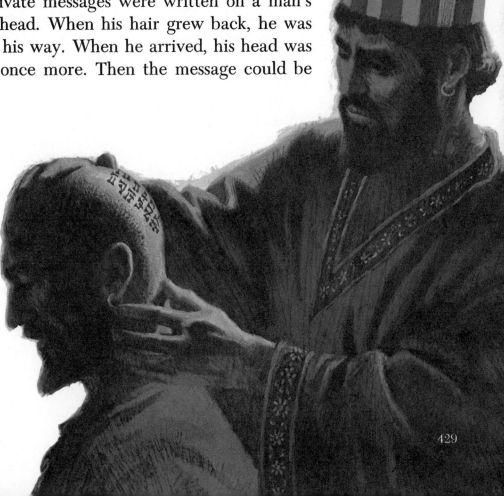

429

During the next 2,400 years, more modern ways of sending letters were developed in many parts of the world. By the 1830's most countries of Europe had ways of getting letters from one place to another within their borders.

But people had a great deal of trouble sending mail out of their own country. International mail was highly taxed. Every nation that a letter passed through wanted to be paid for handling the mail. Many people could not afford international mail service.

In 1874 representatives from twenty-two countries met in Berne, Switzerland. They wanted to solve the problem of high rates. At first they could not agree. Small countries wanted to keep taxes high. They said that they had to handle more letters from larger countries than they sent out. Other countries argued that as many letters were sent out of small countries as passed through. But they all finally came to an agreement. They formed the General Postal Union.

The Union, later called the Universal Postal Union, made some rules that all could follow. Every member nation promised to transport the mail of every other member nation. The rates to be charged for mail of different kinds would be set up by the Union. And the members promised to settle any disagreements in a friendly way.

Today, almost every country in the world uses stamps. There are hundreds of thousands of different ones. Stamps have pictures of many things. They often have pictures of people. Stamps may show plants, animals, or paintings. Or they may picture sports events, spaceships, bridges, maps, and airplanes.

Because of their great variety and beauty, stamp collecting has become a popular hobby. But because of this variety, and the vast number of stamps, it is very hard to collect stamps from all of the countries in the world. Some people collect stamps from only one or a few countries. Some people collect stamps about a certain subject. On page 432, there are stamps arranged by subject. On page 433, you will see stamps from one country—the United States.

### Reflections

1. How many years ago was the year 559 B.C.?
2. Look up the Pony Express in an encyclopedia. How did this American postal system resemble the one that King Cyrus set up?
3. What do you think would happen to everyday life and commerce if there were no mail services?
4. If you could design a new U.S. stamp, what would the stamp look like? In what category would it be? Explain the reasons for your choice.
5. What things might a person learn about other countries just from collecting foreign stamps?

# CHILDREN

Monaco

Maldive Islands

# NATURE

Austria

Czechoslovakia

New Zealand

# SPORTS

Dominican Republic

432

# UNITED STATES

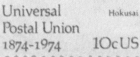

# Wilbur Wright and
# Orville Wright

ROSEMARY and STEPHEN VINCENT BENET

Said Orville Wright to Wilbur Wright,
"These birds are very trying.
I'm sick of hearing them cheep-cheep
About the fun of flying.
A bird has feathers, it is true.
That much I freely grant.
But, must that stop us, W?"
Said Wilbur Wright, "It shan't."

And so they built a glider, first,
And then they built another.
—There never were two brothers more
Devoted to each other.
They ran a dusty little shop
For bicycle-repairing,
And bought each other soda-pop
And praised each other's daring.

They glided here, they glided there,
They sometimes skinned their noses,
—For learning how to rule the air
Was not a bed of roses—
But each would murmur, afterward,
While patching up his bro.
"Are we discouraged, W?"
"Of course we are not, O!"

434

And finally, at Kitty Hawk
In Nineteen-Three (let's cheer it!),
*The first real airplane really flew.*
With Orville there to steer it!
—And kingdoms may forget their kings
And dogs forget their bites,
But, not till Man forgets his wings,
Will men forget the Wrights.

# Daring Flier

PEGGY MANN

*In 1920, a young woman boarded a street car and rode to an airfield near her home. There, she walked over to a pilot standing near his plane and said, "I want to go up." The pilot agreed, and Amelia Earhart took her first airplane ride. This young woman would later become one of the world's finest pilots. It was during this first flight that she made up her mind to learn how to fly. She started taking lessons, and in a few months, anxiously waited for her instructor to tell her she was ready to fly alone.*

The day finally came. John declared she was ready to go "upstairs" by herself. She would solo.

She did not feel much like a pilot as she sat, for the first time, alone in the plane. Would she remember everything? All those instruments! Instructions shot through her head: *revolutions per minute of the motor . . . temperature of the oil . . . compass readings . . . keep your wings level.* How could she possibly remember it all? "Switch off!

Contact!" she shouted. John spun the propeller. And with a thunderous roar, the plane started taxiing across the field. Amelia made an S-turn. She was on the runway. She raced her motor. She checked each dial on the instrument panel. She pulled back on the stick and headed the nose off the ground. The plane rose into the air. But something was wrong! The left wing was sagging!

She landed, dismayed. Her instructor ran up. "Cold feet?" he yelled. She shook her head, climbed out, pointed to the wing.

One of the shock absorbers had broken. The trouble was soon fixed. Amelia climbed back into the cockpit again. But exhilaration had been replaced by clenching fear. The plane suddenly felt so—*fragile*. There were so many things which could go wrong! And before she had even left the ground, her greatest fear was of landing.

She had heard the stories often—beginners going up alone for the first time usually took off with a whoop of joy. But when it came time to land, they developed the shakes. Many stayed up till their gas tanks were empty—simply because of the terror they felt at trying to bring the plane in for a landing. Alone.

Amelia climbed to 5,000 feet. It was a fine day. Visibility was good. As she looked around, all fear left her. It seemed she could see the whole world. Colors stood out and the shades of earth, unseen from below, formed an endless magic carpet.

Trees became bushes. Automobiles were flat-backed bugs. Tiny doll-houses were set out in checkerboard fields.

She played around some in the plane, diving, turning, looping into figure eights. Then she dropped down for a landing. She felt in perfect control now. She was a flier. And—she suddenly decided—soon, somehow she would own her own plane!

But paying for flying lessons had been almost an impossibility. How could she even dream of buying an airplane?

She landed with a huge bump, and jounced along the dusty runway. John was the first to reach her. "That was one rotten landing!" he exclaimed as Amelia leaned out of the cockpit. But he was grinning broadly.

"How do you feel?" one of the mechanics shouted at her.

"Happy," Amelia said, speaking more to herself than to him. "Happier than I've ever been in my life."

*Amelia Earhart went on to break flying records all over the world. In 1932, she took off alone for Europe. People on both sides of the ocean awaited news of her safe arrival. When she landed—in an Irish meadow—she was the first woman to have flown solo across the Atlantic Ocean.*

*In 1937, Amelia Earhart took off for a flight*

*around the world along the equator. With her went Fred Noonan, a navigator. The most dangerous part of the journey came last—the long flight over the Pacific Ocean. During this flight, the plane was lost. Amelia Earhart was never heard from again. But she is still remembered as one of the finest pilots in the history of flying.*

## Reflections

1. Early pilots who broke records and flew dangerous distances were considered heroes. More recently, astronauts have also traveled into space and have been considered very brave. But what are some *differences* between what the early pilots and astronauts did? What are some similarities?
2. What did Amelia Earhart's instructor mean when he asked, "Cold feet?" Have you ever had "cold feet" about something? If so, what?
3. Very few women flew airplanes when Amelia Earhart did. Why do you think this was so? Do you think things have changed since then?

# Sky High

An airport is an exciting place to visit. Many people go there just to watch the planes take off and land. They stand on the roof of an airport building enjoying the thrill of flying—without ever leaving the ground.

The peak of airport excitement comes in the air. But most of the workers in air traffic work on the ground.

Airplane **mechanics** keep the planes in good shape. Their job is to refuel and repair the planes.

Airport **dispatchers** work in the control tower on top of the main building. They plan schedules and watch the weather. They check with pilots on the best altitude, fuel needs, and course of the flight.

**Air-traffic controllers** work in the control tower too. They guide planes to safe takeoffs and landings. They check the radar screen while the planes are in the air.

**Meteorologists** also work in the tower. Using maps and charts, they study weather conditions and make forecasts. Everyone in the tower holds the lives of many people in their hands.

The captain, or chief **pilot,** heads the flight crew. To be a captain takes thousands of hours of flying experience.

The **copilot** helps the captain fly the plane. The third person in the plane's cockpit is the **flight engineer.** The flight engineer checks out all airplane parts, examines the instruments in the cockpit, and keeps the flight log.

When you fly, the **flight attendants** are the members of the crew you see most often. They look after your needs from take-off until landing time at another airport. There, you will probably see a crowd of people on a roof, watching your plane come in for a landing.

# The Would-Be Cowboy

ILSE KLEBERGER

### Where the Cowboys Live

"What are the names of the German tributaries of the Danube?" asked Ingeborg.

Jan drawled in a bored voice, "Iller, Lech, Isar, Inn, thingummy, Nab, and Regen."

"What's thingummy?" Ingeborg asked her brother.

Jan yawned. "I've forgotten."

"But you must remember. When your teacher asks you tomorrow and you don't know, you'll get a bad mark again. Look at your atlas and find the rivers for yourself."

Unwillingly Jan took the atlas out of his satchel. When Ingeborg came back a quarter of an hour later, he was studying a map with glowing eyes.

"Have you found them?"

"Yes, here's Oklahoma and here are the Rocky Mountains, where the big ranches are."

"What sort of ranches? I thought you were looking for the tributaries of the Danube."

"Oh, I don't care a button about the Danube. I'm looking for the territories where the cowboys live in America. Look here."

Ingeborg pushed the atlas aside and scornfully said, "And I don't care a button about your cowboys, and I don't suppose your teacher does either. If you go on being so lazy and learning nothing, you'll stay in the same class *again*."

Jan looked tearful. "Why should I learn all that? I want to go to America and be a cowboy," he sobbed.

"A fine cowboy you'd make, crying like that!" jeered Ingeborg and left the room, slamming the door after her. She went to join her mother and her grandmother, Oma.

Jan dried his tears. She was right; cowboys shouldn't cry. But she was all wrong about cowboys needing to know the names of the tributaries of the Danube. He tucked a book called *As Cabin Boy to America* under his arm and withdrew to the goat shed, where no one would disturb him until the evening milking. He sat on a stool and settled down to read.

> Suddenly they sighted land. It was America! The little cabin boy's heart beat faster. Now he would see the country where the cowboys lived. He would see the country of skyscrapers and Niagara Falls.

Jan looked up from his book and gazed thoughtfully at the goat, which was rubbing against his leg. If only *he* were a cabin boy! But why not?

### A Traveling Companion

Early on Sunday morning Jan dressed quickly, packed his bag, and sneaked out of the house. He did not breathe freely until he got on the train. There he took a seat by the window and looked out. When the train was on its way and the roofs of the village had disappeared, his heart felt heavy. He decided he would come home one day, when he had become rich or famous in America, or perhaps both. Then he would bring his mother a new dress and his father a watch and for his grandmother, Oma . . .

"Good morning!" said Oma cheerfully, sitting down opposite him.

Jan blinked, but there was nothing wrong with his eyesight. Oma was really there, in her black dress with the lilac straw hat on her head. In her right hand was the bird cage with Paul, the parrot, prattling gaily. On her left arm were her handbag and umbrella.

"Where . . . where are you going?" stammered Jan.

"To America," Oma replied.

"America?" Jan gasped for breath. "You want to go to America?"

"Yes, why not?" Oma said. "I've always wanted to go to America. I wanted to go once a long time ago when I was a little girl, but then I got chicken pox, and after that something else always stopped me. When I heard yesterday that you wanted to go to America, I decided to come with you."

Jan stared out of the window in dismay.

"Or don't you like the idea?" asked Oma.

"Oh, yes," answered Jan quickly.

"Well then, everything's all right." Oma took out her knitting, and soon the needles were clicking. She said nothing more.

"How are you going to get to America?" asked Jan timidly.

"Just like you," answered Oma.

"But you can't be a cabin boy!"

"I will peel potatoes in the galley and earn my passage that way," Oma said.

"And what will you do when we finally get to America?"

445

"Perhaps I can work as a cook on the ranch where you're a cowboy."

"Then you could make me macaroni pudding sometimes."

"Of course."

Jan began to be enthusiastic about the idea of Oma traveling to America with him.

"Eberbach—all change!" shouted the guard. Oma jumped up and took her handbag, the umbrella, and Paul's cage.

"Perhaps you would carry my suitcase."

Jan took the suitcase off the rack and followed her out of the train. Outside, in front of the station, they looked at each other.

"Now what?" asked Oma.

"I was going to hitchhike," said Jan.

"All right, let's hitchhike."

They stood on the edge of the broad road. The first three cars Jan tried to stop went racing past.

They waited for half an hour without success.

"I guess we'll have to walk," said Oma.

They set off, but after a few steps Oma stopped. "Are we going the right way?"

Jan shrugged his shoulders uncertainly.

"Where is Hamburg?" asked Oma.

"In—in the north," stammered Jan.

"Northeast or northwest? I'm afraid I was very bad in geography at school."

"Me, too," said Jan in a small voice.

Paul, who had recovered from the shock of the railway trip, shook his feathers and called, "Northwest."

"Paul says northwest," said Oma. "But which way is northwest?"

Jan felt that he couldn't go on making a fool of himself, so he pointed straight ahead.

Oma marched firmly off, singing, "Oh, you'll take the high road . . ."

Jan tried to join in, but soon lost his breath. His Sunday shoes hurt, and Oma's suitcase seemed to grow heavier and heavier.

"What have you got in your suitcase?" he asked.

"Is it too heavy for you?" Oma asked. "There are only a few odds and ends in it. A nightdress, toothbrush, soap, a cookbook, some birdseed, and my roller skates." Oma said that roller-skating kept her young. "That's all. Do you want me to carry it instead?"

"No, no, it's quite light," Jan assured her quickly.

"And what did you pack?"

Jan said, "I packed my water pistol, my comic, a packet of chewing gum, a clothesline . . ." He glanced at Oma. "I need a lasso, you see."

"I understand," said Oma. "Of course, you need a lasso. And what about some soap and your toothbrush?"

"Oh, I forgot all about them."

Oma nodded her head. "That's easily done. You can borrow my soap, and the cowboys clean their teeth with twigs, so I read in a book."

Jan was astonished that Oma knew anything about cowboys. His respect for her increased enormously. Now he was really glad that she wanted to come to America with him.

### Oma and the Bull

It had grown very hot. Jan was sweating. His right arm was numb, and he felt that a blister was forming on his left heel. Yet Oma walked on, still cool and collected. Jan did not want to be the first to suggest a rest.

All at once Oma said, "Now we'll have lunch."

"Where shall we get the food?" asked Jan in astonishment.

"In here." Oma slapped her handbag.

Jan felt much happier. Oma was sure to have something good in her bag, perhaps cakes or sandwiches or even potato salad. His mouth watered at the thought.

Oma looked around for a shady spot. There was a chestnut tree growing on a hill in the middle of a meadow in which two cows and a bull were grazing. Oma began to climb through the barbed wire fence.

"What about the bull?" asked Jan.

"If we leave him in peace, he'll leave us alone," said Oma, stumping across the meadow towards the hill. She was right. The bull and the cows took no notice of them. They sat down in the shade. Oma took a paper bag of birdseed out of her handbag and filled Paul's dish. Then she drew out a napkin and spread it over her knees. Next she took a thermos bottle and a small package out of the bag. Jan watched her greedily. His stomach was rumbling. Next she unpacked a few biscuits.

"What do you think of this?" she asked proudly. "It's real, genuine ship's biscuit, the sort we'll have to eat if our ship is in distress and drifts about for weeks without a rudder. When all the provisions are eaten up, there's always ship's biscuit. It's a good idea for us to get used to the taste."

Jan was rather disappointed. But a cabin boy couldn't be fussy. He began to chew. The biscuit was very hard.

"Tastes a bit like mothballs."

Oma nodded. "Yes, they have been lying next to the mothballs in the drawer for a couple of years, but that's just as it should be. Ship's biscuit always tastes of something else, tar or salt water or shoe polish."

"What's in the thermos bottle?" asked Jan hopefully.

"Water," replied Oma.

Jan drank a little. It was lukewarm and did not taste very good. When his hunger and thirst were barely satisfied, he lay down in the grass. Oma chewed her biscuit with enjoyment and took a sip from the flask. Then she got out her knitting and began to knit. As Oma sang to herself, Jan read his comic.

When he began to fumble in his own bag, Oma borrowed his comic and arranged it on her knee so that she could read while she went on with her knitting. Soon she was so deep in what she was

reading that she did not notice that Jan was un-
raveling the clothesline. Behind them the bull was
grazing peacefully.

In America Jan would have to rope lots of wild
bulls with his lasso. He felt lucky to be able to
practice here! He made a noose and sauntered
towards the bull, which took no notice of him.
Jan threw the rope, standing a little behind so
that the bull could not see him. He wanted to
rope the horns and jerk the bull's head back-
wards, but his throw fell short. Next Jan tried
from the side, and this time the bull turned its
head and glared at him. Jan threw the lasso again.
It touched a horn, but slid down and hit the bull
sharply on the nose. The bull stretched and gave
a bellow that sent shivers down Jan's spine.

"Oma," he shouted, "Oma!" and ran as fast as
his legs could carry him to the tree where Oma
was knitting. Behind him he could hear the bull
thudding along and snorting. When Oma saw
them both coming, she threw knitting and comic
aside and grasped her umbrella. As Jan reached
her, she opened the umbrella and pointed it at
the bull.

"Shoo, shoo, go away, you brute!" she cried.

The animal stopped short. As soon as he moved
again, Oma shut the umbrella and then opened
it quickly. The confused bull watched this strange
game rather nervously.

"Take the luggage," whispered Oma.

Jan grabbed Paul's cage, Oma's suitcase and
handbag, and his own bag. As Oma kept opening
and shutting the umbrella in the direction of the
bull, they retreated.

They were panting as they squeezed through the fence at last. With a furious bellow the bull suddenly charged the fence. When he found the way barred, he rushed back to the tree. He trampled Oma's knitting and the comic, which had been left behind, into the ground. Jan and Oma watched with horror. He could so easily have been trampling *them!*

"Ugh!" Oma said. "We came out of it all right that time. But life is full of dangers. I'm sure it would be best if we went back home again now, before we go any farther. I must fetch some more knitting. What do you think?"

Jan could not speak. The shock had taken his voice away. He only nodded.

As they were walking down the road side by side, Oma said, "I think we'll postpone our journey for a while. Maybe it would be better if we learned some more geography and English first."

Jan's heart suddenly felt much lighter. Only one thing worried him—what would they say to him at home?

To his surprise no one said anything. They arrived just before supper, and the table was already set. Mother asked a strange question: "Well, did you enjoy yourselves?"

No one noticed that Jan was quiet during the meal because his brother and sisters made so much noise. He was very tired and went to bed right afterwards. When he was lying stretched out on the soft mattress, he thought with a shudder of where he might be sleeping now if Oma had not had the idea of coming home.

Oma was helping Mother do the dishes.

"Did you have a nice excursion?" asked Mother.

Oma nodded. "Please, will you give me back the note I left on the table for you this morning? There is something on the back of it that I want."

Mother took a piece of paper out of her apron pocket and handed it to Oma. It said, "I'm going out for the day with Jan. We'll be back in time for supper. Oma."

### Reflections

1. What is a *tributary?* What rivers in the United States have tributaries? Name some of them.

2. How did Jan prepare for his trip and future life in America? Compare his preparations with Oma's. Do you think Oma was well prepared for the kind of journey she was taking? Explain.

3. Why do you think faraway places often seem so desirable? What lands have you wished you could live in? How do you think you might be able to get there?

4. When Jan and Oma returned, why wasn't Jan scolded for running away?

5. What "lessons" do you think Jan learned from his day's outing? How would you like to have someone like Oma as a teacher? Explain your answer.

# He Did It

MARY BRITTON MILLER

Said the dangerous sea,
"You'll not conquer me,
Try as hard as you can.
You are not a whale,
You are not a shark—
You cannot walk
On the waves, young man."

So he made a boat
That was able to float.
"Ho, ho!" said his foe,
"It floats all right
And it's watertight,
But you can't make it go."
"Oh yes I can,"
Replied the young man.
And he made some oars
And learned how to row.

When the sea saw
The boats and the oars
And all the rowers,
He said, "Young man,
They make a fine show,
But what will you do
When they venture out
Where the deep sea swells
Can take them up
And toss them about
Like cockleshells?"

"You can't stump me,"
Said the bright young man,
And cut down a tree
And made a tall mast
And rigged it with sails
To catch the high winds
And weather the gales.

When the ships set out
With their sails unfurled
To cross the Atlantic
And discover the world,
The sea looked them over
From stern to stem
And when he saw,
With considerable awe,
That Columbus himself
Was on one of them,
He said, with a show
Of humility,
"I admit, young man,
You have conquered me."

# The Sailmaker and the Sea Captain

ESTHER M. DOUTY

The early morning sun splashed brightly through the window. James Forten could barely see the outline of the mainsail he had chalked on the floor of the sail loft.

It was the spring of 1793. Young James had come a long way. The son of a sailmaker, James had been one of the first black children in Philadelphia to go to school. At that time few schools took black children. When he was fifteen, during the American Revolution, James signed on a privateer called the *Royal Louis* as a powder boy. The ship was captured by the British, and James was a prisoner on the prison ship *Jersey* for seven months.

When James was seventeen, he signed on another ship bound for England. There he worked for a shipping company as a stevedore. In the English harbors he saw the slave ships which transported kidnaped Africans to America. He met and became friendly with men who deeply believed that this evil practice should be fought.

James Forten returned to Philadelphia a few years later. He brought with him a firm belief that slavery must be done away with. And he felt that free black people had a right to be first-class citizens.

In the next two years James rose from apprentice to foreman in one of the largest sail lofts in Philadelphia. This was a record few twenty-two-year-olds could match.

There were forty sailmakers in the loft. Half of them were white, and half were black. Only James could cut sails all day, stopping only for lunch. It was James, too, who most quickly grasped the principles of sailmaking. He could take a sail from the drawing stage to the great canvasses, all sewn and roped and ready to be bent (fastened) to the mast. No wonder that his employer praised him for his "skill, energy, and good conduct."

One day, James was leaving the loft to do an errand at the waterfront. There he noticed a ship anchored near the public landing. He stopped short and stared. There was nothing unusual about the ship. It was a smallish schooner named *Mary*, of Westport, Massachusetts. It reeked of whale oil and bone. But on the deck he could see the captain and the crew. All were black men.

Before nightfall James met the captain, Paul Cuffe. Captain Cuffe was a tall, broad, kindly looking man of thirty-four. He had just returned from a successful whaling trip to Newfoundland. And he brought with him a cargo of whale oil and bone to sell in Philadelphia.

During the next few days the two men saw much of each other. Although the New England sea captain was modest, James learned his story.

Paul Cuffe's father was a poor farmer who had been born in Africa. He had been brought as a slave to Massachusetts. In time he worked out his purchase price and bought his freedom. Paul's father and mother moved to Cutterhunk Island. There they raised their family.

At thirteen Paul was barely able to read and write. But he kept at his studies, teaching himself. Sometimes he got help from friends on the mainland. Because Paul Cuffe lived in a region that made its living mostly from the sea, he decided to learn the art of navigation.

In 1775, when he was sixteen, Paul became a seaman on a whaling ship. On his third voyage, made at the height of the American Revolution, he was captured by the British. They imprisoned him for three months.

After his release, Paul Cuffe decided to build and sail his own boat. He spent every spare minute

studying arithmetic and navigation. At first
he was unlucky. He built and sailed two boats,
but both were attacked and stolen by pirates.
Then his luck changed. Soon he was making a
profit from his ventures. Cuffe finally had enough
money to be able to build the schooner, *Mary*.
And now it lay at the Philadelphia wharf.

Sailmaker Forten was particularly interested in Captain Cuffe's account of what had happened on the *Mary*'s first voyage. The schooner, accompanied by two boats, had a crew of ten men—all blacks and Indians. It had gone on a whaling expedition to the whaling grounds off Newfoundland. When they reached the Strait of Belle Isle, Cuffe found four other whaling ships already there. They were fully equipped with boats and harpoons.

The usual custom was for whaling ships to share their equipment. But these four New England captains grew angry. They tried to drive the *Mary* away. They thought that Cuffe and the *Mary*'s crewmen were not experienced whalers and that the ship did not have proper equipment.

Captain Cuffe decided that he and his crew would go it alone. His harpooning activities alarmed the other whalers. They were afraid that Cuffe's group would drive the whales away. But when Cuffe's crew caught its first whale, the other captains changed their minds. They decided to share their equipment and to include the *Mary* in the whale hunts. Seven whales were taken, six of them by the crew of the *Mary*. And two of these were harpooned by Cuffe himself!

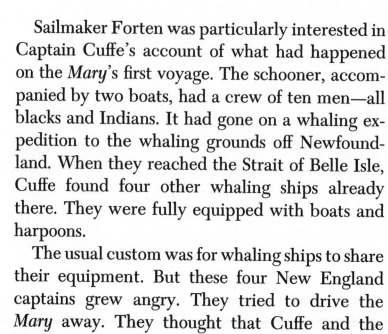

James Forten and Paul Cuffe admired each other at once. The two men became good friends. Both became important figures in black Americans' struggle for equal opportunity, but each in a different way.

Paul Cuffe believed that free black Americans could find greater opportunity in Africa, the continent of their ancestors. He had become a very successful sea captain. At his own expense, he took thirty-eight free black people on his ship to Africa. He had hoped to transport many, many more, but he died before he could make another voyage. At the time of his death, there were two thousand people waiting for Cuffe to take them to Africa.

James Forten, too, wanted to fight for black rights. But he did not believe that black Americans, many of whose families had been in this country for generations, should have to go to Africa to find happiness. Instead, he devoted his efforts and his fortune to changing the lives of black people around him. He held classes where black children, who could not go to school, could learn to read and write. He hid runaway slaves in his home. He donated vast sums of money to *The Liberator*, the famous newspaper dedicated to the idea of black freedom. And in many other ways, Forten used his wealth and influence to make life better for black Americans.

James Forten and Paul Cuffe each came to believe in different ways for black people to search for equality and fair treatment. But at their first meeting they agreed on one thing. Both men felt that they must "cultivate a love to all mankind."

### Reflections

1. What is an *apprentice?* What is a *foreman?* How long did it take James Forten to rise from apprentice to foreman?

2. Why did New England captains at first want to drive the *Mary* away? What made them change their minds?

3. Suppose Paul Cuffe and his crew really had been inexperienced and ill-equipped. Do you think the New England captains would have been right in refusing to cooperate? Be prepared to take either side of the argument.

4. How did Paul Cuffe and James Forten differ in their ideas of what was best for black Americans? How did each man try to carry out his ideas?

5. If James Forten and Paul Cuffe were alive today, what might each be doing in the struggle for equal opportunity? Be sure to consider each man's character and actions in preparing your answer.

# Charlotte Forten: Teacher

ARNOLD DOBRIN

Sixteen-year-old Charlotte Forten was excited. She had never been so far from home before. The trip from Philadelphia, where she had been born in 1838, was long and tiresome. The roads were narrow and bumpy. Even fresh horses couldn't shorten the journey very much. She thought she would *never* arrive in Salem, Massachusetts. Finally, the small New England town came into view. Charlotte breathed a great sigh of relief.

Charlotte was one of the very few children who could afford to go away to school at this time. Her family was rich. Her grandfather, James Forten, had made a fortune as a sailmaker. He wanted his children and grandchildren to have good educations. He knew they would have to be well educated if they were to help their people.

On her first day of school, Charlotte began a diary. And she kept it for many years. In it she recorded her love of nature. She wrote about her

many friends and classes. She wrote about the books she read. But some of the most exciting parts of her diary were written eight years later. In it, Charlotte Forten tells about an important journey she made. She describes her trip to the Sea Islands off the coast of South Carolina.

It was on the evening of October 24, 1862 that Charlotte Forten boarded a ship in New York harbor. She was on her way to St. Helena's Island. There, waiting, were thousands of former slaves who had never been to school. Teachers were badly needed there. And Charlotte Forten was one of the first to volunteer.

### Sea Voyage

The next morning, Charlotte Forten strolled around the deck. She was looking forward to what lay ahead. As the boat pulled slowly away from the pier, she met another passenger—Lizzie Hunn. The two women found chairs on the deck and talked.

Finally, Charlotte Forten began to get sleepy and found her way to her cabin. But when she got inside, the air was so hot and stale she could hardly breathe. After falling asleep at last, she tossed and turned in her bunk all night. As soon as the first light of morning came, she went up on the deck.

Lizzie Hunn was already standing at the rail. "Did you sleep at all?" Charlotte asked.

Lizzie Hunn shook her head. "I never had a more awful night," she said. "Tonight I'm going to sleep in a chair on deck. I feel better when I'm in the fresh air."

"That sounds like a good idea," Charlotte Forten said. "I think I'll join you."

At lunch the two women ate a few apples and dry crackers. When night came they found a little nook on deck. They wrapped themselves in shawls. Together they watched the sea rushing by and the moon reflected in the water. Charlotte Forten said, "I think this is going to be a very happy voyage after all!"

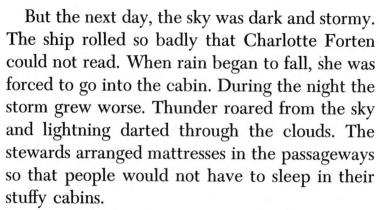

But the next day, the sky was dark and stormy. The ship rolled so badly that Charlotte Forten could not read. When rain began to fall, she was forced to go into the cabin. During the night the storm grew worse. Thunder roared from the sky and lightning darted through the clouds. The stewards arranged mattresses in the passageways so that people would not have to sleep in their stuffy cabins.

As she lay on her mattress, Charlotte Forten listened to the ship creak and groan. Everything that was not nailed down broke away and rolled on the floor. Dishes and glasses shattered. Some passengers began to cry. Others began to pray.

When morning came, the sea was still very rough but Charlotte Forten struggled up on deck. She watched the great white-capped waves as they broke against the bow of the ship. She took deep breaths of the cold fresh air and began to feel much better. She felt well enough to write in her diary, "How grand, how glorious the sea is today! It is far more than my highest expectations of it!"

Just then someone cried "Land, land ho!" and Charlotte Forten saw a faint strip of dark green on the horizon. She rushed to the rail for a better view of the shore.

### The Sea Islands

That night they landed at one of the Sea Islands and took a steamer to Beaufort. But Charlotte Forten's journey was not yet over. From here, a rowboat took her to St. Helena's Island, six miles away.

"The row was delightful," she wrote. "It was just at sunset—a grand Southern sunset. And the gorgeous clouds of crimson and gold were reflected in the waters below . . . It was nearly dark when we reached St. Helena's . . . It is all a strange wild dream, from which I am constantly expecting to awake."

The very next morning, Charlotte Forten went to see the school where she would be teaching. It was filled with children of all ages.

For the next two years Charlotte Forten was very busy. She taught the children during the day

and at night she taught their parents. Men and women, too, were eager to learn to read and write. In 1864, Charlotte Forten returned home, but she never forgot the wonderful years she spent on the Sea Islands.

### Reflections

1. Why did the people on the Sea Islands need teachers so badly?
2. From what you know about James Forten, what effect do you think he had on his granddaughter's life?
3. Many of the things we know about people who lived in the past come from the diaries, journals, and letters they wrote. How might a modern invention like the telephone have changed the way we communicate with each other? If Charlotte Forten had traveled in an airplane, do you think she would have written about the trip in a diary? Why or why not?

# The Summer Sleigh Ride

BETTY ERWIN

*It is the year 1933. Margaret, Emilie, and Polly are riding in a sleigh through the winter countryside. Suddenly the horses pull the sleigh off the road and into a deserted shed.*

## There They Were

There was a rumbling noise, like the beginning of thunder, then a falling feeling, like going down in a fast elevator. Everything tilted dangerously and the girls grabbed each other to keep from falling out of the sleigh. Then everything settled again, and—well, there they were.

There they were. It wasn't cold and dark any more. There was bright summer sunshine, a blue dome of sky arched overhead, trees rustled. There they sat in the sleigh in their winter coats and caps and mittens with the snow still on them. But the sleigh was sitting in a meadow. There were cowslips in the grass.

Who could believe it? They didn't believe it. They just stayed as still as mice on their island of winter and looked around. Then Polly jumped off the sleigh very quickly, grabbed a handful of grass, and jumped back on.

"It's real grass," she said.

"It must be real," Margaret said. "I'm hot and the snow on my coat is melting. I'm getting all wet."

The girls decided to get out and explore. They took off their wet coats and caps and mittens and carried them. In spite of themselves their spirits lifted.

They topped a little rise and looked down into a valley and there was the town.

"Why, it looks just like our town," Margaret said. "There's the courthouse."

"If it's our town how can it be summer?" asked Polly.

They went on, carrying their soggy clothes and treading the springy summer grass with their overshoes. Presently, they entered the town. The sidewalks felt familiar, the houses looked almost right (as though someone had built them from memory—some had too many windows, some had the wrong kind of roofs), and something else was wrong.

"Look at the trees," Emilie said, "those aren't elm trees."

"No, but they're like elm trees," Polly said.

"There's the school," said Margaret, "but there aren't any children."

The whole town, in fact, was empty. They didn't see a soul.

They went up the street and there was Polly's house. They went around to the side and in the kitchen door. There was Mrs. Davidsen's kitchen, with the stove and the worktable and the clock and the blue curtains. But there was no bread rising on the stove, no cakes and icing dishes on the table. There was a woman there, but she was nothing like Mrs. Davidsen, although she was dressed rather like her.

A man stood beside her. And that was how the girls met Jeems. They suspected that he was responsible for their being in this familiar, yet strange, place. But they couldn't understand how he could have brought them there.

"Here they are, Myrtle," the man said. "Here are the children."

The woman named Myrtle was staring and staring. "Why, I had no idea you'd get so many," she said, "and what very nice specimens! Really cunning, aren't they? Do they talk?"

"Certainly they talk," the man said.

"She acted," Margaret said afterward, "like someone at the zoo."

"Now come along, girls," the man said. So they went in the living room and sat on what looked like Mrs. Davidsen's red velvet sofa (only it was a good deal harder).

Then Emilie walked over to the window.

"Who are those people looking in?" she asked.

"Those are the visitors," Jeems said. "Don't pay any attention. They want to see what you look like. I have to go out now, but I'll be back soon."

Margaret went over to the window and stared at the groups of people. They were all the same size and seemed about the same age. They were

dressed in bright-colored, gauzy clothes and their hair was dyed to match. At least she supposed it was dyed. They were beautiful and exotic, like peacocks, only quieter.

"Look, those people have a guide or something," Margaret said. "Let's listen to him."

A man stood in front of the group. He gestured vaguely at the buildings and said, "You'll note that dwellings were made of natural materials, such as wood and clay bricks. Great labor was involved in felling the trees, sawing them, with the most primitive power saws, into planks, and then erecting the buildings. Metal nails were used, and they were actually driven into the wood manually, one at a time, by means of a simple tool called a hammer. It sometimes took months to build a house, and, once built, the walls were immovable so that the room arrangement remained the same."

"Well, naturally," Polly said.

"Sh-sh," Emilie said.

"The larger buildings were dedicated to the primitive social and business life," the guide droned on. Suddenly he caught sight of the girls and interrupted himself to say, "Ladies and gentlemen, if you look behind you, you will see three of the children we have here. They are females of an estimated age of nine or ten years. They retain

**pee·vish·ly** (pē′ vish lē) crossly; fretfully; unhappily

**pen·du·lum** (pen′ jə ləm) hanging weight that swings back and forth, often used to keep clocks running

**per·ish** (per′ ish) to die; to exist no longer

**pet·ri·fied** (pet′ rə fīd) made helpless because of fear, horror, or surprise

**phil·har·mon·ic** (fil′ här mon′ ik) a musical organization such as a symphony orchestra; related to an orchestra

**phrase** (frāz) group of words

**phys·i·ol·o·gy** (fiz′ ē ol′ ə jē) study of the bodies of people and animals

**pin·cers** (pin′ sərz) tool for gripping and holding something, similar in shape to scissors and pliers

**pipes** (pīps) bagpipes

**pit·i·ful** (pit′ i fəl) moving the heart so that one feels sorry

**plan·ta·tion** (plan tā′ shən) a large farm or estate where crops are grown. The people who work on a plantation also live there.

**poach·ers** (pō′ chərs) people who hunt or fish on another person's land without permission or right to do so

**Pol·y·ne·sia** (pol′ ə nē′ zhə) group of islands in the southern Pacific

**pome·gran·ate** (pom′ gran′ it) red fruit having many seeds, which are covered with edible pulp

**por·cu·pine** (pôr′ kyə pīn) animal covered with long spines or quills

**por·ridge** (pôr′ ij) thick, hot cereal

**por·tion** (pôr′ shən) part of a whole; amount; share

**poul·tice** (pōl′ tis) soft, wet mass that is put on the body as a medicine

**prat·tle** (prat′ l) to talk on and on without making sense; to babble

**pre·fer** (pri fėr′) to like one thing better than another; to choose

**pre·his·to·ric** (prē′ his tôr′ ik) of the time before any known history

**pres·ence** (prez′ ns) way of acting; a person's bearing or appearance

**pres·to** (pres′ tō) quickly; right away

**pre·vail** (pri vāl′) to triumph; to win

**pri·ma bal·le·ri·na** (prē′ mə bal′ ə rē′ nə) most important female dancer in a ballet company; ballet star

**pri·va·teer** (prī və tir′) privately owned ship allowed to attack and capture ships of enemy governments

**pro·long** (prə lông′) to make longer; to stretch out

**pro·pel·ler** (prə pel′ ər) revolving fanlike group of blades that moves an airplane, a boat, or some other motor-driven vehicle

**puck·er** (puk′ ər) to form into wrinkles or folds

**py·thon** (pī′ thon) large snake that kills animals by crushing them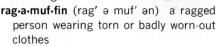

**rag·a·muf·fin** (rag′ ə muf′ ən) a ragged person wearing torn or badly worn-out clothes

**rail** (rāl) a bar of wood or metal around the outer edge of a ship's deck. It serves as a kind of fence.

**Ra·món** (rə mōn′)

**ram·shack·led** (ram′ shak′ əld) likely to fall apart; loose and shaky

**rare** (rer or rar) unusual; not common

**rec·i·pe** (res′ ə pē) set of directions for cooking something to eat

**re·clin·ing** (ri klīn′ ing) leaning back; lying back

**re·flec·tion** (ri flek′ shən) careful thought

**Reg·gie** (rej′ ē)

**rep·re·sent·a·tive** (rep′ ri zen′ tə tiv) person who speaks or acts for others

hat, āge, fär; let, ēqual, tėrm; it, īce; hot, ōpen, ôrder; oil, out; cup, pùt, rüle; ch, child; ng, long; sh, she; th, thin; ᵀH, then; zh, measure; ə represents a in about, e in taken, i in pencil, o in lemon, u in circus.

**re·search** (ri sėrch′ *or* rē′ sėrch′) to hunt for facts about something

**re·sem·ble** (ri zem′ bəl) to be like; to look like

**res·er·va·tion** (rez′ ər vā′ shən) place set aside for some purpose such as for Indian tribes

**rip·ple** (rip′ əl) very small wave; sound of small waves

**Roo·se·velt** (rō′ zə velt) last name of American family that has produced two Presidents

**Rous·seau** (rü sō′) Henri (än rē′)

**roy·al** (roi′ əl) belonging to or like a king or his family

**rum·ble** (rum′ bəl) to make a low, heavy noise

**ru·mor** (rü′ mər) story that people pass along as news without being sure that it is true

**rus·set ap·ple** (rus′ it ap′ əl) kind of winter apple with rough skin

**rus·tling** (rus′ ling) light, soft sound, made when things rub together gently

**rus·ty** (rus′ tē) covered with rust, the reddish substance that forms when iron gets wet

**Saint He·le·na** (sānt hə lē′ nə) one of the Sea Islands

**sal·a·man·der**
(sal′ ə man′ dər) moist-skinned animal shaped like a lizard

**sal·u·ta·tions** (sal′ yə tā′ shəns) greetings

**Satch·mo** (sach′ mō) nickname for Louis Armstrong

**sat·el·lite** (sat′ l īt) something that revolves around a large heavenly body: *A planet, a moon, or a man-made object that has been put into orbit are satellites.*

**sat·is·fy** (sat′ i sfī) to give what is needed; to please

**sa·vor** (sā′ vər) to taste slowly and with pleasure

**Scan·di·na·vi·an** (skan′ də nā′ vē ən) **1.** a native of Scandinavia, which includes Norway, Sweden, Denmark, and sometimes Finland and Iceland. **2.** any of the group of languages of Scandinavia

**scare·crow** (sker′ krō *or* skar′ krō′) stick figure of a person, dressed in old clothes, put in a field to scare birds

**scar·let** (skär′ lit) bright red

**schoon·er**
(skü′ nər) a kind of sailing ship with two or more masts

**scone** (skōn) kind of flat, round cake made from oatmeal or barley flour, cut into triangles

**scrump·tious** (skrump′ shəs) very delicious; good to eat

**sculpt** (skulpt) to carve something from stone or other hard substance

**sec·tor** (sek′ tər) part or piece

**seeth·ing** (sēтн′ ing) bubbling and foaming

**se·ñor** (sā nyôr′) Spanish: **1.** Mr., Mister, or sir. **2.** gentleman

**sen·sa·tion** (sen sā′ shən) something that causes great excitement or very strong feeling

**sen·si·ble** (sen′ sə bəl) showing good judgment; wise

**se·quoi·a** (si kwoi′ ə) extremely tall evergreen tree that grows chiefly in California; also called redwood

**se·vere** (sə vir′) very serious; critical; grave

**shark** (shärk) large rough-skinned fish that eats other fish

**shawl** (shôl) a piece of cloth worn over the shoulders or head

**shriek** (shrēk) to scream loudly and sharply

**shrug** (shrug) to raise one's shoulders to show lack of knowledge or care

**shuf·fle** (shuf′ əl) to drag or push one's feet along the floor

*sí* (sē) Spanish: yes

**Si·a·mese** (sī′ ə mēz′)  from Thailand, which used to be called Siam

**sim·mer** (sim′ ər)  to cook at a heat just below the boiling point

**sit·u·a·tion** (sich′ ü ā′ shən)  the way things are; state of affairs

**slime** (slīm)  soft sticky wet substance; ooze

**slith·er** (sliŦH′ ər)  to move smoothly; glide like a snake

**slot** (slot)  narrow opening

**small pox** (smôl′ poks)  a serious disease that spreads easily

**snore** (snôr)  to make a loud harsh sound while sleeping

**sol·i·tude** (sol′ ə tüd or sol′ ə tyüd)  state of being alone

**so·lo** (sō′ lō)  alone

**sor·cer·er** (sôr sər ər)  person who works magic; evil magician; witch

**Span·ish** (span′ ish)  language spoken in Spain. It is also spoken in Puerto Rico and in most of South and Central America.

**sprout** (sprout)  to start to grow

**squawk** (skwôk)  loud harsh cry

**squirm** (skwėrm)  to wiggle; to twist

**squint** (skwint)  act of looking at something with one's eyes partly closed

**stare** (ster or star)  to look directly at for a long time

**ste·ve·dore** (stē′ və dôr)  one who loads and unloads ships

**stink·bug** (stingk′ bug′)  insect that gives off an unpleasant smell

**stool** (stül)  backless seat, symbol of some African chiefs' power

**straight·a·way** (strāt′ ə wā′)  at once; immediately; without pause

**stren·u·ous·ly** (stren′ yü əs lē)  strongly; with much energy

**struc·ture** (struk′ chər)  arrangement of the parts of something

**stu·di·o** (stü′ dē ō or styü′ dē ō)  room where an artist or writer works

**sub·mit** (səb mit′)  to yield without resistance; to surrender

**sub·stance** (sub′ stəns)  stuff; matter; what a thing is made of

**Sung Dy·nas·ty** (sung dī′ nə stē)  period of Chinese history from 960–1279

**sur·name** (sėr′ nām′)  family name; last name

**sus·pi·cion** (sə spish′ ən)  feeling that someone has done something bad; belief that someone is guilty of wrongdoing

**swoop** (swüp)  to bring down suddenly; to come down suddenly

**sym·pho·ny** (sim′ fə nē)  long musical work played by an entire orchestra: *A symphony orchestra is made up of violins, clarinets, flutes, cornets, trombones, drums, etc.*

**Ta·bas·co** (tə bas′ kō)  hot pepper sauce

**tap·es·try** (tap′ ə strē)  heavy cloth material with a woven design or picture, usually used as a wall hanging

**ta·ran·tu·la** (tə ran′ chə lə)  any of the family of hairy, dark brown spiders with a painful but not serious bite

**tax·i** (tak′ sē)  when an aircraft moves across the ground on its own power

**tee·ter** (tē′ tər)  to rock back and forth

**tel·e·graph** (tel′ ə graf)  way to send messages, usually in Morse code, over electrical wires

**tem·ple** (tem′ pəl)  building used for religious purposes

**ten·ta·cle** (ten′ tə kəl)  long slender part or growth used to propel an animal or to feel or pick up objects

**ter·ri·fy** (ter′ ə fī)  to scare; to frighten greatly; to cause terror

**Thai·land** (tī′ land)  country in Southeast Asia, formerly called Siam

**the·a·ter** (thē′ ə tər)  place where shows are put on

hat, āge, fär; let, ēqual, tėrm; it, īce; hot, ōpen, ôrder; oil, out; cup, pùt, rüle; ch, child; ng, long; sh, she; th, thin; ŦH, then; zh, measure; ə represents *a* in about, *e* in taken, *i* in pencil, *o* in lemon, *u* in circus.

**the·or·y** (thē ər ē or thir′ ē) explanation; probable reason for something

**thong** (thông) thin strip of leather

**throne** (thrōn) fancy chair, like the one a king sits on

**till** (til) to plow; to prepare land for the growing of crops

**tilt** (tilt) to slant; to lean

**to·do** (tō′ dō) Spanish: all, every

**tram·ple** (tram′ pəl) to crush; to step on heavily

**trans·form** (tran sfôrm′) to change form or appearance; to turn into something else

**trib·u·tar·y** (trib′ yə ter′ ē) small river or stream that flows into a larger river; branch of a river

**trough** (trôf) long, narrow, usually shallow container that holds food or water

**u·ni·corn** (yü′ nə kôrn) imaginary animal that looks like a horse but has one horn coming out of the middle of its forehead

**u·ni·ver·sal** (yü nə vėr′ səl) belonging to or true for everyone or everything; having to do with the universe

**u·ni·verse** (yü′ nə vėrs) everything that is; all things that exist everywhere and anywhere

**u·ni·ver·si·ty** (yü′ nə vėr′ sə tē) most advanced school; highest place of study; large college

**vac·cine** (vak′ sēn′ or vak sēn′) medicine given by mouth or needle to keep someone from getting a certain disease

**van·ish** (van′ ish) to disappear; to become invisible

**var·y** (ver′ ē or var′ ē) to differ; to be different

**ven·ture** (ven′ chər) to dare; to explore or go forward

**ven·ture·some** (ven′ chər səm) daring; adventurous

**ve·ran·da** (və ran′ də) large porch

**Ver·di** (ver′ dē) nineteenth-century Italian composer

**vet·er·i·nar·i·an** (vet′ ər ə ner′ ē ən) animal doctor

**vig·or·ous** (vig′ ər əs) strong; full of energy

**vis·i·bil·i·ty** (viz ə bil′ ə tē) distance at which things can be seen

**vo·cab·u·lar·y** (vō kab′ yə ler′ ē) all the words known by a person: *He has a large vocabulary and can make his meaning clear.*

**vol·un·teer** (vol′ ən tir′) to offer to do something for nothing

**Wa–Xthe–Thon·ba** (wash′ te thon′ ba)

**weav·er** (wē′ vər) one who weaves; one who makes cloth

**wee** (wē) very small; tiny

**wheat·en** (hwēt′ n) made of wheat

**wheeze** (hwēz) whistling sound caused by difficult, forced breathing

**whisp** (hwisp) a kitchen tool used to beat eggs and liquids; a whisk

**white·cap** (hwīt′ kap′) white foam at top of a breaking wave

**whoo·zis** (hü′ zis) someone; a person whose name is not remembered

**Wil·liams·burg** (wil′ yəmz bėrg′) town located in the southeastern part of the state of Virginia that has been restored to look the way it did before the time of the Revolutionary War

**wist·ful·ly** (wist′ fəl lē) longingly; with a feeling of mild sadness

**wiz·ened** (wiz′ nd) dried up; wrinkled

**wob·ble** (wob′ əl) to move back and forth unsteadily

**writhe** (wrīŦH) to twist with pain

**yam** (yam) edible root, like a sweet potato

**yearn** (yėrn) to want something very much; to long for

**yon·der** (yon′ dər) at or in a distant place pointed to

**Yo·ru·ba** (yôr′ ü bə) a language spoken in West Africa

**Yo·sem·i·te** (yō sem′ ə tē)

**yuc·ca** (yuk′ ə) large desert plant with white flowers

**zuc·chi·ni** (zü kē′ nē) green squash that looks like a cucumber

their original costumes. They promise to add greatly to our farm exhibition and will be encouraged to gambol freely in an approximation of their native habitat."

"Well," said Margaret, "well! Did you hear that!"

The girls grew tired of waiting for Jeems to return and went back to the kitchen to talk to Myrtle. But Myrtle was gone.

"Polly, have you noticed—this kitchen isn't a working kitchen," said Emilie. "Nothing's in the right place and it's all unhandy. It would take hours to fix a real meal."

"What it's really like is a room in a museum," Polly said, "typical Colonial home. Notice the cobbler's bench, spinning wheel, and flatirons."

"But that's what it is!" Margaret said. "It's just like Williamsburg. And we're the natives in authentic costume."

"It's just like a zoo," said Polly. "You go to some foreign country and get a lion or giraffe and bring it back so people can see what one is like."

"But they come in a ship," Emilie said. "There's no mystery about it."

"Pooh," Margaret said scornfully, "There's no mystery about this either. We came in a time machine."

"Oh, Margaret," Emilie said, "don't be so dumb! That's just in books."

### Polly Catches Cold

Polly woke the next morning in misery.

"I've got the most horrible cold," she said. "I can't breathe, my throat hurts, my head aches, I feel terrible, and I'm not going to get up."

"It's no wonder," Emilie said, "after all that snow, and then being wet, and then hot, and everything happening. Someone was bound to get sick."

"Oh, dear," Margaret groaned, "I suppose they don't have colds here either. We brought this one with us." She paused, reflectively. A ghost of an idea passed through her mind.

"I'll bring you some breakfast, Polly," Emilie said. "You just stay in bed."

When breakfast was over, Margaret said, "I'm going to find Jeems, and ask him some questions." She found him near the house.

"C'mon, Jeems," Margaret said. "Let's sit down. I want to ask you some questions."

"Now, Margaret," he said, "you know I'm not going to answer. I'm not supposed to tell you anything."

"That's all right," Margaret said. "I'll say what I think, and you can tell me if I'm right."

"We can try," he said cautiously, "but don't be surprised if I don't answer you."

They sat down under the apple tree that wasn't quite an apple tree, in the side yard.

"Okay," Jeems said, "shoot."

"Now, I'll tell you what we've figured out so far, and you say if I'm right," Margaret began. "You brought us here in a time machine and this is some time in the future. Right?"

"Well, yes," Jeems said, "about right."

"And this is a museum, isn't it?"

"Yes, it's a museum."

"Well, then, what is it a museum *of?*" Margaret asked.

"Why, the twentieth century," Jeems said.

*Jeems goes on to tell Margaret about this world of the future. Machines do almost all the work. People don't grow food anymore, they just take pills. Nobody gets sick anymore. All diseases were wiped out generations ago.*

### Planning an Escape

"Jeems," asked Margaret, "when they got rid of diseases, infectious diseases, did they immunize all the people?"

"No," Jeems said, "we killed all the harmful bacteria, and all the disease-making viruses."

"Well, in that case," Margaret said, "we've got trouble, because we brought some with us."

"You what?" Jeems said.

"Goodness, you're pale, Jeems. Don't you feel well?" Margaret asked.

"I never thought of that," Jeems said. "And neither did anyone else."

He did look pale. He rubbed his forehead. He's actually sweating, Margaret thought. He's afraid.

"It's just a cold," Margaret said aloud. "I don't suppose it would hurt much if everyone did catch it."

"But we haven't had any sickness for over two hundred years!" Jeems said. "No one has any resistance any more. We'd have an epidemic! Hundreds might die!"

"From a little cold?" Margaret asked.

"We mustn't let anyone else know," Jeems said. "The visitors to the museum mustn't find out."

Margaret hurried back to the house, and she relayed this to Polly and Emilie.

"Serves him right," Polly said. "Let him be frightened!"

"It gives me a sort of an idea," Margaret said.

That night, when the girls were ready for bed, and were holding their usual conference, Margaret spoke. "Now the first part of my plan is this: we've got to act very happy and gay and glad to be here, so no one will have the idea we're plotting anything. We'll keep house like mad, and we'll play games and gambol around. No more sad faces, no matter how homesick we are."

So, for the next couple of days they played games. They played tag, and they danced the Highland fling and they hung by their knees from the branches of the apple tree. They acted out plays and they jumped rope. They talked Jeems into making a teeter-totter (on an old stump) and a couple of swings. The museum visitors increased in number day by day, and though the girls sometimes found it difficult to play naturally with so many people watching, they went steadily on.

But in stolen half-hours, and in the middle of the night, Polly and Margaret, or Polly and Emilie, or Emilie and Margaret were practicing with beet juice, a kind of red clay, sugar, white of egg, and assorted substances.

Then one morning Margaret found Jeems out behind the barn, mending harness. He sat on a bench in the sun. He looked so comfortable and placid, she almost hated to bother him.

"Jeems," she said, "I've got something to tell you, but you won't tell the other girls, will you, because I promised to keep it a secret."

"No, of course not," he said, "what is it, some new game?"

"Oh, no, I wish it were," she said. "You see, Polly has these spots on her neck, and she doesn't know what they are."

"Spots on her neck?"

"Yes, that's why she's been wearing her hair down, so you won't see them. They're scabs, sort of, and they itch, and she doesn't feel very good, either. Why, Jeems, what's the matter? Do you think it might be something—bad?"

"Oh, I was afraid something else might happen," he said. "When things were going so well, too."

Jeems put his hands to his head and moaned.

And the day after that, Margaret said, "Jeems, look at these spots on my arms. They look quite a bit like Polly's. Do you think I could have caught whatever it is?"

Jeems stared at Margaret's arms with horrified eyes. Then he backed away from her until he hit the barn wall and couldn't go any farther. Both Margaret's arms were covered with red crusty spots. They stood up from the skin, like pancakes on a griddle. Each had an angry black pock in the center.

"H-how do you feel, Margaret?" he gasped.

"I'm not so bad, except I have a headache." She rubbed her forehead wearily. "And I'm kind of hot and tired feeling. Emilie's worried though. She tried to make me stay in bed."

She waited a minute to let this sink in. Then she said, "Jeems, have you ever heard of small-pox?"

But Jeems was gone. He just turned and ran.

Then he returned. "Margaret, you just sit tight. I'll have to tell my superior, my boss. There's no way out of it. I'll have to tell him. Luckily, the museum doesn't open till noon today. I'll be back. I'll be back soon."

### Space Men!

Inside an hour, two strange figures appeared at the kitchen door.

"As I live and breathe," Emilie said, "space men!"

From one of the space suits came a familiar voice.

"It's me, Emilie," Jeems said. "We've come to see Polly. We're wearing these suits to filter out the bacteria. We'll go right upstairs."

In the girls' room, the two space suits inclined their helmets over Polly's bed. There was a silence, and then Jeems's boss spoke.

"I can scarcely believe this, Jeems. Her beautiful face, just a mass of runny sores. How could you let it go this far?"

"They kept it from me," Jeems said.

Polly was indeed a hideous sight. As they watched, she rolled up her eyes, and heaved aimlessly about and moaned horribly.

"Yes, yes," the other man said, "awful. The end of an excellent idea. No point in laying the blame. You never thought of this. No more did I. The thing is, what to do? And that's obvious, I think. They'll have to go. They'll have to go back to their own time. You'll have to take them, Jeems."

"I? But I'm afraid—"

"Nonsense. You can wear a space helmet. With your disguise. We'll get an air-car. Destroy it afterward. Get them out to the machine in secrecy. The house will have to be burned."

In a moment, the girls were whisked into the air-car. Quickly, they rode back to the meadow where the sleigh and horses waited.

Jeems sprang to the front of the sleigh. Then there was a rumbling noise, like the beginning of thunder and they were falling. Then everything tilted dangerously and then—there they were. In the shed.

It was dark, and the horses' stamping echoed loudly.

"Here we are, ladies," Jeems said.

The shed door opened and the sleigh moved out. It was night, and bitter cold. All around them the empty snowfields glittered in the moonlight.

The roads were covered with packed snow. Jeems whipped up the horses, and the sleigh sped faster and faster through the brittle air, over the narrow roads, toward home.

### Reflections

1. What is a time machine? Where did a time machine carry Margaret, Emilie, and Polly?
2. Why was a farm exhibit especially interesting to the museum visitors?
3. Why was Polly's cold such an important part of the story?
4. If you could enter a time machine, would you want to be carried into the future, or into the past? Why?
5. What are some things from your home or school that you think would be unusual to people living in the year 2500?

# Where Do I Go from Here?

MARY BRITTON MILLER

Land and sea and earth and sky,
I'm not a bird but I can fly
With the greatest of ease,
I'm not a boat but I can go
Under and over the seven seas,
I'm not a goat but with my skis
I can take a slide down a mountainside,
And also at my very best
Climb to the top of Everest.
Earth and sky and land and air,
I have conquered all of these—
Tell me, children, if you please,
Where do I go from here?

# WORDS AND MEANINGS

Beat the eggs.

Toss the salad.

Put out the lights.

Dress the turkey.

Read the directions under each picture above. Are the directions being followed? How would you beat eggs? How would you dress a turkey? These pictures show that words may have several meanings. Your meaning for a word depends on the way you understand it.

## The Meaning of Words

Words may be tricky. Many words have a number of meanings. What a word means depends very much on the other words in a sentence. Think of words in a sentence as you think of colors in a shirt or dress. Often the colors are woven into the cloth in a careful pattern. In much this way words are woven into sentences.

*Context* is an English word made by borrowing from two Latin words. In Latin *cum* means "with," and *texere* means "to weave." The context, or pattern woven into a sentence, helps us to understand the meaning of a word. Here is how this works.

1. *Spring* is my favorite season.
2. The *spring* is the source of the brook.
3. The pipe may *spring* a leak.
4. *Spring* over the hedge and into my yard.
5. A *spring* in my watch is broken.

How do you define *spring* in each sentence on this page. How do the other words in each sentence help you make your definition? If *spring* could mean only "a season of the year," in which sentence would it make sense? Could you use it in any of the other sentences?

Use the word *scene* in sentences to tell the following:
   a.   where you are
   b.   a favorite part of a TV show
   c.   a temper tantrum

Use the word *legs* in sentences about the following:
   a.   part of your body
   b.   part of a table
   c.   part of a pair of blue jeans

Look at the five meanings for the words *eye* and *root*. See if you can make up a sentence for each meaning.

| **eye** | **root** |
| --- | --- |
| my eye | the root of a tree |
| the eye of a needle | the root of a tooth |
| the eye of a hurricane | the root of a word |
| the eye of a potato | to root for the team |
| my mind's eye | the root of the trouble |

Discuss the different meanings of *eye* and *root*. Could you thread *the eye of a potato* or *my mind's eye* or *the eye of a hurricane?* Of course not. Often we must weave words together with the words near them before their meanings become clear. Context clues will help you break the reading code.

# Glossary

## FULL PRONUNCIATION KEY

The pronunciation of each word is shown just after the word, in this way: **ab·bre·vi·ate** (ə brē′ vē āt).

The letters and signs used are pronounced as in the words below.

The mark ′ is placed after a syllable with primary or heavy accent, as in the example above.

The mark ′ after a syllable shows a secondary or lighter accent, as in **ab·bre·vi·a·tion** (ə brē′ vē ā′ shən).

| | | | | | | | |
|---|---|---|---|---|---|---|---|
| a | hat | i | it | p | paper | v | very |
| ā | age | ī | ice | r | run | w | will |
| ä | father | | | s | say | y | young |
| | | j | jam | sh | she | z | zero |
| b | bad | k | kind | t | tell | zh | measure |
| ch | child | l | land | th | thin | | |
| d | did | m | me | ᵀH | then | | |
| | | n | no | | | ə | represents: |
| e | let | ng | long | u | cup | | a in about |
| ē | equal | | | u̇ | full | | e in taken |
| ėr | term | o | hot | ü | rule | | i in pencil |
| | | ō | open | | | | o in lemon |
| f | fat | ô | order | | | | u in circus |
| g | go | oi | oil | | | | |
| h | he | ou | house | | | | |

The pronunciation key, syllable breaks, and phonetic respellings in this glossary are adapted from the second edition of the *Thorndike Barnhart Intermediate Dictionary*. Users of previous editions or of other dictionaries will find other symbols for some words.

FROM *THORNDIKE BARNHART INTERMEDIATE DICTIONARY* BY E. L. THORNDIKE AND CLARENCE L. BARNHART. COPYRIGHT © 1974 BY SCOTT, FORESMAN AND COMPANY. REPRINTED BY PERMISSION.

**ab·a·cus** (ab′ ə kəs) device, used for doing calculations, which has a frame with rows of beads that can slide back and forth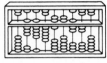

**a·bil·i·ty** (ə bil′ ə tē) skill; power to do something

**ab·sence** (ab′ səns) state of being away

**ab·sent·mind·ed** (ab′ sənt mīn′ did) not paying attention; paying attention to something else

**ab·so·lute** (ab′ sə lüt) complete; unlimited

**Ab·ys·sin·i·an** (ab′ ə sin′ ē ən) from Abyssinia, now called Ethiopia, a country in eastern Africa

**ac·cent** (ak′ sent) **1.** force or stress on the loudest or most important syllable of a word. **2.** particular way of pronouncing a language; speech habits

**ac·cord·ing to** (ə kôr′ ding) based on

**Ac·cra** (ə krä′) capital city of Ghana

**ac·ro·bat·ics** (ak′ rə bat′ iks) difficult turns and twists; tricks

**A·de·ni·yi** (ä′ dā nē′ yē)

**A·de·po·ju** (ä′ dā pō′ jü)

**A·de·yin·ka** (ä′ dā ying′ kä)

*a·dieu* (a dü′ *or* ə dyü′) French: good-by

**ad·just** (ə just′) to make right; to correct

**ad·lib** (ad lib′) stage direction meaning without instructions; made up by actors on the spot

**A·do—I·do** (ä′ dō ē′ dō) small village in Nigeria, a country in west Africa

**a·dopt** (ə dopt′) to take on as one's own

**ad·ver·tise·ment** (ad′ vər tīz′ mənt *or* ad vėr′ tis mənt) notice that gives information about a sale, a contest, etc.

**af·fect** (ə fekt′) to influence

**af·fec·tion·ate·ly** (ə fek′ shə nit lē) kindly; in a friendly way; fondly

**ag·ile** (aj′ əl) able to move quickly and easily

**air·strip** (er′ strip′ *or* ar′ strip′) runway used by planes for landing and taking off

**aisle** (īl) space between rows of seats

**Ak·bar** (ak′ bär) Mogul emperor in the late sixteenth century

**al·fal·fa** (al fal′ fə) plant grown as a food for livestock

**al·le·giance** (ə lē′ jəns) loyalty and duty to one's country

**all·spice** (ôl′ spīs′) spice made from the berries of a West Indian tree, similar to cinnamon and nutmeg

**am·a·ryl·lis** (am′ ə ril′ is) plant with large, usually red, pink, or white flowers

**a·maze·ment** (ə māz′ mənt) wonder; great surprise

**am·bu·lance** (am′ byə ləns) special automobile for carrying sick or injured people

**a·mi·a·ble** (ā′ mē ə bəl) pleasant; friendly; good-natured

**A·nan·si** (ə nan′ sē)

**an·ces·tor** (an′ ses′ tər) any of those from whom one is descended; a parent, grandparent, etc.

**an·chor** (ang′ kər) to keep a boat in one place by throwing overboard a heavy spiked weight attached to a chain

**a·nem·o·ne** (ə nem′ ə nē) sea anemone, a sea animal that looks like the flower with the name anemone

**An·gel** (än hil′)

**An·gel·ique** (än zhe lēk′)

**an·ti·bi·ot·ic** (an′ ti bī ot′ ik) medicine that kills bacteria

---

hat, āge, fär; let, ēqual, tèrm; it, īce; hot, ōpen, ôrder; oil, out; cup, pùt, rüle; ch, child; ng, long; sh, she; th, thin; ₮н, then; zh, measure; ə represents *a* in about, *e* in taken, *i* in pencil, *o* in lemon, *u* in circus.

**a·part·ment** (ə pärt′ mənt) group of rooms for one person or family to live in; part of a larger building

**ap·pa·ra·tus** (ap′ ə rā′ təs *or* ap′ ə rat′ əs) machinery; equipment; any tool used to carry out some purpose

**ap·pear** (ə pir′) to come into sight

**ap·pli·ance** (ə plī′ əns) small machine or tool used for cooking or housework, such as a stove, refrigerator, or vacuum cleaner

**ap·pro·pri·ate** (ə prō′ prē it) suitable; right for the occasion

**apt** (apt) likely to

**a·quar·i·um** (ə kwer′ ē əm) building or glass container in which live fish and water animals are kept

**A·rez·zo** (ä ret′ sō) town in central Italy southeast of Florence

**ar·gu·ment** (är′ gyə ment) reason for a way of thinking; way to persuade someone

**ar·ma·dil·lo** (är′ mə dil′ ō) small animal with a very hard shell, found in the southern parts of America

**Arm·strong** (ärm′ strong′) Louis (lü′ ē)

**ar·ti·cle** (är′ tə kəl) thing; object

**as·sume** (ə süm′) to take on as one's own

**as·sump·tion** (ə sump′ shən) belief

**as·sure** (ə shur′) to guarantee; to convince

**as·ton·ish·ment** (ə ston′ ish mənt) great surprise; amazement

**as·tron·o·my** (ə stron′ ə mē) study of stars, planets, and other heavenly bodies

**a·sun·der** (ə sun′ dər) apart; not together; away from: *The ax split the log asunder.*

**ath·lete** (ath′ lēt′) person who is good at sports or exercise

**at·mo·sphere** (at′ mə sfir) air around the earth

**at·tend·ant** (ə ten′ dənt) person who waits on another; a servant

**Au·du·bon** (ô′ də bon) John James

**Aus·tral·ia** (ô strā′ lyə) island continent southeast of Asia

**au·then·tic** (ô then′ tik) genuine; real

**au·to·bi·og·ra·phy** (ô tə bī og′ rə fē) person's life story written by himself or herself

**av·er·age** (av′ ər ij) usual; like most others of the same kind

**av·o·ca·do** (av′ ə kä′ dō) tropical fruit with dark green or black skin, soft green pulp, and a large pit

**ax·is** (ak′ sis) central line around which an object turns

**ay** (ī) Spanish: oh

**A·yan** (ä′ yan) surname used for Nigerian drummers

**A·yan·ba·mi·ji** (ä′ yan bä mē′ jē)

**A·yan·pe·ju** (ä′ yan pā′ jü)

**A·yan·tun·ji** (ä′ yan tün′ jē)

**ay de mí** (ī deh mē) Spanish: sorrow upon me

**bac·ter·i·a** (bak tir′ ē ə) one-celled plants so small they can only be seen through a microscope

**bac·ter·i·ol·o·gist** (bak tir′ ē ol′ ə jist) scientist who studies bacteria

**baf·fle** (baf′ əl) to confuse

**Ba·ga** (bä′ gä) tribe in Africa

**bag·pipe** (bag′ pīp′) musical instrument having a cloth bag filled with air which the player squeezes to force air through the pipes, making the sound

**bal·ance** (bal′ əns) standing steadily and not falling over

**bal·co·ny** (bal′ kə nē) platform coming out from an upper story of a building

**Ba·lo·gun** (bä lō′ gün) title given to brave African war chiefs

**Ba·mi·ji** (bä mē′ jē)

**Bang·kok** (bang′ kok)　capital city of Thailand, a country in Asia

**ban·nocks** (ban′ əks)　flat cakes like pancakes made of oatmeal, wheat, or barley flour, eaten in Scotland

**ban·ter·ing** (ban′ tər ing)　joking; teasing

**ba·sis** (bā′ sis)　main part; foundation: *His wide reading formed the basis of his knowledge.*

**Bat·ter·y Park** (bat′ ər ē pärk)　park in New York City at the southern end of Manhattan Island

**Beau·fort** (bū′ fėrt)　town on the Sea Island of Port Royal

**be·calmed** (bi kämd′ *or* bi kälmd′)　unable to sail because of a lack of wind

**beck·on** (bek′ ən)　to motion for someone to approach or come nearer to

**be·daz·zled** (bi daz′ əld)　completely confused or overcome by something very bright or splendid

**be·drag·gled** (bi drag′ əld)　wet and soiled

**be·fud·dle** (bi fud′ l)　to confuse; to make someone seem stupid

**be·lit·tle** (bi lit′ l)　to make less important; to insult

**bel·low** (bel′ ō)　loud roar; threatening noise

**be·wil·der·ing** (bi wil′ dər ing)　confusing; puzzling

**be·witch** (bi wich′)　to put under a spell

**bi·ol·o·gist** (bī ol′ ə jist)　scientist who studies living things

**bi·plane** (bī′ plān)　an early airplane, which had two sets of wings, with one above the other

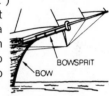

**bit·ter·sweet** (bit′ ər swēt′)　both bitter and sweet

**bless·ing** (bles′ ing)　prayer or wish for someone's luck or happiness

**blue·bot·tle** (blü′ bot′ l)　large bluish fly

**boast** (bōst)　to praise oneself or rave about something one owns

**Boe·ing** (bō′ ing)　name of company that makes airplanes; airplane made by this company

**boil·er** (boi′ lər)　machine that produces steam: *Old fire engines used a steam boiler to run the water pump.*

**Bo·la** (bō′ lä)

**bo·las spi·der** (bō′ ləs spī′ dər)

**bon·net** (bon′ it)　a kind of woman's hat, tied under the chin with a string or a ribbon.

**bow** (bou)　the forward part of a ship

**bow·sprit** (bou′ sprit′) pole sticking out from the front of a sailing ship with ropes attached to it that help to steady the sails

**brack·et** (brak′ it)　shelf that comes out from the wall

**braid** (brād)　trim made by weaving together three or more strands of thread, cord, hair, etc.

**bram·ble** (bram′ bəl)　thorny bush

**brief·case** (brēf′ kās′)　box-shaped bag for carrying books and papers

**brook** (bruk)　small flow of running water; small stream

**bue·no** (bwā′ nō)　Spanish: good

**bulge** (bulj)　to balloon outward; to swell

**bull·doz·er** (bul′ dō′ zər)　large tractor used for moving earth

**Byz·an·tine** (biz′ n tēn)　of or like the ancient city of Byzantium

**ca·ber** (kā′ bər)　tree trunk or large heavy pole weighing about 180 pounds, used in Scottish throwing contests

**cab·in** (kab′ ən)　a private room in a ship

**cab·i·net** (kab′ ə nit)　piece of wooden furniture that holds such things as books, clothing, dishes, etc.

---

hat, āge, fär; let, ēqual, tėrm; it, īce; hot, ōpen, ôrder; oil, out; cup, pùt, rüle; ch, child; ng, long; sh, she; th, thin; ᴛʜ, then; zh, measure; ə represents *a* in about, *e* in taken, *i* in pencil, *o* in lemon, *u* in circus.

**ca·ble·gram** (kā′ bəl gram) telegraph message sent under the ocean through a cable made of many wires twisted together

**cac·tus** (kak′ təs) desert plant with sharp spines

**cal·cu·late** (kal′ kyə lāt) to figure out by arithmetic

**Car·a·velle**
(kar′ ə vel) brand name for a small jet airplane

**ca·ress** (kə res′) to stroke; to pet

**car·pen·ter** (kär′ pən tər) worker who makes wooden objects

**ca·sa** (kä′ sä) Spanish: house

**cat·e·go·ry** (kat′ ə gôr′ ē) group of things that are alike; class

**cat·tail** (kat′ tāl′) tall plant with brown spikes that grows in marshes and swamps

**ce·les·tial** (sə les′ chəl) heavenly

**cell** (sel) smallest complete unit of living matter

**cen·sus** (sen′ səs) official counting of the people in a country or area

**cen·tur·y** (sen′ chər ē) period of a hundred years

**cer·e·mo·ny** (ser′ ə mō nē) act or acts done on special occasions

**chem·i·cal** (kem′ ə kəl) substance made up of elements, often used for a specific purpose

**chick·en pox** (chik′ ən poks) childhood disease that causes a rash and itching

**Chi·nese** (chī nēz′) **1.** a native of China. **2.** language of China

**cin·na·mon** (sin′ ə mən) reddish-brown spice made from the bark of an East Indian tree

**cir·cuit** (sėr′ kit) complete path of wires and plugs for electricity

**cit·i·zen** (sit′ ə zən) one who is a member or native of a nation, state, or city: *The citizens elected a new mayor.*

**civ·il** (siv′ əl) having to do with the citizens of a country: *A civil war is fought between groups of citizens of the same country.*

**ci·vil·ian** (sə vil′ yən) private; not having to do with the armed forces

**clam·ber** (klam′ bər) to climb; to scramble up

**clans·men** (klanz′ men) members of a clan, which is a group of related families

**clench·ing** (klench′ ing) clutching; tightening

**clo·ver** (klō′ vər) low plant with leaves usually arranged in threes

**clue** (klü) item of information that points to the solution of a problem

**clus·ter** (klus′ tər) group of things; clump

**coast·al** (kō′ stl) along or of the coast; very near the ocean

**co·co·nut** (kō′ kə nut′) large round tropical fruit that has edible hard white flesh and nourishing liquid in the center

**co·coon** (kə kün′) case that a caterpillar spins around itself and in which it turns into an adult butterfly or moth

**col·li·sion** (kə lizh′ ən) crash of objects

**col·o·nist** (kol′ ə nist) one who starts or lives in a colony or new community

**col·o·ny** (kol′ ə nē) group of plants or animals of the same kind that live or grow together

**com·mu·ni·cate** (kə myü′ nə kāt) to talk; to exchange news, feelings, beliefs, etc.; to share thoughts or ideas

**com·pa·dre** (kom päd′ rā) Spanish: friend, pal

**com·part·ment** (kəm pärt′ mənt) part of a whole, separated from the rest, meant to hold something

**com·pass** (kum′ pəs) instrument for showing directions

**com·pli·ca·tion** (kom′ plə kā′ shən) something that makes things more confused or harder to settle

**com·pos·er** (kəm pō′ zər) one who writes music

**com·put·er** (kəm pyü′ tər) machine that does arithmetic or calculations

**con·cer·to** (kən cher′ tō) musical work played by a solo instrument accompanied by an orchestra

**con·coct** (kon kokt′) to prepare; to make something out of many ingredients

**con·fi·den·tial·ly** (kon′ fə den′ shəl lē) told or written secretly

**Con·gress** (kong′ gris) the lawmaking body of the United States of America, made up of the Senate and the House of Representatives

**con·ser·va·tion** (kon′ sər vā′ shən) protection of natural resources such as forests, lakes, rivers, wildlife, etc.

**con·stant·ly** (kon′ stənt lē) all the time; without stopping

**con·trast** (kən trast′) to point out differences between two items

**con·trib·ute** (kən trib′ yüt) to add something; to help

**coop** (küp or kůp) pen for chickens, geese, etc.

**co·ral** (kor′ əl) tiny sea animals with hard skeletons that band together to form branches or reefs

**coun·cil** (koun′ səl) group of wise people who advise a king or leader

**co·zy** (kō′ zē) comfortable; snug

**crab** (krab) water animal with a hard shell, five pair of legs, two of which end in large claws

**crim·son** (krim′ zən) deep red

**crock·er·y** (krok′ ər ē) made of baked clay

**crook·ed** (krůk′ id) not straight; bent

**crouch** (krouch) to stoop down with bent legs

**crys·tal** (kris′ tl) clear stone or mineral that looks like glass

**cud** (kud) food brought back up to the mouth of a cow and chewed for a long time

**Cuf·fe** (ku′ fē) Paul

**cui·da·do** (kwē dä′ dō) Spanish: care; used as a command meaning look out or take care

**curb** (kėrb) raised edge between sidewalk and street

**cus·to·di·an** (kus tō′ dē ən) janitor; one who takes care of a building

**Dan·ube** (dan′ yüb) river in Europe

**Daph·ne** (daf′ nē)

**dap·pled** (dap′ əld) spotted

**dazed** (dāzd) confused; stunned; not thinking clearly

**deck** (dek) the floors around the side of a ship

**ded·i·cat·ed** (ded′ ə kāt əd) set apart for a special purpose

**de·li·cious** (di lish′ əs) good tasting

**de·serve** (di zėrv′) to earn; to be worthy of

**des·ti·na·tion** (des′ tə nā′ shən) place to which someone or something is going or being sent

**de·vel·op** (di vel′ əp) to grow; to become more complicated

**de·vise** (di vīz′) to think out or invent

**di·a·ry** (dī′ ər ē) book in which one writes thoughts or feelings about what has happened during each day; an account of each day's events

**dí·as** (dē′ äs) Spanish: days

**di·fí·cil** (dē fē′ sēl) Spanish: hard; difficult

**dis·cov·er** (dis kuv′ ər) to find out; to learn

**dis·pute** (dis pyüt′) to argue

**dog·ger·el** (dô′ gər əl) bad poetry; worthless rhymes; senseless verse

**do·nate** (dō′ nāt) to give

**dou·bloon** (du blün′) gold Spanish coin no longer in use

**drawl** (drôl) to talk in a slow drawn-out way

---

hat, āge, fär; let, ēqual, tėrm; it, īce; hot, ōpen, ôrder; oil, out; cup, půt, rüle; ch, child; ng, long; sh, she; th, thin; ᴛʜ, then; zh, measure; ə represents *a* in about, *e* in taken, *i* in pencil, *o* in lemon, *u* in circus.

**driz·zly** (driz′ lē)  misty; like a gentle rain

**dune** (dün *or* dyün)  hill or mound of sand

**Dun·veg·an Cas·tle** (dun′ vāg′ ən kas′ əl)  home of the MacLeod clan on the western coast of the Isle of Skye

**dwin·dle** (dwin′ dl)  to become smaller; to fade away

**Ear·hart** (er′ härt)  Amelia (a mēl′ ya)

**ear·nest** (ėr′ nist)  real; serious

**ear·wig** (ir′ wig′)  harmless insect, somewhat like a beetle

**Eb·er·bach** (ā′ bėr bäk′)  town in West Germany near Heidelberg

**e·lec·tric·i·ty** (i lek tris′ ə tē)  kind of energy in the form of a current, used to produce light and heat and run motors: *Lightning is a natural form of electricity.*

**em·broi·dered** (em broi′ dərd)  decorated with stitches or needlework

**en·chant·ed** (en chant′ id)  charmed; delighted greatly

**en·dur·ance** (en dùr′ əns *or* en dyùr′ əns)  strength or power to last

**e·nor·mous** (i nôr′ məs)  very big; gigantic; huge

**en·trance** (en′ trəns)  gate or door; way to get into a building or area

**en·trust·ed** (en′ trust′ əd)  given into someone's care

**ep·i·dem·ic** (ep ə dem′ ik)  the rapid spread of a disease

**es·tab·lish** (e stab′ lish)  to set up

**Es·trel·li·ta** (es trə lē′ tə)

**E·trus·can** (i trus′ kən)  of the civilization of the Etruscans, an ancient people who lived in Italy

**ex·ag·ge·rate** (eg zaj′ ə rāt′)  to say something is bigger or better than it really is

**ex·cur·sion** (ek skėr′ zhən)  pleasure trip

**ex·o·tic** (eg zot′ ik)  foreign; strange

**ex·per·i·ment** (ek sper′ ə mənt)  to make tests in order to find out something or to prove a theory

**ex·plo·ra·tion** (ek′ splə rā′ shən)  travel into an unknown place to discover what it is like

**ex·press** (ek spres′)  fastest possible means of transporting something; nonstop or having few stops

**fam·ish** (fam′ ish)  be very hungry

**fangs** (fangs)  long, pointed teeth such as those of a snake, wolf, or dog

**fan·tas·tic** (fan tas′ tik)  very odd; unreal; strange

**fas·ci·nat·ed** (fas′ n āt əd)  very interested in something

**Fe·o·dor** (fē′ ə dôr *or* fē ō′ dər)

**fes·ti·val** (fes′ tə vəl)  special time of rejoicing; celebration; big party

**fes·tooned** (fe stünd′)  decorated

**feud** (fyüd)  quarrel that lasts for a long time

**fire·place** (fīr′ plās′)  framed opening in wall to hold a fire

**flap·jack** (flap′ jak′)  kind of pancake

**flat·boat** (flat′ bōt′)  flat-bottomed large boat used on rivers, similar to a barge

**flat·i·ron** (flat′ ī ərn)  old-fashioned iron

**fledg·ling** (flej′ ling)  baby bird

**Flem·ish** (flem′ ish)  of Flanders, a region in Belgium and France

**flex·i·ble** (flek′ sə bəl)  able to be bent without breaking; able to move in all directions; usable for many purposes

**flo·res** (flōr′ es)  Spanish: flowers

**flum·moxed** (flum′ əksd)  confused or puzzled

**flut·ter** (flut′ r)  to flap back and forth; to wave

**fo·rest·ry** (fôr′ ə strē)  the care of trees and forests; the care of woodlands

**For·ten** (fôr′ tən)  James; Charlotte (shär′ lət)

**frag·ile** (fraj′ əl)  easily broken or damaged; delicate

**fran·ti·cal·ly** (fran′ tik lē)  with great excitement; with panic

**freight·er** (frā′ tər)  ship that carries products, not passengers

**French** (french) **1.** having to do with France. **2.** language of France

**fric·tion** (frik′ shən) rubbing of one thing against another; heat or resistance caused by the rubbing

**fring·ing** (frinj′ ing) bordering: *The flowers fringing the sidewalk are lovely.*

**fron·tier** (frun tir′) border between the settled part of a country and the wilds

**fu·ner·al** (fyü′ nər əl) ceremony held after a person has died

**fun·nel** (fun′ l) a tube that is wide at one end and tapers to a small opening

**fur·i·ous** (fyůr′ ē əs) very angry

**Gal·lau·det** (gal′ ə det′) Thomas Hopkins

**gam·bol** (gam′ bəl) run and jump in play

**gan·der** (gan′ dər) male goose

**ga·zelle** (gə zəl′) small swift antelope of Africa or Asia

**gen·e·ra·tor** (jen′ ə rā′ tər) machine that produces electricity by moving wires very quickly between several magnets

**Ger·man** (jėr′ mən) **1.** a native of Germany. **2.** language of Germany, Austria, and parts of Switzerland

**ghast·ly** (gast′ lē) horrible; awful

**gi·gan·tic** (jī gan′ tik) very large; big as a giant

**gin·ger·ly** (jin′ jər lē) very carefully, so as not to break something

**Glack·ens** (glak′ ənz) William James

**gland** (gland) small part of a spider's body that produces poison

**globe** (glōb) the earth; anything shaped like a ball

**gnats** (nats) small, winged insects, especially ones that bite

**gor·geous** (gôr′ jəs) extremely beautiful; splendid

**gos·ling** (goz′ ling) baby goose

**gos·sa·mer** (gos′ ə mər) soft, sheer lightweight cloth or substance

**grad·u·a·tion** (graj′ ü ā′ shən) ceremony held when one has completed a certain number of courses in school

**Greek** (grēk) language of Greece

**gris·ly** (griz′ lē) frightful; horrible

**grove** (grōv) group of trees that are standing together, without thick underbrush

**gua·va** (gwä′ və) sweet yellow tropical fruit

**guin·ea pig** (gin′ ē pig) small furry animal, kept as a pet and often used for scientific experiments

**Gulf of Guin·ea** (gulf′ ov gin′ ē) part of the Atlantic Ocean along the west coast of Africa

**Ham·burg** (ham′ bėrg′) port city in West Germany

**hand lens** (hand lenz) a magnifying glass to be held in the hand

**har·mon·i·ca** (här mon′ ə kə) small, rectangular musical instrument, played by exhaling or inhaling; mouth organ

**har·poon** (här pün′) barbed spear attached to a rope, used for catching whales

**ha·ven** (hā′ vən) safe place

**heave** (hēv) strong upwards or sideways movement

**He·brew** (hē′ brü) language in which the Old Testament of the Bible was written

**Hemp·stead cart** (hem′ sted kärt) very light two-wheeled cart made of natural wood, used for carrying passengers

**Her·nán·dez** (hėr nän′ dez)

**hin·drance** (hin′ drəns) something that gets in the way; something that creates a difficulty

---

hat, āge, fär; let, ēqual, tėrm; it, īce; hot, ōpen, ôrder; oil, out; cup, půt, rüle; ch, child; ng, long; sh, she; th, thin; ͳH, then; zh, measure; ə represents *a* in about, *e* in taken, *i* in pencil, *o* in lemon, *u* in circus.

**hon·ey·suck·le** (hun′ ē suk′ əl)  shrub or vine with sweet-smelling white, yellow, or red flowers

**hop·scotch** (hop′ skoch′)  children's game in which one player throws a stone into a design marked on the ground and then hops and jumps over the lines to get it

**ho·ri·zon** (hə rī′ zn)  line where the earth and sky seem to meet

*hor·mi·gui·ta* (ôr mi gē′ tä)  Spanish: an ant

**Hum·boldt Cur·rent** (hum′ bōlt kėr′ ənt)  current in the Pacific Ocean that flows north along the west coast of South America

**ice·land** (īs′ land′)  land covered with ice during all or most of the year

**i·den·ti·fy** (ī den′ tə fī)  **1.** to mark a person or thing as separate from others. **2.** to find out what something is

**ig·nore** (ig nôr′)  to pay no attention to

**ig·nor·ing** (ig nôr′ ing)  paying no attention to

**Il·ler** (il′ ėr)  river in Germany

**im·mu·nize** (im′ yə nīz)  protect from disease

**im·per·i·ous** (im pir′ ē əs)  haughty, overbearing, domineering

**im·ple·ment** (im′ plə mənt)  tool

**im·press** (im pres′)  to make others have good thoughts about something

**in·cu·ba·tor** (ing′ kyə bā′ tər *or* in′ kyə bā′ tər)  heated box used for hatching eggs

**in·dex fin·ger** (in′ deks fing′ gər)  finger next to the thumb; also called forefinger

**in·di·cate** (in′ də kāt)  to mark; to point out

**in·dig·nant** (in dig′ nənt)  angry at something unfair

**in·fec·tious** (in fek′ shəs)  spread by germs or viruses

**in·fin·i·ty** (in fin′ ə tē)  state of being without bounds; endless

**in·gre·di·ent** (in grē′ dē ənt)  part of a mixture: *Sugar is an ingredient of candy.*

**in·her·it·ance** (in her′ ə təns)  something which has been passed on from one's parents or ancestors

**i·ni·tial** (i nish′ əl)  first letter of a word or name

**Inn** (in)  river in Germany

**in·sert** (in sėrt′)  to put in

**in·spec·tor** (in spek′ tər)  one whose job is to examine something to see that it is right

**in·spi·ra·tion** (in′ spə rā′ shən)  strong influence; something that causes thoughts or actions

**in·stall** (in stôl′)  to put something into place for use: *The mechanic had to install a new battery in the car.*

**in·stinc·tive** (in stingk′ tiv)  known without having been taught; inborn knowledge: *Fish have an instinctive ability to swim.*

**in·struc·tions** (in struk′ shənz)  directions telling how to do something

**in·ter·na·tion·al** (in′ tər nash′ ə nəl)  having to do with many countries

**in·ter·rupt** (in′ tə rupt′)  to break in on a speech or activity

**in·ves·ti·gate** (in ves′ tə gāt)  to look into closely; to study

**in·vis·i·ble** (in viz′ ə bəl)  impossible to be seen; not visible

**I·sar** (ē′ zär)  river in Germany

**I·sha·ju** (ē shä′ jü)

**Isle of Skye** (īl ov skī)  island west of Scotland

**I·tal·ian** (i tal′ yən)  **1.** a native of Italy. **2.** language of Italy

**I·ya I·lu** (ē′ yä  ē′ lü)

**jeal·ous** (jel′ əs)  wishing to have something that someone else has

**jeer** (jir)  to laugh at; to make fun of

**jel·ly·fish** (jel′ ē fish′) transparent sea animal with long tentacles and no skeleton

**jun•gle** (jung′ gəl) land in a hot, damp climate, completely covered with bushes, trees, vines, etc.

**jut** (jut) to stick out

**Ka•nan•go** (kä näng′ gō)

**kin•folk** (kin′ fōk′) one's family or relatives

**Knize** (nīz) Lili (lil′ ē)

**Kwa•ku** (kwä′ kü) African title similar to Mister

**lab•o•ra•to•ry** (lab′ rə tôr′ ē) place where scientists work

**Las•caux** (las kō′) site of famous caves in France

**Lat•in** (lat′ n) language of the ancient Romans

**Lech** (lek) river in Germany

**le•mur** (lē′ mər) small furry animal; monkey-like animal that lives in trees

***lib•ro*** (lēb′ rō) Spanish: book

**light•house** (līt′ hous′) tower with a revolving bright light on top that warns ships of dangerous waters

**lip read•ing** (lip′ rēd′ ing) understanding someone's speech by watching the lips move

**loom•ing** (lüm′ ing) appearing large and indistinct; appearing mysteriously

**lu•mi•nous** (lü′ mə nəs) giving off light; shining

**lynx** (lingks) any of several wildcats that live in northern North America, Europe, and Asia

**mac•a•da•mi•a** (mak ə dā′ mē ə) large tropical plant that produces an edible nut

***mad•e•moi•selle*** (mad′ ə mə zel′) French: Miss

**mag•nif•i•cent** (mag nif′ ə sənt) marvelous, grand

**main•sail** (mān′ sāl′ *or* mān′ səl) largest sail of a ship

**ma•lar•i•a** (mə ler′ ē ə) serious mosquito-carried disease that causes chills, fever, and sweating

**mam•mal** (mam′ əl) warm-blooded animal that feeds its young on milk: *Mice, rabbits, cats, dogs, cows, and elephants are mammals.*

**Man•dan** (man′ dan) tribe of American Indians who lived in North Dakota

**man•tel•piece** (man′ tl pēs′) shelf over a fireplace

**man•tle** (man′ tl) loose cloak or coat with no sleeves that is worn over outer garments

**mar•i•ner** (mar′ ə nər) sailor

**mar•i•o•nette** (mar′ ē ə net′) string-operated puppet

**marsh•land** (märsh′ land′) land partly covered by water; swampland

**mar•vel•ous** (mär′ və ləs) very good; surprising; wonderful

**May•flow•er** (mā′ flou′ ər) ship in which the Pilgrims sailed to America in 1620

**me•chan•i•cal** (mə kan′ ə kəl) having to do with or like a machine

**med•i•cal** (med′ ə kəl) having to do with medicine or doctors

**mi•cro•scope** (mī′ krə skōp) small device with a lens or several lenses that makes it possible for people to see things too small to be seen with the naked eye

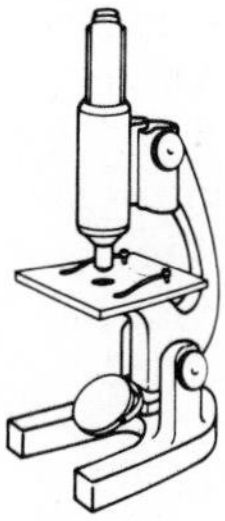

**Mi•de•wi•win** (mi dā′ wə win) secret group of medicine men among the Ojibwa and neighboring Indians

**midge** (mij) kind of tiny insect; also called gnat

---

hat, āge, fär; let, ēqual, tėrm; it, īce; hot, ōpen, ôrder; oil, out; cup, pu̇t, rüle; ch, child; ng, long; sh, she; th, thin; ŦH, then; zh, measure; ə represents *a* in about, *e* in taken, *i* in pencil, *o* in lemon, *u* in circus.

**mi·rac·u·lous** (mə rak′ yə ləs)  marvelous; wonderful; going against the laws of nature

**mis·er·a·ble** (miz′ ər ə bəl)  very unhappy; very poor

**mis·pro·nounce** (mis′ prə nouns′)  to pronounce wrong

**Mo·gul** (mō′ gul)  empire that ruled most of India in the 1500's and 1600's

**mon·sieur** (mə syèr′)  French: Mister

**mon·strous** (mon′ strəs)  very big; huge; like a monster

**mon·u·ment** (mon′ yə mənt)  something such as a statue or a plaque set up to make people aware of the importance of a person, event, etc.

**Mount  Ev·er·est** (mount  ev′ ər ist)  highest mountain in the world, located in Asia

**moor** (mur)  wild grassy land with no trees, similar to a marshland

**mor·ti·fi·ca·tion** (môr′ tə fə kā′ shən)  extreme shame

**mous·tache** (mus′ tash  or  mə stash′)  hair on a man's upper lip

**mu·cha·cho** (mü chä′ chō)  Spanish: boy

**Muir** (myür)  John

**mur·mur** (mèr′ mər)  to speak softly and indistinctly

**mu·tu·al** (myü′ chü əl)  felt or done equally by more than one person; in common

**mys·ter·y** (mis′ tər ē)  something that is not known; something that is extremely puzzling

**nat·ur·al·ist** (nach′ ər ə list)  one who studies animals and plants in their natural state

**near·sight·ed** (nir′ sī′ tid)  unable to see far; seeing clearly at a short distance only

**nook** (nuk)  a small, sheltered spot

**nudge** (nuj)  to poke or push to catch someone's attention

**O·ba** (ō′ bä)  title of Nigerian rulers

**ob·serve** (əb zèrv′)  to look at closely; to study

**O·jib·wa** (ō jib′ wä)  tribe of Indians in the northern United States and Canada

**O·ni·ko·yi** (ō nē kō′ yē)

**op·er·a·tor** (op′ ə rā′ tər)  one who runs a machine

**o·pin·ion** (ə pin′ yən)  belief; feeling that something is true or likely

**or·di·nar·y** (ôrd′ n er′ ē)  average; usual; like most others of the same kind

**or·gan·i·za·tion** (ôr gə nə zā′ shən)  group of people who work together

**o·rig·i·nal** (ə rij′ ə nəl)  not like anyone or anything else; the first of its kind

**O·sage** (ō sāj′)  Indian tribe that lives in Missouri and Oklahoma

**pad·dock** (pad′ ək)  large pen for horses

**page** (pāj)  young man who attends a person of rank, such as a king

**pa·pa·ya** (pə pä′ yə)  yellow tropical fruit that grows on trees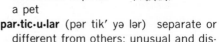

**par·a·chute** (par′ ə shüt)  large cloth shaped like an umbrella, used to bring people or things down safely from great heights

**par·a·keet** (par′ ə kēt)  small brightly colored bird often kept as a pet

**par·tic·u·lar** (pər tik′ yə lər)  separate or different from others; unusual and distinct

**pa·se·o** (pä sā′ ō)  Spanish: walk

**pas·tries** (pā′ strēs)  baked goods, such as pies, made with a rich flour paste

**pea·cock** (pē′ kok′)  blue, green, and bronze male bird with a beautiful tail made of very long feathers that can stand up like a fan